BABY BOOMER BLUES

CONTEMPORARY CHRISTIAN COUNSELING

BABY BOOMER BLUES

GARY R. COLLINS, Ph.D.
TIMOTHY E. CLINTON, Ed.D.

CONTEMPORARY CHRISTIAN
COUNSELING

General Editor
GARY R. COLLINS, PH.D.

BABY BOOMER BLUES
Contemporary Christian Counseling
Copyright © 1992 by Word, Incorporated

Library of Congress Cataloging-in-Publication Data:

Collins, Gary R.
    Baby Boomer Blues : Understanding & Counseling Baby Boomers and
    their families / Gary R. Collins, Timothy E. Clinton.
        p.   cm. — (Contemporary Christian counseling)
    Includes bibliographical references and index.
    ISBN 0–8499–0909–0 (hard)
        0–8499–3373–0 (pbk.)
    1. Pastoral counseling.   2. Baby boom generation—Counseling of.
3. Baby boom generation—Religious life.   4. Baby boom generation—
Attitudes.   I. Clinton, Timothy E., 1960–, Collins, Gary R.,   II. Title.
III. Series: Contemporary Christian Counseling Series.
BV4012.2.C558   1992
253.5—dc20   92–20895
                                                                  CIP

3459 LB   98765432

Printed in the United States of America

Contents

Preface

As every book writer knows, writing a book like this is a major effort. Writing as a team is an even greater challenge. For us it was a great experience, despite the pressing deadlines, the competing demands for our time, and the difficulty of working together when we live half a country apart from each other.

Before we began this book, we had both read widely about baby boomers, and we thought we knew a lot about the subject. Gary has watched the baby boomers from the vantage point of one born before the first boomers arrived. Tim was born near the tail end of the boomer explosion and qualifies as a full-fledged baby boomer himself. When we began writing, however, we realized afresh how massive and significant this movement is—for our society, for counselors, and for the church. We hope that as you read the following pages you will become as enthusiastic about baby boomers as we have become in writing about them. Of course they have problems and blues and struggles, but they are making a significant impact as they move into their middle adult years.

We are grateful to several people, mostly baby boomers and baby busters, who helped with the preparation of this manuscript. Our researchers, Steven Sandage in Illinois and Gary Sibcy in Virginia, spent many hours digging out facts and finding research articles to help with our writing. Kay Milioni compiled the index, and our wives (who have the same first names) were a constant source of encouragement. Without the patience and loving support of Julie Ann Collins and Julie Ann Clinton, we might never have finished the book. We pray that our God will use the following pages to help us all to better understand, counsel, and minister to that diverse group of people who will always be known as baby boomers.

Gary R. Collins
and Timothy E. Clinton

PART ONE

Understanding Baby Boomers

Chapter 1

Who Are Baby Boomers?

Baby boomers belong to one of the most diverse generations in history.

Paul C. Light

Never in the history of our country has a generation been taught to expect more from life. Never has a generation been more disappointed and disillusioned as adults.

Mike Bellah

We are possibly the most spoiled generation ever to come along.

Doug Murren

Baby boomers have not lost the American birthright of optimism about the future.

Time

Why are today's young people about ten times as likely to be depressed as were their parents and grandparents? With too great expectations, the baby boomers are sliding into individualistic melancholy.

Martin Seligman

Baby boomers will be the most important source of church growth in the coming decade.

George Barna

Help! I'm a baby boomer.

Hans Finzel

THEY GATHERED ON September 2, 1945, aboard the battleship *Missouri* anchored in Tokyo Bay. In a solemn ceremony, representatives of the Allies and Japan signed a document that officially ended the Second World War—four months after another signing had ended the fighting in Europe. By Christmas, hundreds of thousands of battle-weary military men and women had been reunited with the friends and families who had carried on the war effort at home.

In the postwar months, marriages boomed and so did pregnancies. In May of 1946, exactly nine months after V-J Day, 233,452 babies were born in the United States. In June the number jumped to 242,303. In October, 339,499 newborns arrived, and by the end of December, the total number of babies born in that one year had reached 3.4 million—an all-time high. And the birthrate kept rising. It peaked in 1957 at 4.3 million but remained in the 4 million range through 1964. This generation born between 1946 and 1964 soon became known as the baby boom. It was a generation that filled the nurseries for twenty years, stretched schools to overflowing (leaving many school buildings empty after the last of the boomers left), and made lasting changes as it passed through adolescence and reached adulthood. Now, the first wave of this nation within a nation has reached middle age, and scholars already are wondering how the baby boomers will change our views of aging when they become senior citizens early in the next century.

Seventy-six million strong, American baby boomers and their children now comprise about half the U.S. population. They control an estimated 55 percent of consumer spending, head roughly 44 percent of households, and make up most of the electorate. Better educated than any previous generation, they are taking charge and changing the face of corporations, politics, education, entertainment, churches, and virtually every other segment of society. They have become a massive power block, voting block, and spending block, both in America and in the three other nations that experienced a similar baby boom—Canada, Australia, and New Zealand.

This is the first generation to grow up on television. Compared to their parents, the baby boomers are less formal and more fitness oriented, aware of computer technology, self-centered, molded by music, and instilled with a deep-seated conviction that the sky's the limit. But as they reach middle age, many are struggling with unstable marriages, career disappointments, problem teenagers, older parents, financial pressures, widespread depression, and questions about their life purposes and beliefs. After ignoring or dismissing the church for decades, baby boomers are now coming back, looking for answers, ultimate values, and help with their continuing problems.

GREAT EXPECTATIONS AND FOUR MAJOR WARS

Thousands of books and articles have attempted to describe and understand the diversified baby boom generation. Woven into most of these analyses are references to the expectations of baby boomers and the influence in their lives of World War II, the Korean War, Vietnam, and the more recent Gulf War.

When the troops came home from World War II, attention shifted from war plants and battlefields to pregnancies and bassinets. Procreation was almost assumed to be patriotic. Childlessness was considered deviant, selfish, and pitiable. Contraceptive devices were awkward and inefficient, but for most that was no problem; having children was seen as a major route to happiness.[1] In those days, nobody had heard of zero population growth.

Demographers note that the baby boom began even before the war's end. During the early 1940s, women in their thirties who had postponed childbearing began having babies, and they had more children than was usual for this age group of mothers. Younger women were marrying earlier and having more babies, with less time between children, than any previous generation in American history.[2] There were no dramatic increases in family *size*. Women who gave birth in the thirties had an average of 2.4 children, and those who reached adulthood in the fifties had an average of 3.2. But the number of children increased significantly because almost everybody was having one more child per family.[3]

Experts have debated why the baby boom was limited to only four countries. Following the Second World War there were "baby boomlets" in Europe, but these lasted for only a year or two, unlike the prolonged birth rise in New Zealand, Australia, Canada, and the United States. These four countries are unique, suggests Landon Y. Jones, who has written what is probably the most definitive analysis of baby boomers. Unlike any others, the four baby boom countries have been nations of hope, with natural resources, open frontiers, widespread mobility, boundless optimism, and great expectations.[4] All four had made substantial recoveries from the Depression era; all had seen increases in their populations during the early thirties (so there were more postwar mothers available to give birth); and none of the four countries had been damaged at home by the ravages of a war that destroyed large parts of Europe and Asia. Hope and high expectations filled the *New Elders*—as parents of the baby boomers are sometimes called (see Table 1). They conceived their children with a sense of optimism, were determined that their kids would have the best of everything, sacrificed to make that possible, and conveyed the message that baby boomers were something special.

Three more wars. In the early 1950s the Korean War cast the first major rays of disillusionment over the baby boomers. Most who grew up in that era knew more about Buffalo Bob and Howdy-Doody than about General MacArthur and the Inchon landing, but the early baby boomers heard much about a different kind of war, a cold war. McCarthyism, the fear of communism, the Russian success in space, the civil rights movement—all of these influenced the first waves of baby boomers as they reached adolescence. The baby boom children discovered that all was not perfect or easy in this life, and they

Table 1
Baby Boomer Definitions

Baby Boomers—People born between 1946 and 1964, in the United States, Canada, New Zealand, and Australia.

Baby Busters—People born following the baby boom generation. Sometimes known as the baby bust generation, this group includes most children of baby boomers.

Dinks—Baby boomers with **D**ouble **I**ncomes but with **N**o **K**ids. Often these people are assumed to have good jobs, career success, and expensive lifestyles.

Early Boomers—Baby boomers born before 1957, most were deeply influenced by the events and social movements of the sixties and seventies including the Vietnam War.

Grumpies—A minority subgroup of baby boomers who are **G**rim, **R**uthless, career-oriented, **U**pwardly **M**obile, most often **P**rofessionals, demanding efficiency and action with little regard for human consequences or personal relationships.

Late Boomers—Baby boomers born after 1957, many of whom feel overpowered and overshadowed by the crowded half generation of early baby boomers.

New Collars—Lower- and middle-class baby boomers, estimated to comprise about one-third of all baby boomers.

New Elders—Parents of baby boomers, sometimes known as the consumer generation because of their purchasing power and spending patterns.

Survivor Generation—Grandparents of baby boomers, known as survivors because this generation was raised during the difficult years of World War I, the Great Depression, and World War II.

Tweenies—Hardworking, often successful baby boomers who resent being called *yuppies*, don't want to be labeled as conspicuous, and often are committed to altruism and traditional values.

Yuffies—**Y**oung, **U**rban **F**ailures, a subgroup of baby boomers with low incomes. Rarely mentioned in the media, this group has been estimated to be eight times as numerous as yuppies.

Yuppies—**Y**oung, **U**rban **P**rofessionals, noted for their affluence and conspicuous consumption patterns. Sometimes this term is used synonymously with *baby boomer*, but yuppies comprise an estimated 5 percent or less of baby boomers.

expressed their outrage in campus protests during the 1960s. They were jolted by the Kennedy and King assassinations and a war in the jungles of Vietnam that tore apart the soul of the nation. The great expectations of the early baby boom years had given way to disillusionment, emptiness, anxiety, and a large scale collapse of traditional moral standards that all seemed to culminate in Watergate.

Almost two decades later, in January of 1991, President Bush ordered war planes to attack Iraq in a U.N.-sponsored but American-led war to liberate Kuwait. Many of the young fighters were children of the baby boomers. Most could be called baby busters, members of the generation that came after the baby boomers. Those men and women of Operation Desert Storm served with distinction and were welcomed home with celebrations and patriotic demonstrations. Perhaps the celebrations meant most to the baby boomers reaching middle age, people born in the years after World War II, raised in the turbulent fifties and sixties, disenchanted by events of the seventies, maligned as the "Me Generation" in the eighties, but encouraged—even briefly—by a faraway war in the early nineties that instilled hope for the future and pride in their nation.

BABY BOOMER DIVERSITY

There are many similarities among baby boomers, but it would be inaccurate to lump them together as if they were all the same. Despite their commonalities, this is a diverse generation, probably more diverse than any generation that has come before or after. Sometimes this diversity is hidden behind a number of myths that can hinder our understanding and reduce our effectiveness in counseling baby boomers.

Baby boomers are not all affluent and greedy. In 1965 and 1986, *Time* magazine published cover stories on the baby boomers, describing them as "cushioned by unprecedented affluence and . . . a sense of economic history unmatched in history . . . often brought up in shiny new suburban enclaves of middle-class comfort . . . [they] moved as a single mass, conditioned to think alike and do alike."[5] Of course it isn't fair to take excerpts out of context, but a careful reading of both articles shows that *Time* made the error of focusing on affluent, trendy, mostly white, success-seeking baby boomers while it overlooked the far larger majority that do not fit this picture. Rarely do we read about black baby boomers who have grown up in ghettos, Vietnam veterans with post-traumatic stress disorders, or deserters and draft dodgers with lingering guilt. Almost everybody has heard about yuppies, but how many are familiar with baby boomer yuffies, young urban failures, of whom four are below the poverty line for every one yuppie above it?[6]

The cover of one otherwise excellent book on baby boom believers shows two youthful hands holding a Bible but also clutching cash, an expensive wristwatch, keys to a luxurious automobile, and the photograph of a large house. The book is described on the back cover as a volume "written for all who expect too much in life—material affluence, fame, or instant spirituality." The person who designed that cover and the Christian publisher who printed it are among those who have fallen into the myth of equating baby boomers with yuppies. Most of the emerging Christian books and articles on baby boomers appear to accept a similar myth.

Baby boomers are not all white and male. This is obvious but frequently overlooked in analyses of baby boomers. African-American baby boomers who were born into poverty have tended to remain in poverty. In 1965, blacks represented 11.6 percent of the total population but accounted for 24 percent of the fatalities in Vietnam. The antiwar protesters were mostly white and so have been the best educated and most vocationally successful of the baby boomers. When most of us think of yuppies, we think of white yuppies.

No accurate analysis of the baby boom generation can ignore the majority of boomers: women. Over half the work force is comprised of women, many of whom are baby boomers juggling careers and family obligations. Many women head families, especially single-parent families, and since baby boomer women have often delayed child rearing until later, many find themselves dealing with younger children and aging parents at the same time. Despite extremes in some segments of the feminist movement, women have made significant progress in their quest for equal recognition and opportunities. Their impact and their emancipation struggles will continue as they move into midlife. As a result, bastions of male dominance, including the leadership councils in thousands of local churches, will not be able to ignore the influence of baby boomer women in the decades ahead. In ways that are consistent with biblical teaching, both women and men must be given responsibility in church leadership and decision making.

"While a male-oriented church used to be acceptable, it isn't anymore," according to one young (male) pastor. "So, if you don't have women in leadership, we boomers will . . . think your church is out-of-date. . . . We will note that no women are leading, evaluate church leadership behavior accordingly, and conclude that such a church is bigoted! On the other hand, if we enter a church where women are openly and strongly involved in all facets of church life, a positive, subliminal message about that church will be evident, stating loudly and clearly: *This church truly represents the whole Body of Christ.*"[7]

None of us who want to understand, counsel, and reach baby boomers for Christ can ignore those who are not white and not male.

Baby boomers are not all highly educated.   Baby boomer parents wanted their children to be the best educated in history. Money was poured into schools, but at least in the United States the baby boom was an educational disaster.[8] Test scores slid and so, it seemed, did the quality of teaching and textbooks. Elective courses replaced many of the educational basics, television replaced books, and a nation that claimed to value education discovered that many of its high school graduates could not read.

The baby boom generation *is* the best educated in terms of years in school and opportunities for education, but the quality of that education has often been lacking. In 1940, 1.6 percent of blacks and 6.4 percent of whites attended college, compared to 11.5 percent college attendance for blacks and 23.2 percent for whites in 1985. But despite these advances, millions of baby boomers have not had the benefits of high quality education.

We are in error if we assume that all baby boomers are highly educated. Most are not.

Baby boomers are not all self-centered.   Parents who gave birth to the first baby boomers were still reeling from the sacrifices and stresses of World War II, but there was widespread optimism and a belief that for these postwar children, life would be better. From the beginning, as sociologists and others have noted, baby boomers were raised with great expectations. "We were raised to be smarter, healthier, and more successful than any before us," wrote Mike Bellah. "We were the luckiest generation alive. That message was not lost on the baby boom. We knew we were special."[9]

Television hammered home the message: life can be beautiful; greed is okay; personal peace and affluence can be expected; you deserve a break; with a college degree and perhaps a little luck, you can make it big. Politicians, advertisers, even churches pushed this message. The relative few who talked to the Jesus People of the sixties, went to church, or watched the televangelists sometimes heard that Jesus could give us a permanent high or make us more successful, healthy, attractive, and Spirit-filled. All we needed was to "name it and claim it." Was it surprising that many baby boomers had high expectations? Is it surprising that many built their lives around the pursuit of luxury and self-centered consumerism? Should we be amazed that a so-called prosperity gospel emerged from some segments of the church?

Many soon discovered, however, that their great expectations were overly optimistic and largely unrealistic.

> If their parents tended to regard happiness as an almost incidental by-product of living by the accepted values of hard work and family obligation, Baby Boomers have relentlessly pursued happiness as an end in itself. Few found it in the dizzying array of self-help movements like est or cults like Synanon and Scientology, which proliferated like weeds in the 1970s. Nor was the sexual revolution the answer. "Casual encounters and open sex left most Baby Boomers with a sense of emptiness, or personal isolation and loneliness. . . ."

Today many Baby Boomers have renounced the lonely pursuit of self. Increasingly, they are groping to find a sense of worth in selflessness.[10]

The so-called Me Generation of the eighties, like the fads and fascinations of the previous three decades, appears to have faded, accompanied no doubt by disappointment and the frequently noted "baby boomer blues."

Baby boomers have not all had similar experiences. The oldest of the boomers are now in their forties; the youngest are still in their twenties. The oldest lived through Kennedy's New Frontier, Johnson's Great Society, the assassinations, the turbulent sixties, the emerging civil rights movement, Watergate, the Nixon resignation, and, of course, Vietnam. They remember Sputnik, two McCarthys (Joseph and Eugene), Kent State, Nikita Khrushchev, the moon landing, Woodstock, George Wallace, Ed Sullivan, and the rise of the Beatles. All of this is ancient history to baby boomers who were born in the early sixties and grew to adulthood in the era of Ronald Reagan.

Baby boomers, then, are a divided generation, sometimes divided even against themselves. Analysts often cite 1957, the peak year of the boom, as a watershed that separates the early boomers from late boomers. In addition to their different experiences in history and positions in the life cycle, the two groups have developed different attitudes and have experienced unequal opportunities.

"The older half of the generation was the most idealistic and the most easily disappointed. They're what people think of as baby boomers," according to Landon Jones.

The second half had diminished expectations. They were more realistic. They looked ahead and saw the world was crowded. They didn't think life would be handed to them on a silver platter. As for their cultural experiences, the older half was more euphoric. They were the youth society, the protesters. They had the sense that youth could take over the world, that rock and roll would bind us. The younger half had no charge. For them, rock and roll is taken for granted, and youth is something you pass through.[11]

In contrast to those who have come later, the early baby boomers were able to experience family life that was more stable,[12] buy houses when interest rates and prices were affordable, get into careers when competition was less intense, and not have to worry about a crowded work force of people who are older and better established. The older baby boomers are more likely to vote, more interested in government, and blessed with higher incomes, lower monthly mortgage payments, and fewer personal debts than their younger baby boom colleagues.

Some of these differences are because the older boomers are further along in the life cycle, but there is evidence that younger boomers will always fall behind. One economist has predicted, for example, that college-educated baby boomers born after 1957 may earn perhaps 10 percent less over a lifetime than those who were born earlier.[13]

Like everybody else, baby boomers are unique. No two are identical. When they appear for counseling, each must be treated individually by counselors whose perspectives are not clouded by stereotypes.

Baby Boomer Similarities

Despite the diversities and the gaps between subgroups of baby boomers, the members of this massive generation have much in common. They are the first generation to grow up with television and computers, with the permissive child-rearing philosophies of Dr. Spock, with the crowding and competition that has come from so many other baby boomers, and with the rapid-fire, never-ending changes in technology. This is a generation that was raised hearing about the Disney worlds, the cold war, the prospects of nuclear war, the harsh realities of civil rights, and the prejudicial treatment of minorities. Despite age differences within their generation, baby boomers have shared some turbulent history. Many hoped for a New Frontier and a Great Society, but their hopes were dashed by the assassinations of and failures in the policies and personal lives of political leaders.

In the midst of these changes and frustrations, baby boomers heard repeatedly that they were special, unlike any who have come before or after. In describing this generation, writers have used the same words repeatedly, words such as *high expectations, introspection, separation,* and *experience.*

HIGH EXPECTATIONS

"It is, above all, the biggest, richest, and best-educated generation America has ever produced. The boom babies were born to be the best and the brightest," Landon Jones wrote at the beginning of his book, which he titled *Great Expectations: America and the Baby Boom Generation.* "Blessed with the great expectations of affluence and education, the boom children were raised as a generation of idealism and hope."[14] Unlike their parents and grandparents who scrimped, saved, and struggled through the Depression and World War II eras, the early baby boomers were told that they could have it all. Nonstop advertising promised instant gratification that could be had now and paid for later. Short-term thinking became the norm. Sacrifice, saving, or lowered expectations have never been prominent parts of the baby boomer philosophy.

By the time they had reached adulthood, the first baby boomers had faced what one researcher has called the "quadruple whammy" of inflation, fierce competition for jobs, exorbitant housing costs, and recessions. Despite what they had been led to expect, many in the postwar generation discovered that hard work and education did not lead automatically to fulfilling jobs and fat paychecks. Many learned the hard way that reality often falls short of youthful aspirations and expectations. Faced with this "expectation bust," some have become cynical, despondent "underexpecters" whose lives are marked by low motivation and disillusionment.[15] When they enter the counselor's office, these people have little hope that life will get much better.

But ingrained attitudes can be difficult to dislodge. Most baby boomers, it seems, still hope—and expect—that life will be better, at least in the near future and in the short term.

INTROSPECTION

Baby boomers tend to look within to find their strength and solution to problems. They sat in crowded classrooms together, protested together in the 1960s, and came together en masse at Woodstock, but they have been characterized as a Me Generation, concerned more about themselves and their own needs or careers than about political parties, church groups, neighborhoods, or families. "When they get into trouble, the baby boomers seek highly personal solutions—for example, individual therapy rather than the comfort of a community."[16] Perhaps in part because of their crowded upbringings, these people have few close friends and minimal involvement in community issues. Politicians, religious leaders, institutions, and (increasingly) therapists are not trusted, so problem solving often depends on individualism, personal journaling, self-reliance, and introspection.

In later chapters we will consider baby boomer spirituality and the return of many to the church. But millions have given up on the church and seek to find direction and solace in eastern and New Age philosophies that promise salvation from within.

SEPARATION

Consistent with their self-focused, introspective mentality, baby boomers resist tradition and are not joiners. In earlier generations there often were lifelong Democrats or Republicans, Southern Baptists or Presbyterians, and people who always drove Fords or Chevrolets. But this kind of loyalty is rare among baby boomers.

Consider their shopping habits, for example. This generation looks for quality and value in their choice of cars, clothes, groceries, or anything else. There is little brand loyalty or blind dedication to one store or manufacturer. Dad may have always driven a Buick and taken pride in his determination to "Buy American." Baby boomers, in contrast, are much more interested in finding value for their dollars. If a foreign-made automobile is better, that is what they buy.

The same attitude extends to religion, politics, communities, and even families. These people have little interest in denominations. They look for churches that will meet their needs, even if this means going to two churches. And if the churches or their pastors change, the baby boomers can leave as easily as they might shift their grocery shopping from one supermarket to another. Since they tend to be skeptical of politicians, there is no party loyalty. Since they have few community ties, they are not hesitant to move from one location to another if this seems to make sense. And for many, there is a willingness to shift from one marriage to another or to risk changing careers—several times if necessary.

These are people who hesitate to make long-term commitments, who applaud innovation, and who tolerate social diversity. They may not want the gay lifestyle, single-parent families, or cohabitation for themselves, but they accept it in others. They may disagree with fundamentalism, liberal theology, Hare Krishna, or eastern mysticism, but they have no problem with allowing these and other religions to exist and grow.

For themselves, however, they demand religion that meets needs, church leaders whose lives reflect what they preach, worship services that show careful planning and quality music, and sermons that connect with the worshiper's daily concerns. When they go for counseling, baby boomers want therapists who deliver what they promise, who provide competent therapeutic services, and who demonstrate psychological stability in their own lives. Many shop for therapists, and sometimes change brands, as they shop for everything else.

EXPERIENCE

Joe Cappo is a business analyst whose book *FutureScope* was written to summarize consumer trends and suggest commercial strategies for the 1990s and beyond. According to his projections, Americans (probably accompanied by people in the other baby boomer countries) want experiences more than they want physical goods.[17]

The generation that advocated free sex, widespread drug use, and a philosophy that said "if it feels good, do it," has given birth to children who have grown up on emotion-packed movies, electrifying rock concerts, and exciting video games. Convinced that doing is better than watching, this whole generation now wants exciting travel and the finest in stereo equipment, health clubs, and experiential religion. All of this has given rise to what Cappo calls an expanding "experience industry," that exists to provide entertainment and other experiences for feeling-oriented baby boomers.

KALEIDOSCOPES AND BOOMERANGS

Before the era of television and VCRs, pre–baby boomer children would sometimes amuse themselves by looking into a kaleidoscope—a narrow cardboard tube with a peep hole at one end, frosted glass at the other, and angled mirrors on the inside that reflected loose pieces of colored glass. As the tube was moved, the glass pieces would shift and show a changing series of colored designs. The designs were never the same. They were always complex, always changing, always beyond description.

The baby boom generation might be described as a multifaceted, multicolored kaleidoscope that is always changing and is never able to be described with precision. For all of the uniquenesses and similarities of the baby boom generation, there are many people who do not fit the descriptions. As this bulky generation passes through life, they look like a massive but moving object that keeps changing like a colorful kaleidoscope.

Some of the pieces in this picture are better described as boomerangs that have flown great distances but are coming full circle back to where they began.[18] Many of the baby boomers are moving to traditional family values, conservative political philosophies, altruistic service to others, and the basics in education. But even these boomerang boomers have been shaped and changed by the experiences of their fast-moving generation.

Never in all of history has the church been presented with so diverse a population to reach and to disciple. And never have counselors encountered so challenging and complex a generation as the baby boomers whom we seek to counsel.

NOTES

1. Elaine Tyler May, *Homeward Bound* (New York: Basic Books, 1988).
2. Landon Y. Jones, *Great Expectations: America and the Baby Boom Generation* (New York : Coward, McCann and Geoghegan, 1980), 25.

3. May, *Homeward Bound*, 136–37.

4. Jones, *Great Expectations*, 21.

5. Evan Thomas, "Growing Pains at 40," *Time* (May 19, 1986), 24.

6. Paul C. Light, *Baby Boomers* (New York: Norton, 1988), 20–21.

7. Doug Murren, *The Baby Boomerang: Catching Baby Boomers as They Return to Church* (Ventura, Calif.: Regal, 1990), 168–69. Italics are in the original.

8. Jones, *Great Expectations*, 51.

9. Mike Bellah, *Baby Boom Believers* (Wheaton, Ill.: Tyndale House, 1988), 24.

10. Thomas, "Growing Pains at 40."

11. From a series of articles by Michelle Ingrassia, published in *Newsday* (Long Island, N.Y.: June 1–3, 1986). This quotation was cited by Hans Finzel, *Help! I'm a Baby Boomer* (Wheaton, Ill.: Victor Books, 1989).

12. Approximately 80 percent of the older baby boomers reached age 18 without experiencing the divorce of their parents; only half of the later baby boomers had a similar experience.

13. Cited by Light, *Baby Boomers*, 78.

14. Jones, *Great Expectations*, 1.

15. Bellah discusses this briefly in *Baby Boom Believers*, chapter 3.

16. Light, *Baby Boomers*, 201.

17. Joe Cappo, *FutureScope* (Chicago: Longman Financial Services Publishing, 1990).

18. This is the emphasis in Murren's book *The Baby Boomerang*.

Chapter 2

Baby Boomer Careers

Dr. Douglas LaBier is a Washington psychiatrist whose patients include some of the most successful up-and-coming young professionals in the nation's capital. Many have good educations, outstanding credentials, high incomes, and important positions in their power-driven careers. On the surface, these people have it all. They are envied by their families, their friends, and their less-successful colleagues. But behind the glittering facades, many are miserable.

In the psychiatrist's office, they describe the loneliness, anxiety, depression, emptiness, and inner conflicts that accompany their fast-track careers. Some have sought relief by working harder or by trying to find peace and happiness through rampant consumerism and glamorous lifestyles. Others have turned to drugs or alcohol as a way of escape. Some have vented their frustrations on their long-suffering families. Almost all feel unbalanced, unfulfilled, and out of control.

LaBier's insightful book[1] describes a seven-year study of these outwardly successful but inwardly unhappy people whose job dissatisfactions have filled their lives with unhappiness, broken relationships, and shattered self-concepts. These are people who expected to succeed—and did—only to find that their lives are filled with futility, endless activity, and emotional turmoil.

BABY BOOMER CAREER TRENDS

Dr. LaBier's patients are a minority. No one group of people in a single locality can represent an entire generation. But the doctor's patients typify millions of others whose lives are deeply affected by their careers, vocational aspirations, struggles at work, employment changes, and (for many) job failures. Baby boomers now comprise over half the work force. They are changing both how the nation works and the way we look at our work.

In contrast to previous generations, baby boomers tend to have much less company loyalty but a greater concern about self-fulfillment and individual career success. Women out-number men in the baby boom work force, and dual career households are the widely accepted norm. As we move toward the new century there will be an upsurge of people who work from their homes,[2] and workers will increasingly change jobs and careers as they get older. Some estimates suggest that by the year 2000, the average adult will make four to six career changes during his or her lifetime.[3]

Whatever one concludes about baby boomers, there always will be exceptions; in their work habits and experiences, for example, this generation is filled with diversity. They are not all white, career oriented, or workaholics. They do not all sacrifice their families so they can get ahead at work, nor has the baby boom generation "withdrawn into its own world of career and condo."[4] As a group, however, baby boom workers tend to show several unique characteristics.

FLEXIBLE SKILLS

None of us needs to be reminded that the world is changing at a rapid pace. Politics, education, families, technology, business, economics, media, medicine, sciences, personal values, religion—all are being transformed at future-shock speed. Baby boomers have triggered many of these changes, have lived through them, and expect to experience increasing change in the future.

Much as Sputnik shocked the west in the fifties, corporations in the baby boom countries have been jolted by the realization that a unified Europe, a highly sophisticated Japan, and a variety of other, mostly Pacific Rim, nations are surpassing us in terms of production, technical know-how, cost control, and product quality.

In response, enlightened organizations in every segment of business are making changes. Corporations are becoming less bureaucratic, hierarchical, and static. Team-based production is replacing more conventional systems in many industries. Robots are taking over assembly lines, and the information explosion is transforming us from an industrial economy to an information economy.[5] Unlike their grandparents and parents, few workers today are able to stay with the same unchanging job throughout life. *Flexible* is the password for the future, according to a *Business Week* report.

> Advancing new computer technology is . . . changing the nature of white-collar and service-sector work. Many formerly fragmented tasks are being converted into jobs requiring multiple skills. Computer networks, integrating diverse functions, also require employees who can work as a team, more often on projects than on tasks. . . . The shift to more complex, project-type jobs should suit well-educated baby boomers, who are demanding broader responsibilities at work as they age. But many workers, particularly younger ones, are deficient in computer literacy or even basic work skills, which places new pressure on corporations to educate labor.[6]

Whether or not they like the idea, workers in the future will have to keep their skills fresh or risk being relegated to menial, low-paying jobs. In an era of swift technological change, experience often counts far less than up-to-date skills and a willingness for workers to keep learning. Like almost everyone else in the society, counselors of the future will have to keep growing, learning, improving their skills, and finding ways to help others do the same.

CHANGING CAREERS

Baby boomers have been described as the first generation whose careers will not last for a lifetime. Some are forced to change because of layoffs and company takeovers. Others, such as the corporate climbers who consult with Dr. LaBier, are dissatisfied and looking for ways to make their own changes. Many shift because they feel blocked in reaching their vocational goals, so they look for better opportunities.

Mindy and Dave, for example, are thirtysomething, parents of two school-age children, residents of a Denver suburb.[7] Both graduated from high school, went to college, married after graduation, and got jobs in different companies. Dave discovered quickly that he did not like business, so he enrolled part-time in law school, eventually became a lawyer, and now works in a downtown corporate office. After helping to put her husband through school, Mindy quit her job so she could be a full-time mother and stay at home with the children. Subsequently she has developed a business that permits her to work out of her home. Both Mindy and Dave are in occupations that they never would have predicted when they married twelve years ago.

A more recent vocational trend is what one writer calls "downshifting."[8] Instead of scrambling for career advancement, some are turning down promotions, moving away from pressure occupations, redefining what it means to be successful, going into business for themselves, or giving up job security for the freedom to pursue dreams and spend time with their families or their hobbies. Downshifters are taking control of their careers instead of being controlled by their work.

This sounds ideal and probably works fine for professionals who are courageous enough and well enough established to make these self-directed changes. But most baby boomers do not have that luxury. Most cannot afford to quit or to downshift, even when they are dissatisfied with their jobs. As a result, thousands face the reality of staying stuck in frustrating work situations that offer little hope for improvement.

Even so, many look for opportunities to change. New York University's Center for Career and Life Planning, which counsels adults on career changes, has seen a 25 percent annual boost in consultations.[9] Many baby boomers realize that they will make several planned or unanticipated changes in their jobs and vocations during their lifetimes. This gives people the freedom to change careers if they get started in a direction that they later dislike. But knowing that change is likely, some baby boomers are reluctant to make long-term commitments to vocations or to job training. As a result, they drift from position to position.

All of this has significant implications for counselors who are trained to help others with vocational guidance and life planning.

WOMEN AND THE MARKETPLACE

World War II made a radical change in the labor force. When the men went off to war, leaving a severe worker shortage on the home front, women went off to work. Previously, working women were mostly single and often in sex-typed positions where they worked as teachers, nurses, maids, librarians, telephone operators, hairdressers, sales clerks, or secretaries. But the war changed all of that.

Women, single and married, young and older, filled a variety of jobs. In the shipbuilding industry, for example, the number of women who held positions as riveters went from 36 to 160,000. When the war ended, many working women stayed at their jobs, and after a brief postwar dip, the percentage of women in the labor force continued to rise.[10]

During the 1980s, two-thirds of the 17 million jobs created in the United States were filled by women, and the fastest-growing segment of the work force was comprised of mothers with preschool children.[11] The gap in earnings between male and female workers has persisted, but with increasing frequency women have moved into significant professional and managerial careers. During the past quarter century, the number of women lawyers, judges, and physicians has more than tripled. Women now hold about one-fifth of all positions in these fields, and an estimated 40 percent of accountants, real estate agents, and elected or appointed officeholders are female. Unlike a generation ago when only one working woman in ten had a college degree, a quarter of today's female workers are college graduates. Women, including many who have raised their children and then gone back to school, comprise over half of all college students.[12]

Most of these women in college and in the work force are baby boomers or the daughters of baby boomers. While many enjoy their work and feel challenged by fulfilling careers, others work because they have to. Their salaries are needed to help their families survive. In single-parent families, women bear the major financial burden, and in almost all families they continue to take major responsibility for running the home and raising the children.

This can lead to worry, tension, and exhaustion. In a recent *New York Times* poll of working women, 83 percent felt torn between the conflicting demands of their jobs and desires to do a better job in raising their children. When asked to name the most important problem faced by women today, the number one issue was the tension between work and family.[13] All of this presents a challenge to counselors and others who are committed to helping baby boomers cope with and avoid work-related stresses.

LIMITED ROOM AT THE TOP

The notion of a middle-age crisis spilled into the counseling literature a decade or so before the earliest baby boomers turned forty. Every year more of this generation enters the middle-age ranks, and by the turn of the century almost one-third of all Americans will be in the 40–59 age bracket. Helping baby boomers face the crises and disappointments of this period in life will be a major task for Christian counselors.

Middle age can be the most productive time in life. Income is highest, and career fulfillment is often greatest. Disappointments hit hard, but if there is good health and hope for better things ahead, the middle aged are able to spring back and keep going. Some business analysts have predicted a coming period of "extended economic prosperity"[14] because middle-aged baby boomers—highly educated, at peak effectiveness, and financially able to make investments—are now entering corporate boardrooms and assuming leadership roles in business.

All of this sounds like fantasy to younger baby boomers or to those who have reached midlife with their aspirations unfulfilled and their lives adrift. Many of those who squeezed into overcrowded classrooms and pushed to enter congested professions now find that there is even less room at the top. A generation that expected to be Chiefs and that studied and worked hard to reach their goals, is discovering that they will forever be Braves. "As each person tries to climb up the business and professional hierarchies, he or she will find other baby boomer competitors blocking the way," according to Landon Jones. "Millions of them crowded on the first steps of management will be forced to stay right there."[15]

This lack of advancement can be devastating to baby boom individuals who base their self-worth on whether or not they are successful vocationally. Of course, some workers never expected to rise in their companies, so they are not surprised or disappointed when their jobs reach permanent plateaus. But for many, the first twenty years of their adult lives have been geared to moving up. When the anticipated promotions do not come and the hoped-for moves are blocked, the psychological blows can be crushing, especially for people who feel they are too old or unmotivated to start over.

BABY BOOMER CAREER GOALS

Perhaps you have attended some. If you are a counselor, you may have led a few. Seminars designed to help people plan and advance their careers have become popular and numerous during the past several years while baby boomers have been growing into adulthood.

The message in these seminars is often the same. Make a list of your goals, long-range and short-term. Decide on the steps needed to get where you want to go. Start working on the list, one step at a time, and reward yourself with each level of accomplishment. Eventually, you will reach the end goals that you set out to achieve.

Advice like this is not bad. It can help people focus their activities and systematically advance their careers. But seminar leaders almost never suggest that some people will not make it. Hardly ever do we hear that the strengths, weaknesses, and realism of the anticipated objectives should be carefully evaluated before one embarks on an ambitious goal-directed program. Even Christian leaders tend to overlook the more basic question, "What does God want me to do?"

MEETING NEEDS: MATERIAL AND EMOTIONAL

Why do people work? For many of us, faced with monthly bills and mortgage payments, the answer is simple. We work to earn money so we can meet our material needs. "I owe, I owe, so off to work I go!" proclaims the bumper sticker. Making ends meet and surviving from paycheck to paycheck are the only goals that some people ever have.

Like the rest of us, baby boomers want to pay their bills, but that is not their primary reason for working. One survey found that 68 percent of the generation wanted jobs in which they could express themselves, and 77 percent were looking for positions that would be challenging and fulfilling.[16]

Regrettably, most jobs are not like that. A lot of work is boring and repetitive, in the company of employers or colleagues who are not especially interesting or stimulating. When baby boom workers encounter this kind of vocational reality, they are less inclined than their parents to stay where they are and stick it out. More often, they begin looking for something new, and they start thinking about changing jobs or careers. Often they look for ways to build stimulating and personally satisfying lives apart from the job. Tennis, weekends away, and a variety of leisure activities replace the dedication that characterized the organization man of the fifties.

People in the nineties want work that will satisfy their emotional needs and give them a sense of being in control of their lives and destinies. "They're questioning, and in many cases jettisoning, their devotion to careers that formed the center-piece of their lives during the workaholic eighties," according to one observer. "Men and women are trying to find a model for their lives that will put them at the helm and eliminate the feeling that they're simply passengers just being carried along."[17] Many are looking for careers that have flexible hours and more free time, even if this means slower advancement. Meeting material needs is important, but meeting emotional needs often is of far greater concern.

REDEFINING SUCCESS

It would be wrong to assume that baby boomers do not want to be successful. Despite dissatisfaction, competition, and frequent frustration in the work place most do want to get ahead, and many still equate success with higher incomes and greater influence. These people do work harder, aim higher, and run faster than before.[18]

But many are reluctant to equate success with long hours, frenzied workaholism, or dedication to climbing some corporate ladder. Baby boomers of all ages have seen the psychological depression, broken families, physical fatigue, and constant pressures that often devastate the lives of those who are driven to get ahead. Climbers who reach the top have money and power, but they might not have much else. In the eyes of some baby boomers, the people at the top are the most persistent, the most ruthless, or the most able to contribute to the bottom line, but that does not mean they are the most qualified, capable, or intelligent. Consider, for example, the widespread belief that anyone who is smart enough to be a competent politician is also smart enough to stay out of politics. In the minds of some baby boomers, the smartest people of all are those who avoid the frenzied career-driven fast-track.

We have become a nation driven by FAX messages, car phones, conference calls, and answering machines. These technical advances are supposed to save time, but instead they have made our lives more complex, more hectic, and more driven. And the pace of life seems to be getting faster. Almost everything seems to get done at the last minute. There is little opportunity for reflection and almost no time to build quality into one's work. Issues of the heart—like compassion, generosity, courage, and the capacity to love—are discouraged in the fast-track world where people are controlled by their own careers.[19] Can any counselor blame baby boomers, especially those who are younger, if they resist stepping on such a meaningless and potentially destructive treadmill?

But if reaching the top is no longer a measure of success, what is?

In the late 1960s, a Columbia University sophomore published a widely read account of the student protests against the Vietnam War. James S. Kunen, who called himself "a college revolutionary," wrote a rambling, often angry, diary account that described the attitudes, actions, and antiestablishment values of the first-wave baby boomers who believed they could change the world.[20] As young adults, they had no concern about getting ahead or fitting into more traditional work roles. These people liked to be known as young radicals, and they were intent on making a difference.

Two decades after his book appeared, Kunen was thirty-seven, working as a professional writer for *People* magazine. Like many of his radical student colleagues, the young Columbia protester had grown up and entered the establishment world that he once so vehemently resisted.

In a brief essay written for *Time* magazine,[21] Kunen looked back to the sixties and noted that for many of his peers, "the greatest concern about a career was how to avoid one." But things changed in the twenty years that followed. "We no longer believe that we can remake the world. Instead we adapt to it," Kunen wrote in his essay. "We have our careers. . . . Our middle-class instinct (subliminal, unshakable) to 'make something of yourself' and contribute to society, has led us down the Establishment road—what we used to call selling out."

Will those who currently try to define success apart from money or power eventually go "down the Establishment road" and get back onto the traditional fast-track? That does not seem likely because so many baby boomers feel crowded out of higher-level positions, and many are resisting the corporate climb. Some may never come to grips with the real meaning of success or self-worth (despite the help of counselors), but few of these people will be content to go on living the way they do, with lives that seem empty.[22] Will any find comfort in looking back, as Kunen did in the last sentence in his article?

He wrote, "It's good that there was a time when we stood up for what we believed in—which, as you get along and go along, is not something you do every day."

BABY BOOMER CAREER PROBLEMS

Adult baby boomers may do little to stand up for what they believe, but they do have to get along from day to day. For most that means dealing with the problems related to work. Like other problems, work-related issues are highly individualistic because no two baby boomers are the same. Their career problems depend on each person's age, sex, level of education, socioeconomic status, aspirations, type of work, personality, race, and ability to be flexible. Often career direction depends on both what you know and who you know. Despite this diversity, there are three common problems that baby boomers and their counselors face: limited opportunities, vocational and financial insecurities, and career-driven lifestyles.

LIMITED OPPORTUNITIES

Richard Majors is a baby boomer with a doctorate in psychology from the University of Illinois, a position on the faculty of the University of Wisconsin-Eau Claire, and a special interest in the problems of black men like himself. Victimized by racism, discrimination, poverty, and limited opportunities, many African-American males have become frustrated, angry, alienated, and distrustful of the dominant white culture. Like others of their generation, black baby boomers were told that they could succeed and attain status, respect, and well-paying positions. But when they reached adulthood many discovered what so many in this generation were learning: their youthful aspirations had far outstripped later reality. Unlike many white baby boomers, however, a much larger portion of blacks did not make it into college, graduate school, professions, or high-status careers.[23] More than others, these black baby boomers have felt squeezed out of the occupations and opportunities that are more available to people with different color skin.

How have these frustrated blacks reacted? How have they expressed their masculinity in a society where they lack access to educational and occupational opportunities? Many develop what psychologist Majors has called "cool pose,"[24] a type of behavior that lets them "act cool and show the dominant culture (and themselves) that they are strong, proud, and capable of survival irrespective of their status in American society." This cool pose is seen in mannerisms, handshakes, speech, gestures, clothing, or hairstyles. Sometimes cool pose is shown by African-American athletes or performers whose mannerisms (like the stylish slam-dunks of a basketball, break-dancing in the end zone, or rap-talking) "empower black males by helping them to appear competent, to satisfy mainstream norms and expectations, and to survive." Regrettably, cool pose also makes its appearance in toughness, excessive risk-taking, substance abuse, sexual promiscuity, and a willingness to use violence in resolving interpersonal conflict.

Discussions of baby boomers rarely touch on the frustrations of impoverished and powerless individuals who want to be good providers, good citizens, and good family members, but who struggle continually with the inability to find a decent job in the marketplace.[25] The frustrations, of course, are not limited to people of any one race, but the problems are greater for those who have less education, lower socioeconomic status, and minority status. For many baby boomers, vocational opportunities are limited because of changing business and economic conditions, job plateaus, and an overcrowded job market.

Despite the optimistic assessments and predictions of many economists or writers in business magazines, adult baby boomers often find that suitable jobs are not available. Mergers, takeovers, budget trimming, attempts to streamline operations, the pressure to compete with lower costs and often higher quality from overseas—all of these have eliminated thousands of jobs in business, industry, government, education, and almost every other segment of society. The unskilled and uneducated suffer most because they are not qualified to find alternative work. But younger baby boomers also suffer when more tenured employees are retained but the newer employees are let go.

Those who keep their jobs are assured of paychecks and worker benefits, but increasingly these employees are forced to face the realities of job plateaus. Baby boomers are accustomed to moving quickly, and most want to move up—fast. In reality, most will be spending more and more time on each plateau. For many, promotions will be slower in coming, or they may not come at all because those at the top are staying on the job longer, there are too many baby boomers scrambling for too few positions, and eager baby busters are entering the job market and adding to the competition. "More and more baby boomers will be trapped in dead-end jobs, or waiting longer for promotions," writes Paul Light in his book *Baby Boomers*.[26] "They will spend more time on each plateau up the promotion climb. They will need to redefine what it means to be successful, to be willing to wait in line for upward movement, and learn to deal with the frustrations of being left behind. . . . No matter how many ways a corporation does it, hundreds of thousands of baby boomers are going to be told they are washed up in coming years."

All of this can lead to profound disappointment, increased depression, damaged self-concepts, painful readjustments, and reduced worker productivity. Will many of these frustrated baby boomers turn their energies and interests away from work and more toward family and leisure activities? Will some withdraw psychologically from their careers, give minimal effort to their work, and move to on-the-job-retirement, at a time when competition from abroad demands more productivity, rather than less, in the baby boom countries? The increasingly prevalent promotion squeeze can have significant impact on the nation's economy as well as on the psychological well-being of baby boomers and their families.

Promotion squeezes and job plateaus never entered the thinking of Michael and Paula Harries when they worked for a computer company in Massachusetts. First-wave baby boomers, they had little concern about the overcrowded competition that was lower on the corporate ladder. Each had enjoyed significant promotions, salary increases, and a variety of business perks.

But in 1989, when Michael and Paula were entering their forties and enjoying peak career success, their company was bought out, four thousand were let go, and the Harrieses were suddenly and unexpectedly unemployed. Finding other work proved to be impossible, and it was not easy to be pinching pennies to make ends meet. Eventually, Michael and Paula joined with two partners to form their own consulting firm. Thus far it has been a successful venture, and the pressures of the corporate world have been gladly abandoned. The Harrieses have more time for their two children and more opportunity to be creative.[27]

This is a story with a happy ending, but what about those who lack the skills, resourcefulness, funding, willingness to take risks, motivation, or know-how to start businesses of their own? These are frustrated, unhappy baby boomers whose hopes and vocational aspirations have been squelched by an overpopulated market of job seekers.

PERSISTING INSECURITIES

After a 10-year bender of gaudy dreams and godless consumerism, Americans are starting to trade down. They want to reduce their attachments to status symbols, fast-track careers and great expectations of Having It All. Upscale is out; downscale is in. . . .

In place of materialism, many Americans are embracing simpler pleasures and homier values. They've been thinking hard about what really matters in their lives, and they've decided to make some changes. What matters is having time for family and friends, rest and recreation, good deeds and spirituality.[28]

Words like these would never have surfaced in a popular magazine during the Me Decade of the 1980s, but some suggest that the 1990s is becoming a We Generation where lifestyles are simpler and less self-centered. This is happening to the burnouts from Wall Street, according to one sociologist, but the return to simpler living appears to be a phenomenon that crosses social lines and is true also of immigrant groups and people who are underprivileged.[29]

Some of these changes surely come from the increasing job insecurities that many workers are facing. Few of us have stable careers, guaranteed high incomes, and certain job security. Economic and political changes are forcing many people, including baby boomers, to face the unrealities of their affluent and free-spending lifestyles. Cutting back, cost accounting, and tightly controlled budgeting have become standard ways of life for individuals and families as well as for corporations, school districts, and local governments. Thousands are being forced to replace their hedonistic, great expectations with pared-down, more realistic aspirations.

CAREER-DRIVEN LIFESTYLES

Cutting back and downshifting is becoming popular even with those whose careers are moving along smoothly and without apparent hindrances. Many baby boomers are still workaholics, engulfed in their careers and pushing for perfection. But grueling hours, ferocious competition, and neglect of almost everything except one's work, can extract a powerful toll from one's health, relationships, sense of well-being, and communion with God. As they reach middle age, many baby boomers see that their heroes at the top often have big offices, plenty of money, and successful careers, but in the process they have lost their marriages, their kids, the joys of living, and often their freedom.

Is the climb worth the effort and the sacrifices?

Several years ago an unimpressive-looking little book became an unexpected best seller.[30] Illustrated with line drawings and written in an easy to read style, it told the story of a caterpillar who found a column of other caterpillars, climbing on top of one another, each struggling to reach the top of the pile. As he made his way up the caterpillar pillar, the hero of the story stepped on faces and sometimes knocked down other climbers with abandon, but eventually he reached his goal. High above the clouds, he looked around from his precarious perch and discovered there was nothing there except other teetering columns of caterpillars, each topped by an insecure climber. Only the butterflies who soared in the sky above seemed to be genuinely free.

The caterpillar hero decided that the climb was not worth the effort, so he started back down the column. As he descended he proclaimed the message that the climb led to nothing, but the upwardly mobile caterpillars mocked him, refused to believe that he was going downward voluntarily, and soundly rejected his message. Eventually, the caterpillar got back to the firm ground, spun a cocoon—as caterpillars are supposed to do—and emerged as the butterfly that he had once hoped to become by climbing.

Trapped in hectic lifestyles, demanding career climbs, and endless pressure, many baby boomers are questioning the wisdom of their upward quests. Many still try to brighten their lives with expensive purchases and affluent lifestyles, but often there is a persisting emptiness. Others discover that stress-dulling addictions or workaholic lifestyles cannot hide their career-related pressures. Occasionally they consult with psychiatrists like Douglas LaBier. Few are likely to remain satisfied at plateau levels, but many are moving back down the ladder, shifting to simpler lifestyles and less demanding vocations.

In the years ahead, many of these career-evaluating baby boomers are likely to look for career-related counseling that will help them get off their vocational treadmills and find fulfillment elsewhere. Christian counselors can help this generation find places of service that will build on their God-given abilities. In part, our work will involve helping baby boomers reexamine and reformulate their values. That is the topic that we consider next.

NOTES

1. Douglas LaBier, *Modern Madness: The Emotional Fallout of Success* (Reading, Mass.: Addison-Wesley, 1986).

2. George Barna, *The Frog in the Kettle: What Christians Need to Know About Life in the Year 2000* (Ventura, Calif.: Regal, 1990), 103. According to Barna, people in 6 million households worked from their homes in 1990. The number is estimated to jump to 20 million households by the year 2000.

3. Barna, *The Frog*, 104.

4. Martin Cetron and Owen Davies, *American Renaissance: Our Life at the Turn of the 21st Century* (New York: St. Martin's Press, 1989), 91.

5. John Naisbitt and Patricia Aburdene, *Megatrends 2000: Ten New Directions for the 1990s* (New York: Morrow, 1990), 40–48.

6. Elizabeth Ehrlich, "How the Next Decade Will Differ: Six Key Trends that Will Shape America in the 1990s," *Business Week* (September 25, 1989), 152.

7. References to people in this book are to real persons, known to one or both of the authors. Unless we indicate otherwise, names and identifying details have been changed.

8. Amy Saltzman, *Downshifting: Reinventing Success on a Slower Tract* (New York: HarperCollins, 1991).

9. Susan B. Garland, "Those Aging Baby Boomers," *Business Week* (May 20, 1991), 109.

10. Landon Y. Jones, *Great Expectations: America and the Baby Boom Generation* (New York: Coward, McCann and Geoghegan, 1980), 166.

11. Sylvia Ann Hewlett, "The Feminization of the Work Force," *NPQ* (Winter 1990), 13.

12. Louis S. Richman, "The New Middle Class: How it Lives," *Fortune* (August 13, 1990), 107–9.

13. Hewlett, "Feminization."

14. See, for example, Karen Pennar, "Economic Prospects for the Year 2000: Surprise—We Could Be Entering the Most Prosperous Decade Yet," *Business Week* (September 25, 1989), 158–70.

15. Jones, *Great Expectations*, 281.

16. Ibid., 285.

17. This is a quotation from Douglas LaBier, cited in an article by Steven Allen, "Working It Out," *Chicago Tribune*, April 24, 1991, section 7, page 5.

18. Saltzman, *Downshifting*, 39. In this section of the chapter we have drawn on some of Saltzman's conclusions in chapter 2, "Images of Success."

19. Michael Maccoby, *The Gamesman* (New York: Simon and Schuster, 1976).

20. James S. Kunen, *The Strawberry Statement—Notes of a College Revolutionary* (New York: Random House, 1968).

21. James S. Kunen, "Strawberry Restatement," *Time* (May 19, 1986), 41.

22. Daniel Levinson, "The Baby-Boomers' Midlife Crisis," *Fortune* (March 26, 1990), 157–58.

23. According to one report, nearly one in four black men in the 20–29 year age group is in prison, on probation, or on parole—more than the number of black men of all ages enrolled in higher education. This information was cited in an article about Richard Majors, written by Peter Freiberg, "Black Men May Act Cool to Advertise Masculinity," *APA Monitor* (March 1991), 30.

24. Richard Majors, "Cool Pose: A New Approach Towards a Systematic Study and Understanding of Black Male Behavior," Ph.D. diss., University of Illinois-Urbana, 1987.

25. With Jacob Gordon, professor of African and African-American Studies at the University of Kansas, Richard Majors has recently published *The Black Male: His Present Status and His Future* (Chicago: Nelson-Hall, 1991). Some of the issues discussed in these paragraphs are dealt with in detail.

26. Paul Light, *Baby Boomers* (New York: Norton, 1988), 257, 259.

27. Gary McWilliams, "How to Fall off the Corporate Ladder—And Thrive," *Business Week* (May 20, 1991), 110.

28. Ann Blackman, Melissa Ludtke, and William McWhirter, "The Simple Life, " *Time* (April 8, 1991), 58.

29. This is the observation of sociologist Stephen Warner of the University of Illinois at Chicago. Cited by Blackman, et. al., "The Simple Life, " 59.

30. Trina Paulus, *Hope for the Flowers* (New York: Paulist Press, 1972) .

Chapter 3

Baby Boomer Values

Has the yuppie generation died?

Since the word *yuppie* first appeared in the early 1980s, an estimated twenty-two thousand magazine and newspaper articles have described, analyzed, criticized, sometimes idolized, and more recently eulogized this prominent minority segment of the baby boom generation. Yuppies were described as consumption-centered people. Some called them fashion conscious, greedy, career driven, self-centered, and ruled by the love of money, success, power, and prominence. They wanted the good life and the finest in quality. *Newsweek* proclaimed 1984 "The Year of the Yuppie," and Christians pondered strategies for reaching this "pin-striped mission field."[1]

Walter Shapiro calls himself a "card-carrying baby boomer" whose values and lifestyle put him squarely in the yuppie camp. "But I was never one of those yuppies; they drove BMWs," he protested. "That was the whole point— yuppies were always somebody else. Almost no one fit all of the requirements of age (young), income (high), geography (urban), attitude (selfish) and affections (Filofaxes and yellow power ties)."[2] Shapiro seems to suggest that yuppies almost never existed, except in the minds of people who were trying to understand the values of a group of people whose image of the good life was far different than that of their parents in the fifties.

None of us can understand or effectively counsel baby boomers without some awareness of their values. These values largely determine how members of this or any other generation perceive the world, act, feel, think, plan for the future, relate to others, respond to religion, or cope with problems.

FINDING VALUES

A person's values are his or her beliefs and standards about what is good, just, right, true, or beautiful. For centuries most people got their values from parents, teachers, or religious leaders, many of whom shared similar viewpoints. But in the late twentieth century, while baby boomers were growing up, many of our long accepted and sometimes cherished values were challenged and thrown to the winds.

This values upheaval arose from a number of sources, including widespread reverence for rational thought and the emerging information explosion. Even before the start of this century, we were becoming increasingly rational and objective. There was fascination with Freud's speculations concerning the unconscious and with Jung's theories about archetypes and the meaning of dreams. But at least in America, people were more impressed with science, technology, logical thinking, empiricism, and the emphasis on objectivity. Behaviorism quickly dominated psychology. Art and architecture became more austere and less an expression of inner subjectivity. For many, the higher criticism, pragmatism, and rational foundations undergirding liberal theology were preferred to a faith that involved "being sure of what we hope for and certain of things we do not see" (Hebrews 11:1 NIV.) Baby boomers began to question and challenge everything.

Along with this shift in thinking came a variety of technologies that have saturated us with the voices and values of others. The media, especially television, have exposed us to values and viewpoints from a variety of sources. As a result, many people have no idea where they (or others) stand on anything. At the barricades in the sixties, the first-wave baby boomers expressed their disdain for traditionalism, absolutes, the morals of their parents, and the intellectual conclusions of their professors. They lauded relativism and embraced a hedonistic morality based on six one-syllable words: "If it feels good, do it!"

As a result, a whole generation now claims to have minds that are open to all religions, all people, all viewpoints, all ideas. University of Chicago professor Allan Bloom has argued convincingly, however, that these same minds are ignorant of the great thinking of the past, intellectually lazy, and closed to any suggestion that some ideas are more true than and superior to others.[3] Often, baby boomers have accepted a philosophy that exalts the most recent thing, "adores today, worships tomorrow, disavows yesterday, and loathes antiquity."[4] On college campuses, many students laud "deconstructionism," a radical viewpoint that encourages readers to look painstakingly at written materials, including classic literary texts, to tear down accepted interpretations and to come up with a nearly infinite variety of meanings that vary from person to person. Deconstructionists shout against elitism, taste, tradition, standards, truth, and accepted certainties of the past. Almost everything is subjected to the same relentless leveling.[5]

Is it surprising that millions of baby boomers feel like they are drifting, with no absolute values or beliefs to which they can anchor their lives? Many feel empty inside, without firm standards of right and wrong, and with no valid guidelines for raising children, maintaining a marriage, building careers, doing business, or finding God. Now, perhaps more than at any time in baby boomer history, these core-less people are looking for truth, identity, and something to believe in that will give their lives a real center.[6] Christian counselors and church leaders bring a biblically based perspective that can meet these baby boomer needs.

MUSIC, MUSIC, MUSIC

If you want to understand a culture, listen to its music. Sociologists, anthropologists, and historians all discovered this many years ago.

Surely no generation in history has been more plugged into music than contemporary baby boomers and their children. Few, if any, past generations have so openly expressed their values through song. Never before have instruments and voices exploded with so many decibels; never before have people been able to surround their brains and their lives with nonstop music. "If you want to understand this generation, you had better give a lot of attention to its music," a long-haired expert in contemporary Christian music told us when we were first thinking about writing this book. "Baby boomers are shaped by their music. Nobody should expect to teach, counsel, sell to, evangelize, or otherwise influence baby boomers, unless their music is taken seriously." Churches that are reaching baby boomers have already discovered that high-quality contemporary music is of crucial importance. Educator Allan Bloom would agree. For "those who are interested in psychological health, music is at the center of education."[7]

Bloom notes that music has had a role in shaping values for centuries, but baby boomer music is in many respects unique. It tends to be so loud—especially among younger baby boomers and baby busters—that conversation is impossible. Frequently it is played through earphones that shut out others and prevent interpersonal interactions. Contemporary musicians often cater to young people whose values are in the formative stages. And many of the values that come through music applaud violence, uncontrolled sexuality, unfaithfulness, relativism, and occultic practices. "Rock gives children, on a silver platter, with all the public authority of the entertainment industry, everything their parents always used to tell them they had to wait for until they grew up and would understand better. . . . The result is nothing less than parents' loss of control over their children's moral education at a time when no one else is seriously concerned with it."[8]

Bloom compares the baby boomer addiction to music with the effects of youthful drug use. In time, but often with difficulty, most get over their exclusive passion for the addiction. Eventually, students "assiduously study economics or the professions and the Michael Jackson costume will slip off to reveal a Brooks Brothers suit beneath. They will want to get ahead and live comfortably. But this life is as empty and as false as the one they left behind."[9] As older baby boomers shift in their musical tastes, the strains of country music reflect the emptiness, lonelines, and unfaithfulness that characterizes many of their lives. The distractions and value messages of nonstop music leave the hearers with little awareness of the great traditions from the past, limited appreciation for the richness of in-depth education, and few solid, time-tested values to guide their present lives or to shape their future directions.

BOOMER-SHAPED VALUES

Ray Dupont describes himself as a baby boomer pastor of a baby boomer church. Probably thousands of others are like him—raised in a baby boomer culture, exposed to baby boomer values, and committed to building a church that nurtures baby boomer spiritual growth. A few of the older members of Pastor Dupont's Ohio congregation worry about the baby boomer presence and wonder if the values of this generation eventually will doom the church to destruction. Others are like the pastor, who has a realistic but generally bright and enthusiastic perception of his postwar parishioners. People who work with this generation know that little is accomplished by bashing baby boomers or condemning them for their values.

In an article describing his congregation, Ray Dupont lists several characteristics that all baby boomer churches share. Summarized in Table 2 , these are really values that determine how many in this generation think, feel, and act. Each of the values listed in the table, and most of those described in the following paragraphs can be positive and healthy. They are not always bad; sometimes they are very good. They do not always undermine therapy; often they keep counselors alert, relevant, and committed to counseling excellence.

Table 2
Common Baby Boomer Values

Relevance—Baby boomers focus on themselves. They constantly ask, "What's in it for me?" and they expect sermons, seminars, educational programs, and reading materials to be both relevant and of the highest quality. They prize excellence and shun mediocrity.

Participation—These people enjoy active involvement in sports, education, entertainment, church activities, and almost everything else they do. Baby boomers like small groups, interaction, and experience. They dislike formal lectures, long sermons, and most other passive spectator activities.

Flexibility—Baby boomers have grown up in a world marked by change. They resist rigidity, traditions, and "the same old church services." They can choose from a variety of menu items, television channels, shopping center stores, and course offerings at the local community college. In a similar way, many shop for churches and are willing to change if the present church does not meet their needs. Few have emotional ties to any one denomination. For this generation, the name of the game is flexibility.

Enthusiasm for Causes—The zeal that fueled the antiwar movement of the sixties is now channeled into other activities. Enthusiasm on both sides of the abortion issue illustrates this. When baby boomer fervor is directed to worthwhile causes, the result can be major positive social and spiritual impact.

Informality—Baby boomers like to go casual. Except for many of their weddings, they do not like to dress formally, interact in formal ways, use formal titles, or participate in formal meetings. Comfort, openness, and casual interaction permit a focus on things other than outward appearance.

Questioning—A generation that grew up with the message that they should ask questions now continues to challenge, scrutinize, and evaluate almost everything they hear. There is little tolerance for authoritarian monologues, sermon oratory, or demands for blind obedience. Clergy, politicians, therapists, and others are examined not only for what they say, but also for their lifestyles and honesty. Leaders and ideas are accepted and followed wholeheartedly, once they pass the evaluations.

Acceptance—Tolerance and equality are widely accepted among baby boomers. They openly accept people of different race, gender, marital status, or lifestyle preferences. Baby boomers, even those who are Christians, readily accept the rights of others to believe what they want about God, religion, sex, politics, or almost any other issue. Because of their tendencies to be accepting, baby boomers are able to show selfless love, although their tolerance also can dampen evangelistic zeal.

Lack of Commitment—Baby boomers have been criticized because they appear to be committed primarily to themselves. As a result, they often do not stay faithful to one church, the same employer, brand names, a lifelong career, or consistent attendance at worship services. Few want long-term commitments to therapy. Transience is common, and often commitments are short-term—even commitments to marriage.

Instant Remedies—Baby boomers have grown up with fast food, one-hour cleaners, drive-through car washes, and television programs that solve even the most involved problems in thirty or sixty minutes. This is not a generation that likes to wait. They want fast service, concise answers to their questions, quick solutions to their problems, immediate spiritual growth, short-term academic degree programs, and brief counseling. With most baby boomers, patience is a drag, not a virtue.

Note: Adapted from Ray Dupont, "Adjusting the Focus: Two ways of Looking at Baby Boomers," *The Evangelical Beacon* 64 (April 1991):15-16.

If they were asked to do so, many people might have difficulty listing their values. Most of us do not give much thought to what we really believe and why we think as we do. Values influence our lives, but we rarely put them into words. To understand baby boomer values, therefore, it is best to observe how members of this diverse generation live their lives and express themselves. We will look at five outward expressions of inner baby boom values.

VALUES ARE SEEN IN BABY BOOMER LIFESTYLES

People change as they get older. Everybody knows that. Long before the time of Freud, philosophers, novelists, and other writers were describing the stages through which we all pass as we move from womb to tomb. The lists of developmental stages are different, but the message of change is the same.

This, in part, explains recent shifts in baby boomer lifestyles. No longer teenagers or irresponsible college students, these people are entering midlife, and some are beginning to think much more seriously about the future. The recently formed American Association of Boomers (AAB) drops the word *baby* and has money management and financial planning for retirement among its top priorities.[10]

A generation that still is caricatured as money flaunting, career-chasing, self-centered, and attached to status symbols is changing its way of living. Trendiness and materialism are being replaced by simpler lifestyles and more time with families. In one recent poll that included many baby boomers, 69 percent of the surveyed adults said they would like to "slow down and live a more relaxed life"; only 19 percent wanted to "live a more exciting, faster-paced life." When asked about their priorities, only 13 percent saw importance in keeping up with fashion or trends, and a mere 7 percent thought it was worth bothering to shop for status-symbol products. But 89 percent said it was important these days to spend time with families.[11]

Recreation, healthy living, exercise, rest, time with the family, product quality, looking for good value, using time wisely, saving money, contributing to the welfare of others, spirituality, and a focus on things that last—these basic values are replacing the race to have it all. Popular and scientific articles on the baby boom culture are agreed: there is widespread slowing down and a shifting away from the relentless pursuit of the good life. This may represent a shift in the baby boom mentality. More likely it reflects the more reasoned thinking of a generation that is growing up and settling down.

In the coming years, counselors (especially those who understand the stages in human development) can play a significant role in helping baby boomers with their downshifting, career reevaluations, and struggles with changing lifestyles.

VALUES ARE SEEN IN BABY BOOMER CAUSES

If you are like us, every month you get letters and magazines from mission agencies describing the needs overseas and calling for new efforts to reach others for Christ. Church mission conferences call for more workers and proclaim a now-familiar rallying cry: "Evangelize the World by A.D. 2000!" More than one hundred "megaplans" have been developed, calling for increased efforts, more financial resources, and missionary volunteers who will expand the cause of world evangelization in this decade.[12]

Have you ever noticed who leads this movement? Most of the calls to commitment come from people with gray hair who are over fifty-five, enthusiastically trying to motivate baby boomers to get involved. Very often the appeals fall on deaf ears.

It would be easy to conclude that baby boomers have no interest in anything other than their own careers and personal agendas, but we have seen that increasing evidence suggests otherwise. A generation that fought the establishment and crusaded against war less than thirty years ago is now coming into middle age, the time of life when people are most determined and able to bring change. Many baby boomers continue to harbor their activist tendencies, and they have the potential to launch powerful efforts directed at improving education, strengthening marriage and families, providing better day-care for young children, dealing with aging parents, coping with the AIDS and drug abuse epidemics, doing something about homelessness or illiteracy, fighting crime and poverty, or dealing with teenage pregnancies and dropout rates. "We'll get national health care out of the baby boomers," predicts a senior fellow at the Institute for Policy Studies.[13] The generation that was committed to social causes in the sixties and early seventies shifted to self-centered causes through the eighties but now is moving back to issues that affect the home, society, and even one's spirituality. This is not a generation characterized by apathy and disinterest.

"Boomers view themselves as problem solvers who, if given an appropriate challenge, are likely to rise to meet it," writes James Engle, head of the Institute of Leadership Development. Every two or three years, thousands of young Christians gather for the Urbana Mission Conference; most are genuinely interested in missions. Many get involved once they sense the need or experience the impact of short-term service abroad.

But baby boomers are not willing to get involved in somebody else's crusade—especially crusades that are mounted
by traditionalists and aging visionaries. "Let's face it," Engle
continues, "Christians are too often viewed as customers for
high-powered, mission-marketing efforts by agencies and denominations."[14] Baby boomers have little interest in denominational loyalty, emotional appeals, or the prepackaged "A.D.
2000" programs designed by older denominational or mission leaders. In contrast, the younger generation can get very
involved in causes that draw on their creativity, stimulate
their entrepreneurial spirits, and involve them in hands-on
strategy development. Once they get a taste of the needs and
challenges in other cultures, baby boomers and their young-
adult children often get very excited about working in part-
nership with nationals, training and equipping others to
present the Gospel, and finding ways to cope with social
needs.[15]

Business leaders agree. They have noticed that baby
boomers

> . . . want to participate in organizations that give them ac-
> cess to activities that are socially worthwhile *and* contribute
> to a satisfactory bottom line. . . .
>
> Boomers also want to be actively involved in shaping the
> policies, procedures, and programs of any organization to
> which they commit. They want to be consulted. They want
> their contributions recognized and appreciated. This group
> insists on participatory management and will look for
> organizations that provide that opportunity. If they don't
> "own" a decision, they tend not to support programs to
> implement it.[16]

All of this may force counselors to rethink their approaches.
People who like hands-on experiences with problem solving
are unlikely to appreciate heavy-handed, directive, Bible-
thumping counselors. A team approach, with the counselor
and counselee working together to resolve troublesome issues,
is likely to be more acceptable and more effective than a doctor-
knows-best type of theological and psychological paternalism.
Counselees may want to know why the counselor uses certain

techniques and whether the methods are succeeding. The baby boomer's questioning spirit is likely to appear more and more in the counselor's office.

VALUES ARE SEEN IN BABY BOOMER INTERACTIONS

Future historians who look back on the twentieth century are likely to conclude that the decade of the sixties was pivotal. This was the time when the baby boomers came of age and shook the foundations of our culture with their intoxicated notions of limitless possibility, unparalleled affluence, unrestricted hedonism, and the dawn of a new age of human relations.[17] But this was also a decade of cataclysmic shock. It was the decade when a young John Kennedy became president and died by an assassin's gun. It was the era when Martin Luther King, Jr., made his "I have a dream" speech but had his expansive dream and his powerful voice abruptly silenced by a small bullet. The sixties was a decade when millions of young baby boomers reached two lasting conclusions: America is not always right or invincible, and political leaders cannot be trusted.[18]

Perhaps it is not simplistic to suggest that disappointed baby boomers abandoned their political agendas temporarily and withdrew into self-centered pursuits. Millions retreated from any sense of community, collective responsibility, or care for one's neighbor. During the Me Decade, there was little interest in politics, international relations, family togetherness, or the church. For a while therapists emphasized group encounters and weekend marathons, but often these were directed toward personal pain or individual emptiness, and the once-popular small group movement eventually fizzled. Baby boomers withdrew into themselves, made few commitments, resisted one-on-one relationships, and worked at building their personal careers. It was a time when privacy was a priority and people built their lives around what Daniel Yankelovich has called the baby-boom anthem: "I want to live my life according to my own lifestyle. Other people ought to live their lives according to their own lifestyles." [19]

Perhaps this generation needed a rest and retreat after the turbulent sixties. Maybe they simply were growing up and, like most young adults, looking to find their own identities and to see where they might fit in the world of turmoil that their generation had helped to create. Now, they are "emerging from the search for and the insistence on identity," to use the words of Erik Erikson, and are "eager and willing to fuse" with others in affiliations and partnerships.[20]

People like this have already begun flocking to recovery groups, embarking on twelve-step programs to get free of addictions, attending workshops to help them overcome dysfunctional family backgrounds, and completing workbooks that help them deal with a whole variety of disorders.[21] Individual counseling will always be needed to help people deal with their problems and get over their painful pasts. But counseling approaches that stress interaction and participation are likely to be preferred.

This may also explain why baby boomers are returning to church, especially to churches that stress high interaction and involvement. In returning to church, writes one baby boomer, "we expect to find a high-touch environment where people are genuinely interested in us as persons. We also hope to find a God we can know on a personal level and who will know us."[22] Once again, it seems, interaction is in.

VALUES ARE SEEN IN BABY BOOMER ATTITUDES

Kip is in his mid-thirties, newly married, working for a small newspaper in the southeast. His career has been a string of big hopes and small accomplishments. As a college student, Kip dreamed of becoming pastor of a big church, so he enrolled in seminary. Part way through, he began to realize that few seminarians get into big churches, at least not early in their careers, so he decided to get a Ph.D. in Britain and become a New Testament professor who would teach young theologians and write scholarly commentaries.

But Kip never studied hard enough to get good grades, and as a result he was unable to get into the desired universities overseas. He did not want to be pastor of any of the small churches that might be willing to take a fresh-out-of-seminary graduate, so he decided to be a writer. At the newspaper he is dissatisfied with his role as a reporter. He sees little chance of reaching his goal of becoming an editor.

Kip wants to reach the top, but he lacks the commitment, the patience, and the willingness to work his way up through the ranks to reach his goals. He sees himself as a good preacher, but he is unwilling to take menial speaking invitations at downtown missions or at small country churches. His dreams of being a professor faded when he demonstrated an unwillingness to plug away at the work needed to get a doctorate. He wants to be an author, but he would like to start by publishing a major book, without honing his writing skills in the crowded offices of bottom-rung newspaper reporters . Kip wants to start at the top, and he continues to be frustrated because opportunities for inexperienced people almost always begin near the bottom. Like many in his generation, Kip wants instant gratification without paying the price to get to his goals.

Disappointments like these have led to considerable depression in baby boomers. Those like Kip expected to reach the top quickly, but they found, instead, that they had to work in the trenches before being promoted to higher levels of influence and prominence. Many were told that hard work and a good education would bring success, so they worked hard and earned their degrees, but the promised success did not come. A few persuasive pastors and televangelists told them that consistent prayer and faithful giving would be returned in manifold material blessings, so some of them prayed and gave, but the blessings seemed to go instead to a few unethical religious leaders.

Despite their frustrations, baby boomers like Kip remain optimistic. Even though they distrust institutions and tend to be cynical, many in this generation respond to optimistic presentations of the Gospel, expressions of hope in counseling, or positive promises for the future. They liked the never-ending optimism of Ronald Reagan, even though they have never cared much for politics or politicians and often have not bothered to vote.

Perhaps it is true that the general negativism of our times has created a hunger for positive messages of optimism. Time will tell if Doug Murren is correct in his speculation that "baby boomers will go to their graves still believing in the dream of a perfect world."[23] Few will come even close to finding it.

VALUES ARE SEEN IN BABY BOOMER SPENDING

"If you want to understand a person's values, look at his or her checkbook." Probably most of us have heard this, and clearly it applies to baby boomers. What they value is seen in how they spend their money.

Baby boomers grew up in good economic times. Money was available through their parents, from the government, or on credit, and there was "so much fat in the American economy that people in their teens and early twenties could lay hands on enough money to create styles of life all their own."[24] This did not apply to all segments of the four baby boom countries, but there was enough money around for many people to live like hippies, Jesus People, preppies, or New Agers. Some even got to the place where they could live and spend like yuppies.

Throughout their lifetimes, millions of baby boomers have responded to carefully crafted advertising appeals directed to their tastes and desires. Most have learned the joys and sense of freedom that come with purchases by plastic. (Worries about paying for the plastic purchases came later.) "Bank cards . . . marketed to the baby boomers may increasingly be the key to a bank's profitability," stated an article in the *Journal of Retail Banking.* "The heart of growth and profitability in bank cards—because of high usage and extended time repayment—is the aging baby boomer."[25]

As they approach middle age, many baby boomers are beginning to notice the exorbitant interest rates and high emotional costs of using credit cards. Many are learning what older and wiser people have known for centuries: money and possessions cannot buy happiness. "We've got all we need," said one young mother who quit her high-paying position as a marketing executive so she could spend more time with her kids. "We don't need a new car every year, dream vacations, and Rolex watches that work as well as a Timex."

Baby boomers still are spenders. They still value comfort and enjoy luxury, but they are most interested in "value" products that offer good quality at reasonable prices.

As we have seen, this demand for quality is already making

its appearance in churches. Busy baby boomers will not tolerate long, poorly prepared sermons or second-rate worship
services. They are willing to give to worthwhile causes, but
they want to be assured that the money is being spent wisely
and not going into somebody's personal bank account.

Will the same be expected of therapists? Counselors already
have the reputation of charging fees that are too high and deliv-
ering services that may be of limited value. Consumer-conscious
baby boomers, who now are shopping carefully for clothes, restaurants, and churches, are likely to demand similar quality
from their counselors—at noninflated prices.

BABY BOOMER DEPRESSION AND VALUES

In one of its final issues before it ceased publication, *Psychology Today* magazine published an insightful psychological
analysis of baby boomer depression. The author, University of
Pennsylvania psychologist Martin Seligman, noted that baby
boomers are about ten times more likely to be depressed than
were their parents and grandparents when they were young.[26]
Despite the optimism that many still claim, thousands of baby
boomers are sliding into melancholy, in part because of
unfulfilled expectations and lives that are empty and meaningless.

According to Seligman, past generations were able to maintain hope through difficult times because they had three
anchors of stability in all of their societies: faith in God, pride
in one's country, and stability in the family. All three of these
anchors seem to have disintegrated during the baby boom decades.

At least until recently, baby boomers as a group have not
been inclined to attend church. In an age of rationality, pragmatism, and busy career-building, God has seemed far away
and largely irrelevant. Christians and their pastors have not
had much of a with-it image, and the Bakker-type scandals
have contributed to the widespread cynicism and distrust of
the church.

In the halls of government, baby boomers have experienced
Watergate, read about sex scandals or misuse of public funds,

and learned to mistrust political leaders. One survey asked respondents to identify the "sleaziest ways to make a living." Drug dealers, prostitutes, television evangelists, local politicians, and members of Congress were clustered near the top of the list.[27]

Families have not fared much better. Divorce, domestic violence, and sexual abuse have reached almost epidemic proportions, and many are coming to realize that they have been raised in dysfunctional families and left with painful pasts and ugly scars that have persisted into adulthood. For millions, the family is no longer a place of calm and stability.

Without God, one's country, or the family, people have turned to the only other available alternative—themselves. When they have found emptiness within and looked at their treadmill lifestyles, many have plunged into depression.

But there is hope. Increasing numbers are returning to the church and finding that God is still alive and remarkably relevant. Patriotism has become fashionable again, especially in light of the Gulf War. As the next chapter will show, families are changing, and family values are returning. The emptiness of individualism is slowly yielding to a greater concern for community.

In the midst of these changes, counselors can play a significant role, not only in one-to-one interactions, but in developing seminars, small group experiences, and other programs for helping people take charge of their lives. Since so many people are giving up on counterfeit religion and looking for God, Christian counselors can play a role of special importance in counseling baby boomers and the baby busters who are now reaching early adulthood.

NOTES

1. This phrase was used by Charles W. Colson, "A Call to Rescue the Yuppies," *Christianity Today* 29 (May 17, 1985): 17–20.

2. Walter Shapiro, "The Birth and—Maybe—Death of Yuppiedom," *Time* (April 8, 1991), 65.

3. Allan Bloom, *The Closing of the American Mind: How Higher Education Has Failed Democracy and Impoverished the Souls of Today's Students* (New York: Simon and Schuster, 1987).

4. These attitudes are at the core of what has come to be known as the philosophy of "modernity." The quotation is taken from a critique of modernity by Thomas C. Oden, *Agenda for Theology: After Modernity . . . What?* (Grand Rapids: Zondervan, 1990), 43

5. Hunter Lewis, *A Question of Values* (New York: Harper and Row), 250–51.

6. These issues are discussed in more detail by Kenneth J. Gergen, *The Saturated Self: Dilemmas of Identity in Contemporary Life* (New York: Basic Books, 1991).

7. Bloom, *The Closing*, 72.

8. Ibid., 73, 76.

9. Ibid., 81.

10. Jeff Ostroff, "Targeting the Prime-Life Consumer," *American Demographics* (January 1991), 30 .

11. Janice Castro, "The Simple Life," *Time* (April 8, 1991), 58. It should be noted that this TIME/CNN poll included only 500 adults, not all of whom were baby boomers. The statistics cited in the text are indicative of a trend that has been widely noted (for this reason they were cited), but the statistics may not be a highly accurate reflection of mainstream baby boomer thinking.

12. This statistic and some of the ideas in the following paragraphs are adapted from an article by James F. Engel, "We Are the World," *Christianity Today* (September 24, 1990), 32–34.

13. Cited by Elizabeth Ehrlich, "How the Next Decade Will Differ: Six Key Trends that Will Shape America in the 1990s," *Business Week* (September 25, 1989), 142.

14. Engel, "We Are the World," 33.

15. At the beginning of his list of suggestions for stimulating baby boomer interest and involvement in missions, Engle writes, "End the all-too-common dichotomy between evangelism and social action. Boomers readily embrace an understanding of the kingdom of God that affirms the lordship of Christ over all phases of life." See Engle, "We Are the World," 34.

16. Irving J. Tecker and Glenn H. Tecker, "Big Boom Theory," *Association Management* (January 1991), 32.

17. Tom Morganthau, "Decade Shock," *Newsweek* (September 5, 1988), 15.

18. Ibid.

19. Cited by Paul Light, *Baby Boomers* (New York: Norton, 1988), 238.

20. Erik H. Erikson, *Childhood and Society*, rev. ed. (New York: Norton, 1963), 263.

21. For further elaboration see Tim Stafford, "The Hidden Gospel of the 12 Steps," *Christianity Today* 35 (July 22, 1991), 14–19, and Margaret Jones, "The Rage for Recovery," *Publishers Weekly* (November 23, 1990), 16–24.

22. Doug Murren, *The Baby Boomerang* (Ventura, Calif.: Regal, 1990), 60.

23. Ibid., 214.

24. Tom Wolfe, "Late Boomers," *The American Spectator* (November 1990), 33.

25. Roger D. Blackwell and Margaret Hanke, "The Credit Card and the Aging Baby Boomers," *Journal of Retail Banking* 9 (Spring 1987): 17.

26. Martin E. P. Seligman, "Boomer Blues," *Psychology Today* (October 1988), 50–55. (*Psychology Today* resumed publication in 1992.)

27. James Patterson and Peter Kim, *The Day America Told the Truth* (New York: Prentice Hall, 1991), 144.

Chapter 4

Baby Boomer Families

As an artist, Norman Rockwell was in a class all by himself. His highly detailed, realistic paintings of middle-class American life were sometimes criticized for being sentimental and homey, but thousands delighted at his often humorous depictions of ordinary people in everyday situations. As a cover illustrator for *The Saturday Evening Post* and other magazines, Rockwell soared to great popularity, and his work still is recognized and admired, even by people who have no special interest in art.

Rockwell's meticulously crafted paintings often portrayed small town scenes, patriotic events, and family incidents. Today, less than twenty years after the artist's death, those Rockwell-illustrated families seem woefully out of date. Clothing styles have changed, of course, but so have families. Gone is the old image of one breadwinner husband and one homemaker wife, living without divorce for a lifetime, while they raised two or more children who regularly attended church, knew little about drugs, and believed that sex was for married partners only. It might be argued that such families never did exist, but most of us would agree that the baby boomer generation has forever exploded our oldest ideas about marriage and the family. Within the space of a few years, family life has been revolutionized, and hardly anybody has been left untouched by the changes. Norman Rockwell might have great difficulty illustrating family life in the present baby boom generation.

In contrast to the more traditional living arrangements and family compositions that existed following World War II, this is the first generation to:

- think of the *traditional family* in terms of two wage-earner parents with one or two children who are cared for outside the home during the day;
- widely accept (without criticizing) the right of couples to live together and to have children without the restrictions or the securities of getting married, to marry but remain child-free, to abort unwanted pregnancies, and to delay childbearing until the midthirties or later;
- accept the reality of homosexual partnerships, roommates of the opposite sex sharing living quarters, widespread divorce and remarriage, and the adoption of children by single and/or homosexual parents;
- have *boomerang kids*—young adults who leave home, launch out on their own, and then return to live with their parents because it is cheaper and more convenient (about one in nine adults between twenty-five and thirty-four now lives in a parent's home); and
- have almost half the families in America headed by single parents, raising children without the help of a spouse.

Statistics change so rapidly that they quickly are out of date, but a few of these can illustrate the changes that have come by way of baby boomer families. Roughly one-fourth of the baby boom married couples will remain childless, either by choice or because of infertility. Another fourth will have only one child. Half of all baby boomers' children will spend part of their childhood living with a single parent (in nine cases out of ten that parent will be female) after watching their parents get a divorce. About 70 percent of baby boom women work outside the home and of those who have children, roughly half are back at work before the child's first birthday.

There can be no accurate statistics to document incidence of domestic violence, verbal and sexual abuse, alcohol-related home problems, or other ongoing tensions that disrupt lives behind the closed doors that hide millions of dysfunctional families. Is it any wonder that we have had an avalanche of books, seminars, and workshops dealing with children and adults who have suffered through incapacitating family abuse? Is anyone surprised at the upsurge of interest in family counseling?

WHAT IS A BABY BOOMER FAMILY?

In a widely read book published several years ago, Edith Schaeffer wrote that a family is "a changing life mobile," the birthplace of creativity, a formation center for human relationships, a shelter in the time of storm, a place where truth is relayed, and a museum where memories are built.[1] It would be easy to smile at Schaeffer's description and dismiss it as being more outdated than a Rockwell painting. We are bombarded with media reports of family violence. Our movie and television screens portray family dysfunction with increasingly explicit visions of abuse and maltreatment. Every counselor hears repeated stories of domestic unhappiness and turbulence in the home. It is easy to conclude that Schaeffer's vision describes an unusual family, her own, that is seldom duplicated.

Even so, before we look in more detail at the changes and weaknesses in baby boomer families, honesty demands that we pause to consider the strengths. There *are* good marriages and stable homes among us.[2] Many children do grow up in modern families without being emotionally and psychologically wounded. Despite the plethora of books that might suggest otherwise, baby boomer families are not all dysfunctional, disruptive, or decaying. Many baby boomers and their children move through the teenage years and become healthy adult children of *functional* families. In some homes, the family members might be more, rather than less, healthy because of the changes in family living that the baby boom generation has introduced.

Of the many changes, good and bad, that have redefined baby boomer families, three issues are prominent. These concern baby boomer views of marriage, family stability, and the roles of women.

CHANGING VIEWS OF MARRIAGE

Baby boomers are not opposed to marriage. Despite high divorce rates, widespread cohabitation, a greater acceptance of singleness, and frequent sex without commitment, more than nine out of ten baby boomers believe that marriage is the best lifestyle. According to demographic predictions, 90 percent of baby boomers will marry, at least once; about one-third will marry twice.

But half will get at least one divorce, one in five will get two divorces, and 5 percent will divorce three times or more.[3] By the time the older baby boomers complete their marriage course, an estimated 60 percent of women who have ever married will also have been divorced at least once.[4] Baby boomers think marriage is great, according to one observer. It is their partners they do not always like.[5]

In previous generations, divorce was scorned socially, and couples were inclined to stay together, even when their marriages were dead and their lives at home were miserable. Baby boomers can see no sense in pretending to be happy and fulfilled in marriage when they are not. They realize that marriages often turn sour, but many go to the altar with expectations of never-ending romance and with the belief that their love is different from all others. Christian couples take these hopes one step further. They plan their weddings with confidence, expecting to stay together for life, because they know that Christian marriages have a greater likelihood of survival.

When problems come, few couples are surprised. But when the problems get progressively worse and threaten to undermine the marriage, there can be dismay, disappointment, deep discouragement, and sometimes a decision to bail out. When separation and divorce do occur, there often is intense psycho-

logical pain, spiritual emptiness, a sense of failure, and feelings of insecurity—especially in the children of divorce.[6]

Family breakups are never easy, and often the pain is made
worse by the social stigma that long has plagued divorced
people. But this attitude is changing in the baby boomer generation. Many believe that life is too short to stay in a bad
marriage, so changing partners has become more acceptable.
Marital breakdowns have become so common that most of us
know and better understand divorced people and their children. As a result, we have learned to be more sympathetic and
tolerant of divorced people. Many can now find support and
help for healing, even in the church.

Based on an informal survey of six hundred people who had
maintained successful marriages, psychologist James Dobson
arrived at "three tried and tested, back-to-basics recommendations" for reducing the chances of divorce and for
maintaining marital stability:

- A Christ-centered home where the husband and wife are
  deeply-committed to Jesus Christ;
- A committed love in which nothing short of death is permitted to come between the couple (in contrast to the idea
  that "I'll stay with you as long as I feel love for you"); and
- A never-ending willingness to work at maintaining good
  communication.[7]

Dobson notes that "people are not looking for perfect marriages, but [for] marriages that keep working." But even these
less-than-perfect marriages have evaded many in the baby
boom generation. Marital instability has been taken for granted
in this low commitment era, and divorce has come to be seen
as a reasonable way to get out of an unhappy marriage. As a
result, the United States has the highest divorce rate in the
world.

Will this change as baby boomers mature and develop a
greater willingness to work on keeping their marriages together and growing? As we have seen, many are beginning to
realize that staying with a marriage and trying to make it succeed is often preferable to the stresses that come with
separations. With their open attitudes about counseling, baby
boomers are willing to get help, to attend marriage enrichment

seminars, and to make a commitment to building their family relationships. Christian counselors and local churches have a growing opportunity to help strengthen marriages and build better family relationships.

CHANGING FAMILY STABILITY

According to a report from the Census Bureau, over one-quarter of all homes in the United States are "nonfamily households." These are maintained by individuals who live alone or by unrelated people who live together. The latter category has been growing dramatically since the baby boomers reached adulthood. The group includes same-sex college roommates, single people who share an apartment, and members of religious communities who live together. Homosexual couples are also included in the listings of nonfamily households and so are the increasing numbers of unmarried opposite-sex partners involved in cohabitation.

According to one statistical analysis, baby boomers have, "to a large extent, established the now familiar notion that cohabitation is an extension of courtship, a precursor to a wedding, an interval in a stage following separation or divorce, or an arrangement of permanence."[8] The number of cohabitants has more than tripled since 1970, and the trend shows no sign of diminishing. Far from being treated as outcasts, these people — most of whom are assumed to be sexually active — are widely accepted in the society. Many bear children, and few see anything wrong with a living arrangement that once would have been generally scorned by society.

Churches with ministries to singles often encounter cohabitation among the membership. Some of the cohabiters, especially those who are new Christians, express surprise when church leaders question the morality of this increasingly accepted type of living arrangement.

Cohabitation is only one of many nontraditional family lifestyles that characterize baby boomers. In mobile societies like ours, we see relatively few three-or four-generation families living together or family members who never move from the communities where they were born. But we do see more female-headed homes, more never-married mothers remaining single and raising their out-of-wedlock children, more busy couples who decide to delay or forgo childbearing (the fertility rate has dropped significantly since the 1950s), and more blended families. These "Brady Bunch" households usually consist of one previously married husband presently married to one previously married wife. This couple lives together with the children that each has brought from previous marriages, and in time the new marriage gives birth to children of its own.

Are these new arrangements more stable than traditional marriage? For many, the answer is *no*. Cohabitants, for example, do not have the restrictions of marriage, but they also lack legal ties and emotional security. Single-parent families frequently struggle with the pressure and confusion of one parent trying to fill the roles of both parents. Many have financial stresses that lead to extra work for the parent and extra responsibilities for the older children. There can be continual struggles to find adequate child care, and often developmental problems come in the wake of a divorce.[9] Blended families can have unique difficulties of their own. Often the children feel ill at ease in the new family setting, struggle to relate to the new family members, and continue to wrestle with the stresses and conflicts that tend to persist long after their real parents divorce.

Following several decades of trying to convince ourselves that divorce really does not leave psychological trauma, many people—including baby boomers—are discovering that family instability and separation often take a toll.

Divorced men are more likely than married men to have psychiatric problems, serious accidents, and to be in poor health generally. Divorced women often experience depression and frequently suffer from markedly reduced and even impoverished economic circumstances. The children of divorce become more vulnerable to developing a wide variety of social, behavioral, emotional, and academic problems.

The risks to healthy, wholesome child development that appear linked to divorce include an increased probability that the following problems may emerge: (1) angry and aggressive behavior; (2) sadness, low self-esteem, and depression; (3) impaired academic performance; and (4) trouble with intimate relationships in adolescence and adulthood.

For some youngsters these difficulties are short-lived, and within a year or two of the parental separation they regain their developmental stride and are able to put the problems behind them. However, there is mounting evidence now that a substantial number of children, perhaps as many as 30 percent to 50 percent, bear the painful and disruptive legacy of their parents' divorce for years.[10]

Most of these victims of divorce are baby boomers and their children. Evidence suggests that despite their problems, some children of divorced, separated, or nontraditional families are better adjusted than children from intact but unhappy traditional families.[11] Sometimes a single-parent family brings more security than a highly tumultuous two-parent household. Even so, the personal experience of having lived in dysfunctional and disintegrating families often carries into adulthood, hinders subsequent personal or family stability, and sends thousands of people to seek the help of counselors and family therapists.

Alex Kotlowitz is a baby boomer, a writer, and an investigative reporter for the *Wall Street Journal*. After writing an award-winning story about inner-city violence and the toll it takes on families, Kotlowitz decided to write a book about two children who live in Chicago's Henry Horner Homes. Their mother agreed to cooperate, but she made a sobering observation about the kids in her neighborhood. "There are no children here," she said. "They've seen too much to be children."[12]

Writing about kids in the suburbs, family therapist James Coyne made a similar observation. Childhood depression has become common, most often in baby boomer families "characterized by tense emotional uproars in which family members trade verbal abuse." These are homes where disagreements are rarely resolved and hurts seldom understood.[13] Children want their parents to get along and their families to be secure, but many homes are storm centers rather than shelters from the times of storm outside. Ours is an era where values are molded by television violence, illicit sex and foul language are glorified in videos and music lyrics, and perhaps millions of homes are marked by frustration and conflict. Many baby boomers and their children appear in one respect to be like those inner-city black boys. Maybe there are no baby boomer children. They have seen too much to be children.

CHANGING ROLES OF WOMEN

Two separate trends have changed the nature of parenting among baby boomers, according to Landon Jones. One of these is the widespread divorce that is creating so many one-parent families—almost half of all children now spend a significant portion of their growing up years in single-parent homes. The other trend is the massive entry of baby boom women into the work force.[14]

"Married women should stay home with their children," an older businessman stated recently. "If they want to get involved with the community, they should serve as volunteers instead of working all the time." Thirty years ago such an attitude might have been widely accepted, but not anymore. Today most women work outside the home, not as volunteers, but in jobs that provide income. Most women are in these jobs for one or both of two reasons: they have to work, and/or they want to work.

For many baby boomer women, employment is not an option. Poor and middle-class women, women whose husbands are sick or out of work, women who head single-parent homes—these people do not have the luxury of deciding whether they should stay at home with their children or serve as volunteers. Older people, like that businessman, fail to appreciate the struggles that many individuals and couples face in providing for their families. These people are not greedy. Often they live from paycheck to paycheck, stretching the family income to make ends meet. For women in these homes, working is essential.

Working is not always bad, however. Many women enjoy their work, like being involved in their communities, and find fulfillment in building careers. In one survey of middle-class working women, 57 percent said they wanted careers as well as families; only 27 percent wanted to be "traditional house-wives."[15]

All of this has affected baby boom families in a variety of ways.

- Some homemakers have become convinced that their work is of secondary importance, although increasing numbers are coming to recognize that few roles are as important as being a mother.

- Some working women and their husbands worry about their children, especially their latchkey children who come home to an empty house and spend a part of every day without adult supervision.[16] Many of these kids are lonely, starved for affection, and searching for intimacy. With no adults around they turn to each other and often get into various kinds of trouble.

- The roles of husbands and wives have changed and often undergo continual role negotiation as each tries to juggle work, child rearing, and family responsibilities. This can leave children confused, but there are benefits. For example, fathers often take over some of the nurturing of children rather than leaving all of this to the overburdened mother.

- The baby boom ethic expects young mothers to return to work (over half do so), but child care has become a major problem. There are too few day-care centers, and often there is great difficulty in finding and paying for alternate child care.

- Millions of children grow up in homes where there are frequent parental absences, parents who are too busy, television sets that baby-sit, and a lack of good adult role models.

- Continuing family violence and child abuse are dramatic examples that many families explode in rage because they cannot cope with the stresses. "Parents don't cause child abuse; stress does," Jones writes. "And the families of the baby boom have experienced more marital stresses than any generation in history."[17]

It is not difficult to understand why God hates divorce (Malachi 2:16), why the scriptures teach the importance of sexual faithfulness and marital stability, and why churches and Christian counselors are faced with a continuing need to help baby boomer families deal with their stresses, prevent problems, and learn to apply biblical guidelines for family living.

What one influence or event has had the greatest impact on molding the baby boom generation? Some might answer television. Others would point to the Vietnam War or to the assassinations of the Kennedys and Dr. King. But a writer named Ann Marie Cunningham has a different answer: the contraceptive pill.

The Pill "transformed our lives like nothing before or since," wrote Cunningham in *Ladies' Home Journal.* "In this age of AIDS, when the very idea of Sexual Revolution seems both archaic and dangerous, it's easy to forget how truly liberating the Pill seemed to be in 1960. Nothing else in this century—perhaps not even winning the right to vote—made such an immediate difference in women's lives. Overnight, the Pill gave women control of their reproductive systems; no longer was biology our absolute destiny."[18]

For the first time in history, women on the Pill could plan or delay childbearing, have the children they wanted, prevent the pregnancies they did not want, determine the size of their families, and build their careers without fear of an intervening pregnancy. The Pill significantly lowered the birthrate and ended the baby boom in 1964, according to Cunningham. "It allowed women to think seriously about careers because they could postpone childbirth. And it sparked the feminist and pro-choice movements; once women felt they were in charge of their own bodies, they began to question the authority of their husbands, their bosses, their doctors and their churches."[19]

Among the people in those churches were Catholic women, 80 to 85 percent of whom approve of contraception. They used the Pill in defiance of the church's centuries-old prohibition against birth control. "It prompted them to question the church," according to one prominent priest. "Their attitude toward the church's teachings on other matters will never quite be the same."

Effective contraception has done much to free women so they can move into the work force, build their careers, and take leadership roles in society. Other important influences have also contributed to the changing roles of women, including legalized abortion and the women's liberation movement. Unlike many of their parents, baby boomers no longer assume that women will play secondary roles or remain content to let their husbands fill the professions, build fulfilling careers, or take all the active leadership roles in the church.

BABY BOOMER PARENTING

The homes where we grow up can have a powerful effect on shaping the homes that we establish as adults. Children who grow up in abusive families often abuse their own children. Adult children of alcoholics have a higher than average likelihood of ruining their own homes with alcohol. Parents who provided good models often discover that their children, in turn, are good parents. When we become parents, probably most of us are determined to avoid the failures of our own parents and to do the things that our parents did right.

Baby boomers grew up in homes that were characterized by entitlement, entertainment, enlightenment, and enchantment with independence. Each of these has been modified over the years, but each still has a significant impact on baby boomer parenting.

ENTITLEMENT

In the postwar days that gave rise to the baby boom, young parents were buoyed with optimism and with visions of a prosperous future, if not for the world then at least for their kids. Nothing was too good for the baby boom children. They were entitled to have the best and to have it all—the best toys, the best medical care, the best education, the best opportunities for the future.

Reality did not always follow these high expectations, but young baby boomers gave little thought to this. In the student unrest of the sixties, they considered themselves entitled to take over university buildings, flaunt the establishment, and do whatever felt good. By the mid-eighties, many baby boomers had become part of the establishment, seeking the good life, still assuming that they and their children could have it all, even if some of their pleasures had to be charged now and paid for later.

Someone has suggested that many early baby boomers made a religion out of caring for their children. When these children reached adulthood and brought great disappointment, parents became disillusioned and put more focus instead on caring for themselves. Today we have parents torn between meeting their own needs for fulfillment and concerned about raising their children effectively. The golden attitude of entitlement has been tarnished a little by reality, but the old idea has not died. Many baby boomer parents still want the best for themselves and the best for their children.

ENTERTAINMENT

Several years ago a New York critic and communications professor wrote an insightful but scarcely noticed book that gave a powerful and sobering critique of television. The book, poignantly titled *Amusing Ourselves to Death*, carefully documented how our politics, government operations, legal system, businesses, religion, and education have all been shaped by television.

"Sesame Street," for example, appeared to be a creative way of teaching young people how to read and encouraging them to love school. In fact, it encouraged them to expect that school would be like "Sesame Street," and in so doing the program undermined much of what traditional schooling has represented.

Whereas a classroom is a place of social interaction, the space in front of a television set is a private preserve. Whereas in a classroom, one may ask a teacher questions, one can ask nothing of a television screen. Whereas school is centered on the development of language, television demands attention to images. Whereas attending school is a legal requirement, watching television is an act of choice. Whereas in school, one fails to attend to the teacher at the risk of punishment, no penalties exist for failing to attend to the television screen. Whereas to behave oneself in school means to observe rules of public decorum, television watching requires no such observances, has no concept of public decorum. Whereas in a classroom, fun is never more than a means to an end, on television it is the end in itself.[20]

Baby boomers, of course, were the first generation to be raised on television. In many homes television has become the every present baby sitter, filled with cute puppets, catchy tunes, enticing advertisements, rapid-fire editing, and the undocumented assumption that the best learning is visual and presented in dramatic form.[21] Weaned on these attitudes, millions of baby boomers became addicted to television, glued to the screen, flipping from channel to channel until they find the most exciting presentations, oblivious of the violence, immorality, and self-centered values that have filled their living rooms and have been imprinted literally thousands of times on their minds.

In themselves, of course, there is nothing wrong with entertainment or with television. Life can be stressful and boring, and we all benefit from things that are interesting and pleasant to experience. Every parent enjoys taking the kids to a circus or making the long-anticipated trip to one of the Disney attractions.

But the baby boomer has become engulfed with a let-us-entertain-you mentality and is annoyed when entertainment is taken away. At a beautiful vacation resort in northern Michigan a man was overheard expressing his opinion of the idyllic setting. "I hate this place," he said. "They don't have any television here and no video tapes!" He might have sympathized with the parents who recently howled in protest when a local school board stated that vacationing students would be required to read one book during the summer. In an incident that attracted wide media attention, some of the parents complained bitterly because reading would interfere with their children's summer vacation.

Baby boomer parents and their children are not the only ones who expect to be entertained. Most of us want entertainment from our political leaders, teachers, business presentations, and church services. Enjoyment is in; discipline is not. Immediate gratification and innovation are still highly regarded values; we do not care much for long-term planning and waiting for results. These attitudes are carried into counseling sessions, and they permeate the home. And because they cater to our self-centered and sinful natures, they are likely to be passed on to subsequent generations.

ENLIGHTENMENT

Entitlement says we can have it all. *Entertainment* says we can enjoy it all. *Enlightenment* says we can know it all—or at least get any information we want.

No one person can absorb everything in this information age, but baby boomers have more accessible information at their fingertips than any prior generation. One recent book on the baby boom generation pictures two young people on the cover, both in front of a computer screen. Their kids are likely to know a lot about computers at an early age, and few of us are far from data bases that we can access or from libraries that stock some of the over fifty thousand new book titles that appear every year.

How has this influenced baby boomer families? In many homes, the information explosion makes no difference. Education is not emphasized. Serious discussions are rare, and people are intellectually lazy. They can get information if they need it. Why think and stuff our heads full of learning if everything anyone needs to know is in a computer anyway?

In contrast, other baby boomers have become pushers—not pushers of drugs but pushers of their own children. Kids are pushed into high pressure athletic programs, music lessons, cram courses to help them do better in school, science fairs, and other activities designed to enrich, stimulate, and motivate. Highly energetic parents push their children to become "superkids" who sometimes respond with ulcers, childhood depression, compulsivity, subsequent rebellion, and the embittered attitudes that we are warned against in Scripture (Colossians 3:21). Some parents need to be reminded that children can be pushed to grow up too fast, knowing more than they need to know, sooner than they need to know it.

ENCHANTMENT WITH INDEPENDENCE

In 1924, two sociologists began what came to be known as the Middletown study of a community later identified as Muncie, Indiana. Mothers were asked to rank the traits that they most wanted to instill in their children. The winners: loyalty to the church, strict obedience, and good manners. It is not surprising that the results were very different when a much more recent generation of mothers in the same community listed their child-rearing goals. Independence and tolerance topped the list; the original three preferences were not even selected by three-fourths of the sample. As baby boomers have become parents, conformity has slipped in significance. Independence, self-reliance, the ability to solve problems and take care of one's self—all of these have risen to prominence. And as baby boomers recognize the dangers in me-first individualism, there appears to be greater emphasis on teaching interdependence, cooperation, and mutual support.[22]

Every generation of parents has passed its own values on to its children. Baby boomers are no different, but some of their values emphasize an individualism that leaves people with few supports except what they find within themselves. Thousands follow New Age teachings, eastern religions, or humanistic values in a vain attempt to find who they are. Many are finding that independence can give a sense of freedom, but often this leads to an alienation and isolation that can give a sense of despair. The increase in depression among baby boomers and their children may not be all that surprising.

More surprising, perhaps, is the increasing tendency of adult baby boomers to move back home with their parents. Some analysts wonder if these young adults are ambivalent about taking on adult responsibilities. Many find their parents' home a secure and inexpensive place to think through careers or to save money that might be used to get one's own accommodations later. But never-departed and boomerang adult children can bring tensions into their parents' homes. There can be struggles over space, rules, control, and issues such as who gets the meals, pays for the electricity, or does the laundry. For parents there is a struggle with balance—treating their children as adults but feeling reluctant about suggesting guidelines for family living.

Young adults who live at home often want the privileges of adulthood without the financial responsibilities, the sensitive communication, and the common courtesies that adults who live together need to show to one another. Coming home and living with parents, according to one counselor, should not be too attractive. But few parents are inclined to push their adult children from the nest, forcing them to face cold, present-day realities.[23]

WHAT ABOUT GRANDMA?

While baby boomers have been busy building their careers and raising their children, something has been happening to their parents: they have grown older. People who were in their early twenties when the baby boom began will be in their sixties and early seventies during the 1990s. These older parents, who gave unselfishly to raise their baby boomer children, are now reaching the time in life when there are many physical, emotional, and financial needs. Because of better health care, many of these older people are living longer. Already there is evidence that the baby boom is encountering a senior boom that will put added pressure on both groups.[24]

It is never easy to recognize that our parents are getting old and looking to us for guidance, help with decisions, and sometimes long-term care. The oldest baby boomers have already entered the sandwich generation of adults who are squeezed between the demands and needs of teenage children and the problems of older parents.

Neither churches nor counselors have given a lot of attention to the sandwich and elderly generations. Our focus still is on young people and their baby boomer parents. To counsel and minister effectively with baby boomers, we must understand their parents, their children, and their perspectives on religion. That is the topic of chapter 5.

ISN'T IT AWFUL?

Looking at families today, there is reason to despair.

Domestic violence and abuse do seem to be on the rampage. Dysfunctional families do exist in abundance. Divorce statistics are still high, and so are costs for health care and rates of poverty, suicide, and depression. The state of the family in the four baby boomer countries is not healthy.

While this chapter was being written, one of the authors came across a new book by baby boomer Joni Eareckson Tada, who was writing about some of her challenges of building a marriage as a wheelchair-bound quadriplegic. Shortly after the accident that left her paralyzed, a stranger wrote with some good advice: "Many believers gaze at their problems and glance at the Lord. But I tell you to gaze at the Lord and glance at your problems."

"Too many of us fix our eyes on our problems—the hurdles— and we start measuring the height of the next jump," Tada wrote. "In so doing, we glance occasionally at the Lord only to make sure He's aware of all the hardships these hurdles are causing."[25] Instead, as counselors, church leaders, baby boomers, or concerned Christians, we need to keep God's sovereignty, power, and compassion in clear view.

Many baby boomer families *are* in bad shape. But the Christian knows that Christ brings hope and healing, even in the midst of abundant difficulties.

NOTES

1. Edith Schaeffer, *What Is a Family?* (Old Tappan, N.J.: Revell, 1975).

2. Jim and Sally Conway, *Traits of a Lasting Marriage: What Strong Marriages Have in Common* (Downers Grove, Ill.: InterVarsity, 1991).

3. Cheryl Russell, *100 Predictions for the Baby Boomer: The Next 50 Years* (New York: Plenum, 1987), 91–95.

4. Paul C. Light, *Baby Boomers* (New York: Norton, 1988), 147.

5. Hans Finzel, *Help! I'm a Baby Boomer* (Wheaton, Ill.: Victor Books, 1989), 115.

6. Judith Wallerstein and Sandra Blakeslee, *Second Chances: Men, Women and Children a Decade after Divorce* (New York: Ticknor and Fields, 1989).

7. James C. Dobson, *Love for a Lifetime: Building a Marriage that Will Go the Distance* (Portland: Multnomah, 1987), 49–66.

8. Esther Wattenberg, " The Fate of Baby Boomers and Their Children," *Social Work* (January/February 1986), 20–28.

9. Leroy G. Baruth and Margaret Z. Burggraf, "The Counselor and Single-Parent Families," *Elementary School Guidance and Counseling* 9 (October 1984): 30-37.

10. Neil Kalter, *Growing Up with Divorce* (New York: The Free Press, 1990), 2.

11. I. Nye, "Child Adjustment in Broken and Unhappy Homes," *Marriage and Family Living* 19 (1957): 255– 61.

12. Alex Kotlowitz, *There are No Children Here* (New York: Doubleday, 1991), x.

13. James Coyne, "Old Before Their Time," *Family Therapy Networker* 15 (July/August 1991): 50-51.

14. Landon Y. Jones, *Great Expectations: America and the Baby Boom Generation* (New York: Coward, McCann and Geoghegan, 1980), 207.

15. Louis S. Richman, " The New Middle Class: How It Lives," *Fortune* (August 13, 1990), 107.

16. Mary Lou Padilla and Garry L. Landreth, "Latchkey Children: A Review of the Literature," *Child Welfare* 68 (July/August 1989): 445–54.

17. Jones, *Great Expectations*, 212.

18. Ann Marie Cunningham, "The Pill: How it Changed Our Lives," *Ladies' Home Journal* (June 1990), 123.

19. Ibid.

20. Neil Postman, *Amusing Ourselves to Death: Public Discourse in the Age of Show Business* (New York: Penguin, 1985), 143.

21. Ibid., 151. Postman cites a review of 2,800 studies on the impact of television's influence. Together they are unable to point to persuasive evidence that "learning increases when information is presented in a dramatic setting."

22. Anne Remley, "From Obedience to Independence," *Psychology Today* (October 1988), 56–59.

23. Jon Anderson, "Boomerang Kids," *Chicago Tribune,* June 23, 1991.

24. Jane E. Myers, "The Mid/Late Life Generation Gap: Adult Children with Aging Parents," *Journal of Counseling and Development* 66 (March 1988), and Lee Smith, "What Do We Owe to the Elderly?" *Fortune* (March 1989), 54–62.

25. Joni Eareckson Tada, *Seeking God: My Journey of Prayer and Praise* (Brentwood, Tenn.: Wolgemuth and Hyatt, 1991), 135.

Chapter 5

Baby Boomer Religion

Baby Boomers Rediscover Church.

A Generation Warms to Religion.

The Boomers are Back!

THESE HEADLINES, TAKEN FROM RECENT magazine articles, point to a trend that some Christians find surprising. The same baby boomers who dropped out of the church in record numbers are now coming back.

This is not a mass movement. Most church pews are not filled and overflowing with baby boomers. Some denominations, mostly liberal in theology, continue to lose members,[1] and an estimated 40 percent of the postwar generation still show no interest in organized religion.[2] Those who do return are mostly married couples with children and high incomes; childless married couples are the least likely to come back.[3] The younger baby boomers are less likely to return at present than those born before the midsixties. And the returnees have many friends who still prefer New Age crystals to age-old commitments to Jesus Christ. Even so, large parts of the generation that dropped out in the sixties are coming back.

More surprising than the return of the baby boomers may be the fact that so many observers did not expect it to happen. For decades, young adults have dropped out of the church in their late teens and twenties, but an estimated 80 percent come back later. Shouldn't we have expected that something similar would occur among baby boomers?

One report has divided church members into five categories.[4]

- People age 65 and above are the servants and the served who have reached retirement age and eventually drop out of active church involvement because of deteriorating health and limited mobility as they get older.
- People in the 56–65 age group are the loyalists who have made church a habit and continue to be involved, but as they move toward retirement, they are progressively more inclined to turn their responsibilities over to younger members.
- The age 41–55 group holds most positions of church leadership and provides most of the financial support.
- The 26–40 year age group is comprised of people who often have returned to church when their children became toddlers. The parents of these children are active as volunteer workers in the nursery and Sunday School. And despite their busy lives, many are involved in evangelism, youth programs, and other areas of service.
- The youngest group, those who are 25 and under, often are church dropouts. For many, the church seems irrelevant and unimportant, even though most continue to believe and show no hostility to organized religion. As they move through the twenties, this group begins drifting back.

It should come as no surprise, therefore, that older baby boomers are returning to church. As the following pages will show, however, they are not returning to just any church. This is the generation that still insists on quality, that is bored with irrelevance and traditionalism, that distrusts televangelists but wants contact with sensitive mentors, that dislikes taking orders but thrives on entrepreneurial hands-on approaches, that likes small groups, and that demands practical answers to problems of the nineties. These people want solid moral values for their children and intimate spiritual experiences for themselves. And they will shop from church to church until they find what they are seeking.

BABY BOOMER THEOLOGY AND THE CHURCH

What do baby boomers look for in a church?

This generation that has a lot and expects a lot is not interested in boring services, dead music, sermons that do not meet needs or relate to life, unfriendly people, poor quality child care, or talk about money. They do not want to be embarrassed, so they do not like being singled out as visitors or having to stand to introduce themselves. They have little interest in heavy theology, denominational loyalty, church jargon, or congregations that have authoritarian leaders. They are highly sensitive to hypocrisy and intolerant of theological arrogance. Instead, these people want a church that emphasizes people over doctrine and denominations, that has a high commitment to quality, and that knows what it is *for* instead of emphasizing all of the people and things that it is *against*.

In the weeks following her diving accident, Joni Eareckson Tada often prayed, "God, if I can't die, show me how to live!"[5] Baby boomers have a similar desire. They seek churches that offer experience, participation, and challenges, all of which teach *and* show people how to live.

EXPERIENCE

It took place on Mr. Yasgur's farm in upstate New York over twenty years ago. A crowd of five hundred thousand young people gathered in the summer of 1969 for a raucous, drug-infested, orgylike celebration of rock 'n' roll music. Every news organization in the country covered the event, and an older generation watched their television screens in disbelief often mixed with disgust. Why, they wondered, would thousands roll about in the rain and mud for several days, expressing their frustrations and disdain for the values of a society that had tried to give them everything they could ever want? Why did so many of the participants sense an unexplainable chord of unity in a rain-soaked event that would come to be known as Woodstock?

Doug Murren, who pastors a baby boomer congregation on the west coast, has written a sobering commentary on that famous gathering in Mr. Yasgur's fields.

For us, Woodstock proved that religious citadels and stained glass weren't necessary in order to have a "religious experience" of unimaginable proportions. Yet at Woodstock, there were no laws, no priests, no Bibles—just a lot of music, mud, drugs, sex, and people.

From that powerful experience emerged the theology of Woodstock: human love and unity, equality, respect, and appreciation for differences, and a total abandonment to celebration. People needed and helped each other; camaraderies were formed. For those present, Woodstock was a fantasy dream world for a few mesmerizing days.

Secretly, I think we thirty something folks believe that the myth of Woodstock is what the Church, in a certain sense, ought to emulate. Church ought to be celebrative, informal, and spontaneous. People sharing and helping each other should not only be an expectation, but a reality.

The theology of Woodstock is the dream of a generation. We hope it is possible to have religion without formal titles and without unnecessary rules. Isn't there some place where people simply need each other for survival? Isn't there a place where each individual is important and respected? Can't I know God as a person? Isn't it possible for us humans to relate to God without all those official channels?

The Church's failure to appreciate the impact of Woodstock could cause it to miss a wonderful opportunity in communicating the Gospel intelligibly to an entire generation. . . .

We baby boomers aren't coming to church to become members. We're coming to experience something. Yes, even to get something. What we're hoping for is some kind, human touch in these churches we're checking out.[6]

From this it should not be assumed that baby boomers are seeking a feelings-only theology that has high emotion and low content. In a world of hyperactive lifestyles and widespread insensitivity, they want caring relationships, love, respect, and an intimacy that is something more than yet another social club activity such as one might find at the local workout center. They want the freedom to sing and to celebrate God's person and presence, but they have little time for eighteenth-century hymns with archaic language. They look, instead, for a faith that makes sense; a belief system that is both practical and relevant for people who live in a modern, high-tech world. Despite their desire for experiences, they are not resistant to clearly stated, logically presented, biblically based challenges, packaged in language that nontheologians understand. And they are willing to get involved in service projects that make sense.

PARTICIPATION

Books and articles about baby boomers sometimes present a mirage of contradictions. Often pictured as a Me Generation of self-centered, acquisition-oriented, career builders, baby boomers from the beginning have been concerned about social causes and sticking up for the underdog. Living miles from their families and in communities where they feel no roots, many feel lonely, even though their lives are filled with people and people-centered activities. They rarely join churches and are not very religious, but most claim to believe in God and are concerned about spirituality—a vague term that can have various meanings. They have high tolerance for differing theological perspectives (in part because they are tolerant of diversity in all areas of thinking), but they look for clear religious and moral values for their children. When they come to church, baby boomers expect high quality programs and meaningful, well-articulated sermons, but they also want small-group sharing and the opportunity to be involved in making things happen.

"Having been herded together from their childhood on, boomers are forever searching for the contribution they can make as individuals," states Paula Rinehart, who has been writing a book on baby boomer spirituality. "Largely responsible for the 600 percent increase in the number of private business ventures begun in the last 30 years, this age group favors a hands-on entrepreneurial approach to meeting needs."[7] Churches that minister effectively to baby boomers emphasize small groups, active involvement, meeting needs, and helping people find and use their spiritual gifts.[8]

The pastor of one large baby boomer church summarizes much of our discussion thus far. "The organization that wants to relate well to boomers will promote variety, treat everyone as a professional, value straight talk and truthfulness, encourage participation, minimize layers of management, and be sensitive to individual needs and relationships."[9] These conclusions can provide clear guidelines for church leaders and business managers; counselors are likely to have more difficulty applying similar principles to our work as people helpers.

CHALLENGE

Churches that attract baby boomers are often criticized, sometimes with justification. Congregations that develop high quality programs designed to attract the unchurched, to meet needs, and to stimulate involvement, often are guilty of playing down biblical teachings about self-denial, sacrifice, commitment, and costly grace. In their efforts to accommodate the returning generation and to increase numbers, some church leaders drop *sin* from their vocabulary,[10] make little call for commitment, and turn worship services into showmanship pieces that end with beautifully crafted talks about coping with stress, succeeding in life, and becoming more loving. Critics charge that baby boomer churches kick aside virtually every conventional expression of worship, turn Sunday services into "first-class musical-comedy-drama productions," avoid Bible teaching or expository preaching, and permit nothing that would challenge church goers or make them feel uncomfortable. And it is true, no doubt, that some pastors do stay with a weak theology or an emasculated half-gospel that hides the reality of sin, confession, self-denial, and commitment.

But the critics are wrong (sometimes they are also naive and ill informed) if they assume that such weaknesses apply to all baby boomer churches. This is a generation that "instinctively gravitates toward the opportunity for personal challenge." They have to be convinced that the cause is worthwhile, and, as we have seen, it helps if they can own issues and not have them imposed from above. But these people are willing to make commitments. They admire and are willing to be led by Christian leaders who are faithful to Christ and who do not water down the message of the Gospel in order to give humorous pep talks with minimal Bible exposition. Churches, educational institutions, or counseling approaches that meet the baby boomers' high expectations will flourish, and baby boomers, in turn, will respond well to approaches that have high expectations of them.[11]

This generation has lived long enough to encounter strong doses of realism, but many still are intent on changing the world. Now they are reaching the time in life when they have the financial resources and the positions in society to turn some of their long-frustrated dreams into reality. That can be good news for the society and for churches that dare to be challenging.

BABY BOOMER CONSUMERISM AND THE CHURCH

Are we preaching Christ or packaging Jesus?

This was the lead question in a series of magazine articles that focused on ways to reach a culture that is steeped in consumerism. One article, appropriately titled "The Marketing of a Boomer Church," described how a large midwestern congregation has attempted to reach a generation that has been raised to think continually like consumers.[12]

"The average boomer is a consummate consumer," according to Doug Murren. This is true "even when it comes to religion. We've been reared as the focus of the advertising sector of our society; the media have aimed at us and so has the military. We've been taught to look for products and services that interest us the most. We tend to view churches from this perspective as well."[13] Baby boomers inspect churches like restaurants and they do not return if they find nothing to their taste. The generation that has no brand loyalty and little inclination to join anything is a generation that has no hesitation shifting from one congregation to another and no desire to become members of any church. People who value the one-stop shopping convenience of suburban malls and supermarkets often like a one-stop church complex that offers a variety of groups and programs, high quality programming, and the opportunity to identify with a large and successful enterprise.[14]

In an earlier chapter we summarized Neil Postman's insightful analysis of television's role in American culture. Postman writes as a journalist, not as a church leader, but his observations about religious television have great relevance for the church that seeks to minister to baby boomers.

Television viewers must be captured and held, according to Postman. They are free to leave the room at any time, to turn away from the television screen, or to flip channels. To prevent this, television producers and performers strive to keep their programs interesting, visually appealing, focused on personalities, and above all, entertaining. To keep them watching, viewers have to be offered something they want, and modern marketing methods must be used abundantly. If television is to be successful, these principles must be applied to soap operas, sitcoms and comedy shows, televised sporting events, news reports, documentaries, and every other type of presentation including religious programs.

Postman's commentary on all of this is sobering.

There is no great religious leader—from the Buddha to Moses to Jesus to Mohammed to Luther—who offered people what they want. Only what they need. But television is not suited to offering people what they need. It is "user friendly." It is too easy to turn off. It is at its most alluring when it speaks the language of dynamic visual imagery. It does not accommodate complex language or stringent demands. As a consequence, what is preached on television is not anything like the Sermon on the Mount. Religious programs are filled with good cheer. They celebrate affluence. Though their messages are trivial, the shows have high ratings, or rather, *because* their messages are trivial, the shows have high ratings. . . . The preachers . . . control the content of their preaching to maximize their ratings. You shall wait a very long time indeed if you wish to hear an electronic preacher refer to the difficulties a rich man will have in gaining access to heaven. . . .

I believe I am not mistaken in saying that Christianity is a demanding and serious religion. When it is delivered as easy and amusing, it is another kind of religion altogether.[15]

Baby boomers, of course, have been raised on television. The consumer mentality that they accept without question has been accompanied and reinforced by a television mentality that carries into the church building. Attendees expect worship services to be more appealing and entertaining than the Sunday paper or the convenient television competition that is available at home with the press of a button. And all of this is complicated by the oft-noted baby boomer demand for relevance, quality, credibility, need-satisfaction, and practical help in solving problems.

Churches that succeed in reaching baby boomers try to understand the generation, seek to maintain credibility, strive to meet needs, carefully plan services that evoke a sense of community involvement in worship, present well-prepared sermons and relevant teaching, provide quality child care and children's programs, and offer a variety of options in terms of church programs, meeting times, styles of music, and types of worship—all without compromising the church's message. That, of course, is a tall order.

Several years ago a television program dramatized the struggles of a young seminary graduate who was torn between an opportunity to join the staff of a large and influential television ministry or to pastor a small local church. For two hours, viewers watched the young man's struggle. The mega-ministry had fine programming and great impact in the lives of thousands, but the small church pastor was available to care for the hurting, to comfort the grieving, to talk with those who had doubts, and to model authentic Christianity for the seekers and younger believers. The fictional young preacher in the television drama eventually elected for the local church. Baby boomers, we suspect, would prefer to have both types of ministry rolled into one consumer-sensitive congregation.

BABY BOOMER MENTALITY AND THE CHURCH

"We possess an uncanny belief in our ability to make the world better," one baby boomer wrote. "We are simply waiting for the leadership and occasions to ignite us to action."[16] Have you ever noticed, however, that baby boomers do not have any heroes and appear to be without any leaders? Dan Quayle was the first baby boomer to reach the highest ranks of government, but he quickly became the brunt of criticism and jokes. It is difficult for any person to give leadership to a generation that has limited loyalty, a reluctance to take direction from others, widespread distrust of existing leaders, and a tendency to believe that truth is relative—all depending on one's perceptions.

As they move into middle age and take increasing leadership roles in business, professions, and educational institutions, baby boomers seem likely to emphasize team approaches, innovation, quality of product, acceptance of diversity, and increasing places of influence for women. Churches and religious organizations that welcome these changes and make room for the baby boomers will have a leading edge in attracting their participation and meeting their needs. "Those that are slow to open leadership to this generation will face constituency defection, internal revolution, or even institutional death."[17] Everybody knows that baby boomers cannot be ignored. They are too numerous and too influential.

For Christian counselors, these changes raise two significant issues. They deal with the effects of baby boomer thinking on Christian theology and on Christian counseling.

BABY BOOMERS AND CHRISTIAN THEOLOGY

Faced with the return of baby boomers, the church is in danger of making two major errors. First, we can ignore the baby boomers and go about doing our religious business as usual. But churches will be bypassed by the baby boom generation if they stick with old traditions and old style music, stress denominationalism and church membership, give little heed to quality of worship or accountability, stay with authoritarian (mostly

male, mostly older) leadership, show little awareness or interest in the needs of people with high-tech and high-pressure
careers, or de-emphasize small groups, shared responsibilities,
and relevance. In time, these are the churches that will fade to
insignificance or be filled with self-congratulating traditionalists who have lost touch with both their culture and their Lord
who was actively involved in reaching the people of his society.

A second, more dangerous error, is the temptation for
churches to wrap themselves in the baby boomer mentality
that puts high value on tolerance, experience, entertainment,
stress management, intimacy, narcissism, and meeting
needs. Buoyed by the consumer mentality of our constituents, we could be in danger of subtly papering over those
parts of the biblical message that might offend or drive away
our baby boom parishioners. With little conscious awareness of the shift, we could change the Gospel from a
message that saves to a message that sells. In doing so, we
would not be the first to be guilty of proclaiming a watered-
down Christianity.

In our determination to be relevant and consumer conscious,
we must not forget that the biblical message is revolutionary
and commitment oriented. It is sensitive to needs and filled
with compassion, offering genuine good news of hope and forgiveness for people of all ages in the midst of a chaotic and
populous generation. But it demands that people make decisions, and its "Thus says the Lord" goes against the grain of
those who deny classical logic, assume that all truth is relative, or base conclusions solely on what they experience.

Some things in this world are true and some are false, regardless of our experiences. We may stand at the shore of an
ocean, look at the straight line along the horizon, and conclude
that the world is flat. Hundreds may stand beside us and agree.
We may all be convinced, based on our experience, of a conclusion that is not true, regardless of the popular vote. The
Christian message assumes that some things are true, regardless of what we feel, perceive, endorse, or accept as a group.

Baby boomers who could agree with the above paragraph
might disagree with biblical assertions that there is only one
God, sovereign and eternal, who exists in three persons—

despite New Age declarations that we are all gods, within ourselves. Baby boomers who tolerate different beliefs may resist the idea that we are saved by grace, through faith, and not as a result of our own efforts (Ephesians 2:8–9). Steeped in their own conclusions, experiences, and desires to be tolerant, many might disagree that salvation comes through belief in Christ alone (Acts 4:10–12), but that is true whether or not anyone believes it. Baby boomers, like generations that have come before, may resist the declaration of Jesus that any person who follows him must deny oneself, take up a cross, and follow him (Matthew 16:24–27).

God does not alter truth to fit the spirit of the times or the thinking of a contemporary generation. He has not done so in the past; he does not do so today. Methods can be altered but the basic content of the message cannot.

Churches that call for confession of sin and commitment to Christ will lose some of the baby boomers who came because of the contemporary music and practical messages. But the baby boomers who stay often are willing to make commitments and to grow as followers of Jesus Christ. They are grateful to have something solid to believe, and they are willing to invest their energies and their money into Christian service that will make a difference.

BABY BOOMERS AND CHRISTIAN COUNSELING

Nobody needs a graduate degree in counseling to realize that many baby boomers are hurting people. They have grown up and live in an era of unfulfilled expectations, high rates of depression, family breakdown, the creeping influence of AIDS, domestic violence, and sexual abuse that is estimated to affect one-fourth of all women by the time they reach adulthood. This is a generation that was born with the highest of hopes but has watched many of its dreams die. These are people who have grown up disillusioned and wounded. They have been hurt too much to tolerate simplistic answers, catchy self-help formulas, hypocritical advice givers, irrelevant sermon topics, or churches where everybody wears a plastic smile and pretends that Christians never have doubts or problems.

A few angry critics may fire their darts at Christian counselors, but the baby boomers whom we seek to help are oblivious to squabbles over Christian psychology. People in need want help with their problems, answers to their questions, and reductions in their stresses. They have fueled a boom in Christian counseling, but they will not go to just any counselor. Consumer-conscious baby boomers will shop for help and helpers until they find what they seek.

Like pastors and other church leaders, Christian counselors must be aware of baby boomer thinking, knowledgeable about baby boomer needs,[18] sensitive to baby boomer consumerism, and careful not to water down our *Christian* counseling so that baby boomer preferences weaken our therapeutic interventions. We will be expected to give help with family issues, career frustrations, and feelings of resentment—sometimes directed at God or against the pathological religious upbringing that has brought suffering to many.

To work effectively with people in this generation, we may have to make adaptations that are similar to those being made by the church. Consumer-conscious counselees might not be loyal enough to stick with long-term counseling if they do not see any improvement. Experience-preferring, participation-oriented, highly relational baby boomers may not be satisfied with authoritarian approaches to therapy. Our methods may be challenged by people who want to have ownership in the therapeutic process. A generation that values sharing and small group experiences has already shown their liking for mutual aid and specialized support groups. People who want answers and formulas for improvement are flocking to workshops, seminars, and a host of eight- or twelve-step programs that deal with issues ranging from drug abuse and bulimia to spiritual growth and career management.[19] Baby boomers want helpers who have the ability to understand and deal sensitively with painful issues and hurting people.

But like the church, we too must take care lest we embrace a secular psychology that glosses over sin, gives psychological explanations to excuse unfaithfulness and disobedience, never challenges self-centered values, or fails to call counselees to account for attitudes and behaviors that are inconsistent with biblical teaching. A watered-down Christian counseling is no more excusable than preaching or church programs that cut out much of the bite and commitment that is at the core of biblically based Christianity.

The Wooddale Church in the Minneapolis suburb of Eden Prairie, Minnesota, has been on the cutting edge of meeting the needs of baby boomers. The congregation has grown through a mixture of innovation, dynamic leadership, and healthy caution lest there be theological compromise in the midst of a rush to be relevant. To keep the church on track and true to its biblical roots, the congregation has employed core guidelines. Each of these could apply equally well to Christian counselors who work with baby boomers.

First is a commitment to Scripture. When changes are proposed, the members go to Scripture for guidance, and even then they move cautiously. "I find baby boomers appreciate intentional and analytical change," the pastor told a recent interviewer.[20] It is easy, and dangerous, to let enthusiasm and creative planning run ahead of intensive periods of Bible study and prayer for guidance.

Second, the church constantly examines its programs and methods, tries to evaluate what it is doing and why, and ponders other approaches or techniques that might be better—or worse. To help with this process, the church invites consultants and critics to give their evaluations. Such openness extends to the secular press, which has free access to the church's activities and books.

Third, since independence can be a hazard, the church remains attached to a denomination, is affiliated with the National Association of Evangelicals, and strives to build accountability into its structure.

To this list we might add the importance of clear mission statements. Why does the local church exist? What is the purpose of each of its ministries? If the local church has no clear direction, it is likely to flounder, adrift in a sea of innovations or irrelevancies.

Christian counselors who work with baby boomers might apply similar guidelines to themselves. Is what you are doing consistent with Scripture? Are you willing to be critiqued, to learn, and to change? Are you accountable to anybody? And do you have a personal mission statement that guides your work and your ministry?

Churches and Christian counselors will face unprecedented opportunities as they work with the baby boom generation. And as we work, all of us will have to keep aware of an emerging group that affects the lives of many baby boomers. This is the generation of baby busters that we discuss in the next chapter.

NOTES

1. "Baby Boomers Rediscover Church," *Christianity Today* 34 (October 22, 1990): 58.

2. Kenneth L. Woodward, "A Time to Seek," *Newsweek* (December 17, 1990), 50–56.

3. Wesley G. Pippert, "A Generation Warms to Religion," *Christianity Today* 33 (October 6, 1989): 22.

4. Robert L. Bast, *Attracting New Members* (Monrovia, Calif.: Church Growth, Inc., 1988), 32.

5. Joni Eareckson Tada, *Seeking God: My Journey of Prayer and Praise* (Brentwood, Tenn.: Wolgemuth and Hyatt, 1991), 4.

6. Doug Murren, *The Baby Boomerang: Catching Baby Boomers as They Return to Church* (Ventura, Calif.: Regal, 1990), 53–54. Italics are in the original.

7. Paula Rinehart, "The Pivotal Generation," *Christianity Today* 33 (October 6, 1989): 25.

8. One of the authors regularly attends such a church, Willow Creek Community Church in South Barrington, Illinois. Worship services are characterized by a high level of excellence, sermons are consistently relevant to baby boomer needs, and a significant proportion of attendees are involved in small groups and volunteer activities. See, for example, Verne Becker, "A Church for Bored Boomers," *Christianity Today* 33 (October 6, 1989): 25. It is NOT true that this church offers no challenge to its communicants. Weekend services are designed for "seekers," but the heavily attended midweek services (held on two nights because there is not sufficient room in the 4650 seat auditorium for everyone to gather on one night) are consistently focused on worship, expository teaching, and challenges for costly commitment.

9. Leith Anderson, *Dying for Change* (Minneapolis: Bethany, 1990), 94.

10. Kenneth L. Woodward, "A Time to Seek," *Newsweek* (December 17, 1990), 56.

11. Anderson, *Dying for Change,* 85.

12. James Berkley, "The Marketing of a Boomer Church," *Christianity Today* 35 (February 11, 1991): 34–36.

13. Murren, *Baby Boomerang*, 139.

14. Woodward, "A Time to Seek," 53.

15. Neil Postman, *Amusing Ourselves to Death: Public Discourse in the Age of Show Business* (New York: Penguin, 1985), 121.

16. Murren, *The Baby Boomerang*, 59.

17. Anderson, *Dying for Change*, 93.

18. This explains, in part, why we have devoted five chapters in this book to helping counselors understand baby boomers.

19. Tim Stafford, "The Hidden Gospel of the 12 Steps," *Christianity Today* 35 (July 22, 1991): 14–19.

20. Berkley, "The Marketing," 35. The church pastor is Leith Anderson whose book, *Dying for Change*, was consulted repeatedly as we prepared this chapter.

Chapter 6

Baby Boomer Followers: The Baby Busters

W HEN THE FIRST BABY BOOMERS were ten years old, an insightful and disturbing critique of American business people was published by a *Fortune* editor named William H. Whyte, Jr. Even readers who cared nothing about business were fascinated with the author's thesis that many people were giving up the personal hopes and ambitions that had dominated earlier generations and were looking for jobs that would promise security and a high standard of living under the protection of big organizations—the corporation, the government, the university, or the labor union. In exchange for security, workers at all socioeconomic levels were abandoning individual aspirations and becoming what Whyte termed "organization men."[1]

One of these organization men was Ray Myers, an official of Continental Bank in Chicago. His three sons were baby boomers, and the youngest, Scott, grew up to become a businessman himself. But unlike his father, Scott Myers refused to become an organization man. "I don't have any loyalty to the company," he told a reporter for the *New York Times*. "I'm in it for me." Unfortunately for Scott Myers, the company president read the quotation, and three days later the young man was fired.

His story attracted national attention, not only because the company president was well-known, the former treasury secretary of the Carter administration, but also because Scott Myers articulated what many of his colleagues had been thinking: the individual rather than the organization should be paramount.

This is the theme of a book that appeared thirty-five years after Whyte's famous description of the organization man. The authors, both baby boomers, interviewed 175 of the people whose careers were described in the original book and an equal number of their offspring, including Scott Myers. Their conclusion: the "generation after the organization man" is composed of "new individualists" who distrust and disdain people that sell out to organizations.[2] The new individualists, instead, use the organization for their own purposes and want to work either for themselves or for companies that recognize their contributions, allow individuals to determine how their work should be accomplished, and create an atmosphere where knowledge and skill are considered more important than issues of authority and rank. When compared to their parents, these baby boom individualists are indeed "a different crop."[3]

If the baby boomers differ so significantly from the generation that came before, isn't it logical to assume that an equal or greater gap may separate those same baby boomers from the generation that is growing up in their wake? Often known as *baby busters*, these are the people who were born in the decade or so between the midsixties and the midseventies and before the baby boomers began producing their own "baby boomlet" of children.[4]

What are these baby busters like?

They were raised in smaller families, attended schools with fewer classmates, and experienced much less competition than the baby boomers, in whose shadow they will always dwell. This is a generation that grew up in an era of drugs, divorce, and economic strain, according to *Time* magazine.

They "virtually reared themselves" in a time when "TV provided the surrogate parenting, and Ronald Reagan starred as the real-life Mister Rogers, dispensing reassurance during their troubled adolescence." Now as adults they feel paralyzed by the social problems they see as their inheritance, and many seek to avoid risk, pain, and responsibility. The world seems out of control, and some might identify with the twenty-three-year-old college student who concluded "it is almost our role to be passive."

As a result, many baby busters

> . . . have trouble making decisions. They would rather hike in the Himalayas than climb a corporate ladder. They have few heroes, no anthems, no style to call their own. They crave entertainment, but their attention span is as short as one zap of a TV dial. They hate yuppies, hippies and druggies. They postpone marriage because they dread divorce. They sneer at Range Rovers, Rolexes and red suspenders. What they hold dear are family life, local activism, national parks, penny loafers and mountain bikes. They possess only a hazy sense of their own identity but a monumental preoccupation with all the problems the preceding generation will leave them to fix. . . .
>
> But here they come: freshly minted grownups. Anyone who expected they would echo the boomers who came before, bringing more of the same attitude, should brace for a surprise. This crowd . . . scornfully rejects the habits and values of the baby boomers, viewing that group as self-centered, fickle and impractical.[5]

Baby boomers have attracted considerable attention since they began arriving over forty years ago; baby busters largely have been overlooked or ignored. But these are the people who will be expected to fill high-tech jobs, to pay taxes, to be church leaders, and to cope with escalating social programs, including the aging of the baby boomers. In the next several decades, the country will need more baby busters than we have and present them with more demands than they want. Perhaps it is not surprising that so many of them resist growing up.

THE BABY BUSTERS: A CHARACTER SKETCH

Like the baby boomers who came before, baby busters are a diverse lot. They are not cookie-cutter organization men and women. They are more like new individualists, but as a group they show unique characteristics that counselors and others might find helpful to recognize.

ENTITLEMENT

In one of the books in his *Children of Crisis* series, Harvard psychiatrist Robert Coles wrote that children of the very rich have a "narcissistic entitlement" type of thinking. They have grown up in the midst of prosperity, with seemingly endless provisions coming from their two working parents. This is a generation that has been given much but has not been expected to give much in return. Many have come to expect that life will be fulfilling, that opportunities will be abundant, and that everything is going to be okay.

This kind of thinking is not limited to young adults who were raised in affluence. Like the baby boomers who came before, the baby buster generation has been given the same message. Life will not be hard. Competition will not be intense. Careers, when they come, will be fulfilling, and the rewards will be immediate. Unlike baby boomers who entered schools that were crowded and faced daily competition, the baby busters had a life that was easier. They learned to expect that their needs should be met, jobs would be provided, money would be available, and problems would be solved. The result is a generation of young adults who want and expect everything right away. Life is to be lived for the present. There is little awareness of a philosophy that says we should make long-range plans, or work hard today so things will be better tomorrow. This is a *now* generation that has little interest in any religion that talks about sacrifices, heaven, or "the sweet bye and bye." They want to hear about a faith that works now and brings immediate benefits.[6]

As they move into the marketplace, many of these baby busters are encountering a devastating shock. There *is* competition in this world, and it often is accompanied by aggressiveness, scarcity, limited employment opportunities, and even hostility from the baby boomers who have been around longer. Most jobs—at least most beginning jobs—do not give immediate fulfillment, meaningful work, instant status, opportunity to make a difference, freedom to work with minimal supervision, and salaries that support affluent lifestyles. The emphasis on self-expression and feeling good that many baby busters learned in school, does not fly in a real world that puts more emphasis on demanding work, solid training, the hard knocks of experience, and the ability to produce.

In a sobering cover story, *Business Week* magazine documented the difficulties that many people under thirty face as they seek to make ends meet and to get affordable housing. For the first time in our history, a generation is reaching adulthood and discovering that they may have to work harder but settle for a lower level of affluence than their parents have experienced. On the average, young men today earn 17 percent less, in inflation-adjusted dollars, than they would have earned in 1973. When compared with their less-educated peers, college graduates are more likely to reach their goals, especially if both spouses work, but the process will take longer than it did for baby boomers. High school graduates have less chance of winning the race for prosperity, and there is even less hope for high school dropouts. The greatest struggles occur among African-Americans, Hispanics, single mothers, and others who do not have the benefits of more prolonged education. It is not surprising to read the business analyst's observation that "some busters may end up as depressed as their incomes, spawning a higher incidence of psychological and medical problems" in themselves and among their children.[7]

Despite these dire predictions, baby busters have not given up the idea of entitlement. They still hope to have it all and to have it soon. And they might get what they want. Since they are few in number, the demand for workers will increase in the coming years, and frustrated company executives may have to give previously unheard-of perks to entry-level baby busters.

But for now, many are frustrated. Like millions of others whose dreams have been thwarted, numerous baby busters have fallen back into age-old defensive ways of thinking and living. Some have postponed their full entrance into adulthood. Others have responded by returning to traditional values or by finding ways to react against the frustrations. Confusion is widespread, but increasing numbers are facing the cold waters of reality and learning to swim in a murky ocean of adult responsibilities for which they have been poorly prepared.

Postponement

Melissa was one of our students—bright, articulate, poised, and so attractive that she was runner-up in a statewide beauty contest. She was also single. "I've had opportunities to get married, and I want to get married," she said, "but quite frankly I'm afraid of divorce."

Melissa is a devoted Christian who has struggled to get free from the grasp of her divorced mother. When she was twenty-three, Melissa was maid of honor at the marriage of her best friend and college roommate. The newlyweds were intent on serving Christ and went off to seminary where their marriage ended in divorce two years later. Melissa, now thirty, expects to get married, and she probably will. But she has been stung by the experiences of others, and she wants to delay her trip to the altar until she can be more sure of marital success.

Most of us know people like Melissa. They postpone marriage, career choice, further education, and childbearing. Some leave the homes of their parents, go to college for a while, or get a job, but then they come back home where living is cheaper. In most cases, parents are willing to take in their boomerang children, are reluctant to push them out, and tend to make few demands while they remain at home. According to one recent report, 75 percent of U.S. males eighteen to twenty-four years of age are living at home, the largest proportion since the Depression.[8]

In an article about these baby busters, a national magazine described them as adults who want to postpone growing up; a generation that is proceeding with caution. These are people who:

- are not in any rush to get married, hoping that by waiting, time will bring a more compatible mate and the maturity to avoid divorce;
- are reluctant to get close to others lest somebody gets hurt;
- are willing to postpone child rearing, hoping that eventually they will have families that are more stable than the families in which they grew up (an estimated 40 percent of people in their twenties are children of divorce);
- are not finding, settling into, or remaining with previously chosen careers;
- have a strong desire to travel and see the world before they settle down for further education, career building, or marriage; and
- recognize the importance of getting a college degree but are willing to delay schooling and go back to college later.[9]

All of this has led one writer to call baby busters "the postponed generation" of young adults who are still growing up.[10] These are not children; they are men and women in their twenties who are reluctant to take adult responsibilities. Some may be trying to deny the reality of adulthood, but others are realistic enough to know that marriages fail, that independent living can be expensive, that long-term commitments can be confining, and that career advancement takes hard work. For the first time in our history, a significant part of a generation has the privilege of changing majors, wandering around the world, living at home with one's parents, postponing marriage, spending endless years in school, getting help with financial struggles, and delaying childbearing. The postponed generation is waiting to settle down, perhaps with the hope that if they wait on life's big decisions, they might get a better and more secure deal later.[11]

NEOTRADITIONALISM

Following his first visit to the United States, a recent visitor described his impressions. "I didn't expect people to be so friendly or to have any manners," he confessed. "I thought I might see some muggings in the city, and I was surprised that we didn't see any police chases. The only policemen I saw were drinking coffee in a donut shop."

Where did the visitor get these and other assumptions about the United States? His expectations came from watching television, listening to the lyrics of American performers, and observing American clothing styles and popular expressions. In two words, he learned from our *pop culture*. This is the second-largest U.S. export, according to *Fortune* magazine, and it largely forms the basis of how we are seen by people in other countries.[12]

And what do they see? What is the message that pop culture conveys? According to one analyst, we "may sometimes be banal, our taste isn't the most refined, and sometimes we're downright crude. Like Bart, we can be comfortable and underachieving." In addition, we tend to be mindless, relaxed, nonrebellious, and settled into what someone has called "neotraditionalism." This is a way of thinking that combines traditional values—such as stability, the home, family—with the personal freedoms that have come as a result of the sexual revolution, feminism, and the civil rights movement.[13]

This return to more traditional values is seen most clearly in the baby busters. Like all generational groups, they have their own language, music, attitudes, perceptions, and behaviors that separate them from the generation that came before. In one study of AIDS-related risk-taking behavior, for example, baby boomers were compared with the pre-baby boom generation that proceeded them and with the baby busters who came later. On several measures—including involvement with multiple sexual partners, having intercourse without using condoms, or the use of drugs injected through unsterilized, previously used needles—the baby boomers were significantly more likely to engage in higher-risk behavior than were older or younger generations, both of which tended to be more conservative.[14]

Many baby busters might agree that

> we have left the sixties behind, with shaggy hair and Hula-Hoops, and we have returned to a neater, more traditional life-style. . . . Education has gone "back to the basics," and we don't mind uniforms and strict requirements. Our politics are more conservative. In fact we are almost apolitical. . . .

The wealth and sense of entitlement linger in memory as a basic standard. The hippies are gone and so are the rap groups, but we still believe that there are alternatives to the middle-class life-style and that we have a right to self-fulfillment, choice, power, even the right to transcend ordinary life.[15]

In places there still are rebels in the streets, and baby busters still get involved in crusades—as young adults have crusaded for centuries. When compared with their grandparents, this generation is more promiscuous and more open about their sexuality,[16] more aware of violence and problems in the world, and more crude in their talk. But many of their basic values are more traditional and closer to those of the pre-baby boomers than to those of the intervening baby boomers. You can see this for yourself if you listen to their music or talk with them about the values that guide their lives.

REACTION

As a generation of individualists, baby busters have found a number of ways to express their frustrations about the adult world that they are having to enter.

Some react with anger and resentment. They dislike being compared with baby boomers, resent the self-centered and seemingly fickle values of those who came before, refuse to be caught in the pursuit of materialism or ambition, and do not appreciate the massive social problems that have been dumped on the world by free-spending older generations. It is characteristic of young adults to be optimistic and idealistic, but baby busters recognize that problems do not have easy solutions, and many feel ill-equipped, unable, and unmotivated to build adult lives or to solve problems that others have created.

As a result, many have become passive, isolationist, and reluctant to form close relationships that involve trust, vulnerability, and the possibility of rejection.[17] Some are discovering that the parents who invested heavily in their adolescent children now expect their adult offspring to fend for themselves. Many respond with humor and suggest that while "baby boomers get depressed; baby busters laugh." Others are like the

Washington Post writer who described her generation as "25 and pending." We are "grown-up but still children," she wrote, in an article that some of her same-age peers might challenge. We are "seeking experience without responsibility," wearing suits but keeping our ponytails. "We are undecided, leaving the doors open," and uncertain how to respond when there are more choices than anyone can make.[18] Perhaps we should not be surprised that this is a generation of ambivalence, indecision, and confusion.

CONFUSION

The message is heard frequently: we are living in a time of rapid change perhaps unmatched by any previous generation in history. "America will be substantially different in the year 2000," according to futurist George Barna. "Unparalleled change will sweep the nation, and transform every dimension of life in this country."

When change is sudden and *revolutionary*, there is always confusion until the dust settles and the new order emerges. But contemporary change is more *evolutionary;* a slow process that brings continual but incremental changes in our values, beliefs, perspectives, lifestyles, institutions, and ways of doing things. Revolutionary changes attract everybody's attention, but incremental changes often slip by unnoticed. Like unobserved ripples of water that in time can alter a shoreline, constant evolutionary changes can undermine and radically transform cultures, institutions (including churches), and individual lives. Barna is not being overly dramatic when he calls the nineties "the pivotal decade in the history of American Christianity."[19]

Where does this leave baby busters? Many are confused. They have learned to live with change and endless choices. They are reluctant to make firm commitments lest they overlook something or make a mistake. Instead of trying to integrate all aspects of life into a consistent philosophy, they have learned to live with contradictions. Choices are made one at a time, on the basis of feelings or what makes sense *now*. Even baby boomers who are tolerant of diversity and comfortable with change do not like internal contradictions. But this,

it seems, is no problem for many baby busters. "They may op-
pose abortion but have one, believe in both the Bible and
reincarnation, or register Republican and vote Democrat. There
is little felt need for cohesion, consistency, or overall integrity."[20]

Is it surprising that many in this generation feel a sense of
confusion? They have few good role models, little reason to
trust political or corporate leaders, not much faith in the
church, and plenty of uncertainty about the future. So they
float from one job, one living arrangement, one goal, one belief, one college major, or even one sexual partner to another.
Nothing about life seems permanent or certain, so these people
keep their options open and live with indecision, ambivalence,
and uncertainty.

Action Oriented

Counselors must remember, however, that baby busters are
also young adults who show many of the characteristics that
people in their twenties have always shown. They are molded
and perhaps restrained by world events and the cultures in
which they have been raised, but they are also idealists, activists, willing to take risks, and often convinced that they can
make a difference.[21] Many are cynical, and few have causes to
match the antiwar movement, feminism, or civil rights
struggles of the sixties. But they do want to give something
back to society and to make an impact. Regrettably, they have
no leaders, overarching causes, or clear directions about how
they can get started. For many, it is hard to be assertive. So
their lives are on hold.

Baby Buster Aspirations

As university professors, the authors of this book have a lot
of contact with baby busters, and one of us teaches a weekly
Sunday School class of mostly baby buster couples. Our contacts with this generation do not leave us discouraged. On the
contrary, we see great potential in this generation and in the
baby boomers that they are following. Each generation has
unique problems, but both have goals and hopes that can give

us cause for optimism. But perhaps our enthusiasm is colored by the fact that we work mostly with Christian baby busters.

Whether or not they are believers, many baby busters are willing to work hard. Some, of course, have no alternative but to work at whatever job they can get. But when they have the choice, these young people are unwilling to be organization men or women, workaholics who are driven by their careers, corporate climbers who burn out and lose everything in the process, or mindless employees who settle for routine work schedules and inflexible hours. They like performance evaluations and involvement in short-term tasks where results are observable.

Some evidence suggests that the baby busters see careers differently than the older baby boomers.[22] The younger generation does not much believe in the likelihood of job security or instant wealth. Instead, many seek job gratification, even if this means lower pay and less prestige. There has been an upsurge of interest in teaching (long disdained as an underpaid and underappreciated profession), in public service careers, or in other activities that will make a difference to society. Corporate ladder climbing is out; work that allows people to have flexible lifestyles and to have an impact is in.

Baby busters are still willing to get college degrees, despite the escalating costs of tuition, uncertainty about the future, and a suspicion that a university degree might not really be worth much. Without a degree, fulfilling and decent paying jobs are difficult to find, even though much of the education process is likely to be seen as irrelevant. For many, college is a necessary evil and a time of intense anxiety that sometimes spills over into excessive drinking, ugly fraternity parties, degrading—sometimes violent—sex,[23] and acts of vandalism. Only a minority may be involved in such actions, but these behaviors can create psychological and physical wounds that last for life.

For many baby busters, life in the future will involve families. When compared to the older generation, baby busters appear to be more family oriented and concerned about their future children. Many want to spend more time with their kids, in part because they felt neglected by their own parents and do not want to make similar mistakes. "When I raise my children, my approach will be my grandparents', much more serious and conservative," said one twenty-four-year-old. "I would never give my children the freedoms I had."

Where are the baby busters spiritually? As we have seen in earlier chapters, they are living at a time of life when many people drop out of the church. But like the baby boomers who are returning to church, the younger generation has no time and little interest in religion that is irrelevant, dull, and not abreast of the times.

Jim, twenty-six, recently left his well-paying job with a big city ad agency to work for a Christian organization that is involved with poverty-enslaved kids overseas. Jim and his wife both became Christians while they were in college, and their commitment to Christ has led them to make a career decision that neither of their families can understand or appreciate. But Jim is frustrated with the church. "I've been attending here for three years," he told a church leader before he left. "I want to serve Christ, but neither the music here nor the messages speak to a twenty-six-year-old. I feel like I'm forgotten, out in left field someplace."

One pastor has called his work of leading a multigenerational church as a "glorious challenge."[24] It is a challenge that many churches rise successfully to meet. But baby busters who live in an age of change and contradiction have little interest in a God or a religion that seems rigid, static, and outdated. The solutions that worked even ten years ago may not work with baby busters. While we must keep the same timeless message, we need approaches to ministry, and approaches to counseling, that are creative, relevant, and able to reach both baby boomers and baby busters.

RESPONDING TO BABY BUSTERS

Perhaps every generation has worried about its young people who, in turn, grow to middle age and then worry about their own children. Baby busters, it seems, are postponing adult responsibilities, are overwhelmed with choices, find themselves in a world of unusual change, are aware that life is tough, and face a world where there is instability and few widely admired models. But this generation is highly educated, willing to be flexible, open to change, inclined toward more traditional values, and determined to proceed cautiously in an effort to avoid mistakes of the past. If we believe that God is sovereign, then all of us, baby busters included, can move through the nineties with confidence, despite the ominous trends in the culture.

When we look at them closely, baby busters may be heralds of things to come. In a study conducted for Hilton Hotels, 50 percent of the people polled said they would sacrifice part of their pay for more time off. And the more time pressured they felt, the stronger their desire to take time off. Given their choice of eight goals for the future, 77 percent said "spending time with family and friends" was a priority, 74 percent cited intellectual, emotional, or physical improvement, and 66 percent wanted more time to "spend any way you please." In contrast, 61 percent cited "making money" as a goal and only 29 percent said they would like to spend more money on material possessions. One in five complained that they "had no time for fun anymore."[25]

Baby busters do not want these kinds of time pressures. Unlike many of the baby boomers that came before, the younger generation seems willing to flow with the changes without the constant stresses, many self-imposed, that have made life miserable for many who are moving into middle age.

NOTES

1. William H. Whyte, Jr., *The Organization Man* (New York: Simon and Schuster, 1956). A fascinating appendix to Whyte's book is titled "How to Cheat on Personality Tests."

2. Paul Leinberger and Bruce Tucker, *The New Individualists: The Generation After the Organization Man* (New York: Harper Collins, 1991). The book was written after William Whyte declined an invitation to update *The Organization Man*. Whyte made his original notes available and gave his full cooperation and encouragement as the Leinberger-Tucker volume was being written—even though Whyte disagrees with many of the conclusions in the more recent book.

3. Bill Barnhart, "A Different Crop," *Chicago Tribune*, August 11, 1991.

4. There are different definitions of baby busters. We have chosen to limit our definition to the group that was born in the decade following the last of the baby boomers and before the first large wave of baby boomers' children began appearing around 1975. Others have used the term *baby buster* to describe people born between 1965 and 1985 (a twenty-year span) or between 1960 and 1980 (this technically includes some baby boomers). Occasionally the term has been used—too broadly in our opinion—to refer to all people born after 1965.

5. David M. Gross and Sophfronia Scott, "Proceeding with Caution: The Twentysomething Generation Is Balking at Work, Marriage, and Baby Boomer Values, " *Time* (July 16, 1990), 57.

6. These views are discussed further by Leith Anderson in *Dying for Change* (Minneapolis: Bethany, 1991), chapter 6. See also Leith Anderson, "The Next Generation: Baby Busters Come of Age," *The Evangelical Beacon* 64 (April 1991): 9–11.

7. Aaron Bernstein, "What Happened to the American Dream?: The Under-30 Generation May Be Losing the Race for Prosperity," *Business Week* (August 19, 1991), 80–85.

8. Gross and Scott, "Proceeding with Caution, " 58.

9. Ibid.

10. Susan Littwin, *The Postponed Generation: Why America's Grown-Up Kids Are Growing Up Later* (New York: Morrow, 1986).

11. Anderson, "The Next Generation," 10.

12. For an insightful Christian analysis of pop culture, see Kenneth A. Myers, *All God's Children and Blue Suede Shoes: Christians and Popular Culture* (Westchester, Ill.: Crossway, 1989).

13. John Huey, "What Pop Culture is Telling Us," *Fortune* (June 17, 1991), 89–92.

14. Duane C. McBride, "Generational Differences in HIV Risk and AIDS," *American Behavioral Scientist* 33 (March/April 1990): 491–502.

15. Littwin, *The Postponed Generation,* 24–25.

16. According to one recent survey, 61 percent of baby busters had lost their virginity by the age of sixteen; more than one in five had intercourse by age thirteen or earlier—mostly as a response to peer pressure rather than for the pleasure of sex itself. For this generation, like the baby boomers who are older, sex outside matrimony is generally considered acceptable. See James Patterson and Peter Kim, *The Day America Told the Truth* (New York: Prentice Hall, 1991), 101–102.

17. When a first draft of this chapter was completed, we gave it to an expert to read—a baby buster, the daughter of one of the authors. Carefully she read what we had written and gave a number of thoughtful and useful suggestions for revision. She strongly challenged the suggestion of passivity in baby busters (this led us to insert *many* in the text), and she disagreed with the reporter who is cited later in this paragraph of the text. "You make us look worse than we are," our critic suggested, and as a result we have

altered portions of the chapter. Regrettably, because of her own pressures as a student, our evaluator did not have time to write a rebuttal to the chapter that we hoped to publish. Nevertheless, both of us want to thank Lynn Collins for her helpful critique of baby busters.

18. Nancy Smith, "25 and Pending: Getting Out of the Shadow of the Baby Boom Generation," *The Family Therapy Networker* 13 (September/October 1989): 15–17.

19. George Barna, *The Frog In the Kettle: What Christians Need to Know About Life In the Year 2000* (Ventura, Calif.: Regal, 1990), 223, 224, 226.

20. Anderson, "The Next Generation," 11.

21. Gene Bocknek, *The Young Adult: Development After Adolescence* (Monterey, Calif.: Brooks/Cole, 1980).

22. Gross and Scott, "Proceeding with Caution," 60.

23. Date rape, often occurring in student settings, has been described as an epidemic in America. An estimated 19 million women have been victims of date rape. See Patterson and Kim, *The Day America,* 128.

24. Robert Page, "The Glorious Challenge of Pastoring a Multigenerational Church," *Evangelical Beacon* (April 1991), 12–14.

25. Carol Hymowitz, "Trading Fat Paychecks for Free Time," *The Wall Street Journal*, August 5, 1991.

PART TWO

Counseling Baby Boomers

Chapter 7

Connecting with Baby Boomers

In 1955, when the oldest baby boomers were only nine years old, a spectacular amusement park opened in Anaheim, California. Disneyland was an immediate success; a clean, wholesome, fantasy world that appealed to people of all generations.

Walter Elias Disney was an innovative genius whose creative mind had given birth to Mickey Mouse, Donald Duck, Goofy, and Pluto prior to World War II. In 1937, Disney produced the first full-length cartoon film ever made, *Snow White and the Seven Dwarfs*. This became one of the most popular movies in history and was followed by *Pinnochio, Fantasia, Bambi,* and *Cinderella*. All appeared before the first baby boomers were born. *Lady and the Tramp* was released in the same year that Disneyland opened, and in 1964, while the last baby boomers were making their appearance, the Disney studios released what may have been their most successful film of all, *Mary Poppins*.

Few baby boomers can remember a world without Mickey Mouse and Walt Disney's influence. Many have visited one of the Disney theme parks, and the entire baby boom generation has been influenced by Disney creations, movies, television programs, and commercial ventures. Decades of children's television programming, cartoon characters, puppetry, and fantasy movies have all been shaped in some way by the trailblazing work of Disney illustrators, artists, and business entrepreneurs.

A sobering story, perhaps apocryphal, describes a time when a very young Walt Disney went to Sunday School, years before he achieved his fame. The experience must have been boring because the boy is reported to have concluded that church is a place where they do not care about children.[1]

Is church today a place where they do not care about baby boomers? Has business not cared about baby boomers? Have educators, politicians, and even counselors gone about their work without taking much notice of the baby boomer generation in our midst?

In the preceding chapters we have considered the complexities, expectations, disappointments, characteristics, and aspirations of the baby boom generation. We have looked at baby boom careers, values, families, beliefs, and trends. We have learned, in the words of Landon Jones, that "no single generation has had more impact on us than the baby boom, and no single person has been untouched. The baby boom is, and will continue to be, the decisive generation of our history."[2] No counselor, pastor, advertiser, political candidate, educator, artist, publisher, or business person can hope to influence this generation without some awareness and understanding of baby boomer distinctiveness.

Compared to generations that have come before, baby boomers are more open about their problems, more willing to ask questions, more inclined to seek and benefit from counseling. To reach baby boomers, to communicate with them, to minister to their needs, and to counsel with them, we must learn to connect with their thinking and ways of viewing the complex, often disappointment-filled world in which they live.

CONNECTING

In your entire lifetime, how many sermons have you heard? Of these, how many have made a lasting impact?

Most of us are likely to answer "many" to the first question, and "few" to the second. Even carefully crafted, laboriously prepared, precisely exegeted sermons often fall on deaf ears because the messages do not connect with the people who listen.

When two people connect—a husband and wife, a preacher and parishioner, a writer and reader, a counselor and counselee—there is something more than intellectual comprehension. When we connect with another person, we both have an inner awareness that we are together, on the same wave length. There is a mutual perception that we understand one another and are able to communicate openly.

In many relationships, even in those that are intimate, this rare sense of connectedness never emerges, and it seldom is seen in speakers or other public communicators. When a pastor, advertiser, or counselor connects with us, we each conclude that this person "knows where I am coming from, what I struggle with, the things that I need." The best communicators, including the best counselors, are able to make this kind of connection.

How do we connect with baby boomers? Walt Disney was able to do it with loveable cartoon characters, but Disney was in a class by himself. Few have matched his creativity and communication capabilities. No one person can comprehend the diverse cultural values and characteristics of an entire group of seventy-six million people.[3] Not many of us, especially those who are older, are able to recognize the significance to baby boomers of all the terms or people listed in Table 3. This special generation has been called a mosaic society, a kaleidoscope of changing social roles, ages, races, value systems, wealth patterns, lifestyles, cultures, beliefs, passing heroes, fads, and expectations, all existing within the confines of one monolithic group. It is not surprising that so few nonboomers really connect with the diversified baby boom generation.

But connecting is possible. It begins with the helper.

As most counselors are aware, psychologist Carl Rogers advocated a person-centered approach to therapy that stressed

Table 3
Baby Boomer Buzz Words

This is a partial listing of terms that have emerged and been used at different times during the baby boom era and are somewhat descriptive of the generation.

against all odds	fitness	Monkees
Beach Boys	flower power	Moonies
Beatles	feminism	Muhammed Ali
bell-bottoms	Gilligan's Island	natural foods
Big Bird	Hair	nifty
Black Friday	health nut	Nolan Ryan
blue jeans	high	nukes
Bobby Vinton	hula hoop	peace
Bonanza	Jane Fonda	Peter, Paul, and Mary
boss	Jesus Freaks	the Pill
cartoons	Jefferson Airplane	Pogo
Charles Manson	John Denver	pot
Chicago	Jimmy Carter	POWs
chick-a-boom	Jimmy Connors	Reagan
clogs	JFK	Rocky
coonskin caps	jogging	rock and roll
cool	J. T.	sexual revolution
cold war	Kenny Rogers	slinky
credence	Kent State	smiley faces
cruisin'	Kentucky Woman	Sonny & Cher
Davy Crockett	LBJ	spaced-out
drugs	lite	tanning spas
dude	love	Three Dog Night
Doonesbury	macho	Tina Turner
Elton John	Madonna	Tom Cruise
Elvis	making love	U–2
establishment	M*A*S*H	Watergate
far out	MIAs	Woodstock
Far Side	miniskirts	Vietnam

the counselor's use of accurate empathic understanding, congruence or genuineness, and unconditional positive regard for the counselee. According to Rogers, this therapeutic triad of characteristics was assumed to be necessary and sufficient if therapy was to be effective.

Rogerian therapy emphasized self-actualization and the goal of helping counselees get in touch with their innate capabilities and potential for growth. The therapist and his or her client were assumed to be coparticipants in a process of change and discovery. The relationship was expected to be equalitarian, informal, and nonauthoritarian. "Active listening, clarification and reflection of feelings, personal presence and 'coparticipation' . . . coupled with a profound respect for process and inner-directedness" were seen as the only methods that any counselor needed.[4]

Rogers's humanistic approach presents some serious problems for Christian counselors, but his emphasis on being genuine, showing respect, and looking within ourselves to find solutions for our problems are all attractive to Me Generation baby boomers. These are people who like to stand on their own. They value autonomy, personal freedom, and self-assertion. Turning to a counselor for help is the antithesis of baby boomer independence and determination to keep going when the going gets tough. For many, even for those who understand and appreciate the value of psychology, it is difficult to expose one's weaknesses and inadequacies before another individual. It is not hard to understand why these counselees would respond positively to a therapy that gives them the freedom to find solutions for their problems by looking within themselves.

Christian counselors, among others, recognize that such person-centered approaches often fail. Lasting change only comes from God, even though he often works through human beings who are his instruments in bringing change. But most Christian counselors agree with Rogers on the need for genuineness and sensitivity in any effective people helper. These attributes were seen often in Jesus, whose compassion and concern for others made a difference in many lives.

More recently, counselors have stressed the importance of showing respect and genuineness,[5] getting on the same wavelength with a counselee,[6] and building a relationship that elicits and permits consideration of feelings and ways to change behavior.[7] In themselves, these do not always lead to change, but helping is difficult and often not successful if the helper has not made the effort to be sensitive and to get in touch with the counselee's struggles and ways of looking at problems.

Effective counselors—like effective preachers, marketers, or educators—recognize that each baby boomer is unique. Each has a distinctive life history and a particular set of needs, struggles, expectations, beliefs, and concerns that vary from those of others. But each baby boomer also is a product of his or her culture and each has been influenced, in unique ways, by the thinking and values of the baby boomer generation. Table 4 summarizes some of these attitudes. Often they form the background for the specific needs that individual baby boomers are facing.

Table 4
Baby Boomer Attitudes

To connect with baby boomers, remember that this generation:

- Still has high *expectations*. Many are disappointed with the reality of their lives, but the dream of "making it" still lives.
- Values *autonomy*, individualism, and self-reliance.
- Is *nontraditional*, resistant to authority or institutions, disinterested in political parties or church denominations, and inclined to question and challenge establishment values at every opportunity.
- Has high *tolerance* for diversity, including nontraditional lifestyles.
- Tends to be *self-centered* and lacking commitment, but often feels isolated, alone, and yearns for a cause to commit to.
- Is characterized by a *microwave mentality* that wants immediate gratification and quick results.
- Is *driven*, perhaps in an effort to prove themselves, although there is a recent tendency to downshift to simpler lifestyles.
- Is looking for fulfillment, still *searching* for their own values or worthy causes, but not much interested in churches or world evangelism.
- Is *nostalgic*, looking back to the good days in the past, and facing middle age with uncertainty and insecurity.

People who ignore these issues are unlikely to connect with baby boomers. Neither will we connect if we imply that we have all the answers, demonstrate a lack of trust or respect, fail to listen, or show by our words or actions that we are not aware of baby boomer struggles. Baby boomers will excuse ignorance or misunderstanding in a person who shows a willingness to learn, but this generation has little time or regard for anyone who does not know what is going on among baby boomers and does not care to learn. In time you can challenge baby boomer values, especially if you portray an attitude of sensitivity and respect, but you will get nowhere if you display a know-it-all, my-way-is-better authoritarian mentality. That is true of anyone who has contact with baby boomers—including their parents, employers, and counselors.

GUIDELINES FOR CONNECTING

Counselors and others who seek to understand and help baby boomers should be guided by several principles.

- Remember that we will never reach baby boomers unless we make the effort to understand them. Following a session with a marriage counselor, a baby boomer husband refused to return because the counselor "floated a lot of garbage. The jerk didn't even know what was going on!"
- Give them space. Baby boomers value freedom to make decisions and most want to feel in control. They resist pressure including sales pressure, sermonic demands, or marketing hype.
- Do not make statements that you cannot back up with good reasons. Generalizations, pigeonholing, personal biases, or pontifications about what is right or wrong can all backfire with baby boomers unless you can support your opinions and observations with fact.
- Show genuine interest, both in the counselee and in life. Baby boomers resist narrow-mindedness.
- Be real. Never compromise your values or pretend to be something that you are not. Phoniness and hypocrisy will quickly undermine your credibility with baby boomers. Be down to earth, even in the way you dress. For most baby

boomers, casual is in, formal (i.e., the conservative striped suit with a power tie) is out.

- Do not pound them with Scripture. There is great value in using Scripture, but weave this into your conversation instead of reading from a big Bible. And do not use the Bible primarily as a hammer or wedge that attempts to force change.
- Try to discover what the baby boomers whom you work with really want. This generation tends to be cause directed.
- Be flexible. Boomers are accustomed to change. Their lives change rapidly, and they shift easily between television channels, restaurants, and sometimes jobs. They resist rigidity.

THE HIGH RISK GENERATION

In a survey conducted by the Graduate School of Business at Eastern College, a sample of baby boomers from fifteen evangelical churches in Philadelphia was asked about reaching the poor. Ninety-eight percent agreed that the church should be involved in helping poor people, but few were involved in such ministries. Most were busy with their lives and careers, puzzled about the relationship between social action and evangelism, convinced that the government should have primary responsibility for helping the poor, and inclined to place poverty ministries low on the list of important programs for the local church.

World Vision magazine, which commissioned the study, concluded that baby boomers are a "generation confused about the causes and cures of poverty and doing little about it."

"Who is going to solve the problems of poverty in the 1990's?" the magazine editors asked in an article titled "The Rich Young Rulers." "Who is going to house the homeless, feed the hungry, and lift the crushing weight of destitution off the backs of 1 billion men, women, and children around the world? *It won't be Christian baby boomers!*"[8]

Why do these people express concern about needy people but do very little to make things better? Are many baby boomers so engrossed in their own problems and life demands that they have little time or energy to get involved with anyone else?

POPULATIONS AT RISK

Psychologists sometimes write about special groups of people within a society that are populations at risk. Individuals who are members of these groups are "more at risk or more vulnerable to psychological, interpersonal, and economic difficulties than people outside that population."[9] People in these groups have a heightened vulnerability to stress, crises, and personal turmoil. Sometimes they are vulnerable because of past abuses, present failures, current environmental pressures, or personality factors such as low self-esteem or feelings of powerlessness. Many people move in and out of at-risk populations as their environmental circumstances, resources, or support systems change. Others—poor people, the homeless, some disabled persons, the chronically ill, drug users, school dropouts, some members of minority groups among others— are at risk throughout their entire lives.

People at risk often show stress-related physical symptoms, mental disorders, depression, chemical dependency, family difficulties, and abusive behavior. Many have limited access to counseling or to other mental health services, and often these people are trapped in their circumstances, with little hope for change.

How does this apply to baby boomers?

Many are members of these special populations at risk. They have grown up in alcoholic, abusive, or other types of dysfunctional families, and they continue to carry the scars. Others are homeless, unemployed, trapped in self-perpetuating poverty, unskilled, persons with AIDS, or members of oppressed minority groups. Far removed from the so-called yuppie mentality, these often-forgotten people are also baby boomers—boomers at risk.

BABY BOOMERS AT RISK

Although some baby boomers are members of the generally accepted populations at risk, it could be argued that the entire baby boom generation is a population at risk—at risk of facing intensified stress, crises, turmoil, and disappointment as they grow older. This conclusion is suggested by at least four observations.

1. *Baby boomers are primed for disappointment.*   Michael Landon was an actor and television performer known to millions because of his roles in "Bonanza" and "Little House on the Prairie." Like John F. Kennedy, Martin Luther King, Jr., Elvis Presley, James Dean, and John Lennon, Michael Landon died too soon. His death, at a relatively young age, was another reminder to baby boomers that dreams collapse, superstars fade, and disappointments abound in this life.

The deaths of heroes, economic realities, public scandals, and deep disillusionment have all jolted baby boomer idealism, but deep within, the psychology of entitlement still lives. The generation that expected the best has encountered the realistic. The gap is widening between what they had hoped for and what they have achieved. Victims of their own great expectations, baby boomers are twice as likely as their parents to be disappointed with their accomplishments.[10] But do they harbor a latent idealism that is fueled by isolated survivors—Jimmy Connors, Nolan Ryan, Kenny Rogers, or even Perry Como and George Burns—who show that the dream of making it still lives?

Without hope, most of us would give up and quit trying to reach goals or to improve life. There is encouragement in the realization that some baby boomers have succeeded, that many people do get their acts together later in life, that some who fail in the beginning experience later comebacks. Of course there is widespread loneliness, long-term disillusionment and longing for improvement, but the generation that microwaves its pizza and faxes its messages, still hopes for quick solutions that will melt its disappointments.

Do many in the baby boom generation still have a mindset that is a setup for a big letdown? If so, how will the entitlement generation cope? How many will discover that hope in oneself is ultimately disappointing? Perhaps the writer of Psalm 42 was baby boomer age when he (or she) wrote that downcast souls must learn to hope in God.

2. *Baby boomers are self-oriented, and many are driven.* From the beginning, baby boomers have focused on themselves. There are exceptions of course (the Peace Corps is a good example), but many who disrupted the universities in the sixties and early seventies and became the much-analyzed Me Generation of the eighties[11] have downshifted and drifted into New Age subjectivism and deconstructionism in the nineties. A generation that once resisted war is now dedicated to saving the environment (both of which are worthy causes), but New Age philosophies encourage people to look inside themselves to tap inner potential and get in touch with the god that is within. The prevailing philosophies still focus on *me.*

And while some meditate and seek to accumulate good karma, others are caught in workaholic lifestyles driven in the pursuit of career success, affluence, power, and fulfillment. The old idea that hard work and good education lead to eventual success is an idea that still lives and drives many baby busters, baby boomers, and their parents.

Throughout history, people without God have found that life ultimately is disappointing when we try to make it on our own. Self-oriented and self-driven people are always populations at risk. They risk facing failure and existential despair.

3. *Many baby boomers are rudderless and searching.* When he published *The Closing of the American Mind,*[12] Allan Bloom triggered a groundswell of discussion. Some condemned the book and others sang its praises, but most heard the messages that the author was trying to convey: hedonism, promiscuity, moral illiteracy, spiritual emptiness, relativism, and the fulfillment of one's own passions have become the hallmarks of our society and our educational institutions. In academic communities, Bloom wrote, reason has been replaced by "mindless commitment, consciousness raising and trashy sentimentality." Words such as *caring, self-fulfillment,* and *consciousness,* have become excuses to keep us from thinking.[13] Our only principle of justice is the self-centered little phrase "I've got my rights."[14] While we pride ourselves on being tolerant and open-minded, we have abandoned the effort to evaluate different viewpoints critically, to decide what we

believe and to know why. The generation that is called the most educated in history really is adrift on a sea of noncommitment and relativism.

It is always tempting to look for examples of people who disprove social critics. Certainly Bloom's scholarly book cannot portray an entire generation; there are many exceptions. But the writer's insightful observations suggest that many who have passed through the American education system in the past forty years have come to adulthood floundering, unable to think clearly, inclined to reject parental values, but still searching for values of their own.

Many do not even know where to look for values and do not know how to decide what they do and do not believe. So they drift from fad to fad, from idea to idea, or from one television image to another. Is it surprising that many are finding themselves unprepared to face the realities of midlife, the meaning of suffering when it comes, and ultimate conclusions about life's purpose and one's ultimate destiny?

In a special issue of the *Family Therapy Networker* journal, editor Richard Simon noted that therapy, despite all its fascination, has "no answers to the ultimate mysteries that surround our lives. However intricately a clinical theory can help us analyze a client's dilemma, it cannot tell us why any of the various dramas in anyone's life is worth caring about, or what meaning our lives have. . . . 'We can do therapy, come up with clever interventions, but we're going to die anyway, just like everybody else.'"[15]

The baby boomer population, including many of its therapists, is at risk of increased spiritual floundering as it grows older.

4. *Baby boomers tend to be reactive.*   In chapter 1 we noted that the countries where baby boomers live—the United States, Canada, Australia, and New Zealand—all developed as frontier societies. Each nation was built on the idea that problems could be fixed and that solutions could be found. Each was on the winning side during the Second World War, and each launched a generation of baby boomers who were raised with the mindset that winning is to be expected.

When they do not win, baby boomers are frustrated and often inclined to react. Doing something, short-term thinking, or hands-on entrepreneurialism can lead to problem solutions, but when things do not get better, people often express their frustrations through abuse, violence, crime, impulsivity, or withdrawal with the aid of substance abuse.

Quick, short-term reactions often lead to persisting, long-term pain.

THE HELPING RELATIONSHIP

To connect with any high risk population, the helper must learn to develop therapeutic relationships. Most counseling courses teach how this is done:

- by demonstrating empathic understanding, compassion, warmth, and therapeutic genuineness;
- through active listening, gentle probing, and limited questioning;
- by showing respect and occasionally engaging in limited self-disclosure;
- through providing a safe, therapeutic environment where a counselee finds freedom to discuss issues without feeling a need to be defensive or guarded in what one shares;
- by guiding counselees to move away from generalities and to deal with specific issues and concerns.[16]

With baby boomer counselees there is an additional need to understand how people in this generation think and perceive the worlds in which they live. This leads to the first of several helper attributes that build good relationships and stimulate connectedness.

RELEVANCE

How would you react if a counselee responded to you as the following man did to his real counselor?

"Come on," he stated bluntly. "Are you sure you really know what's going on in the real world: where I'm from, the world of drugs, prostitutes, and crime? This is the twentieth century. Get real!"

Therapists tend to dismiss such responses and assume the counselee is resisting. That may or may not be true, but it is possible that a counselee like this is also saying something important about the women and men of his peer group. This is a generation of authenticity. Baby boomers resist clichés, out-of-date terminology, and helpers who fail to appreciate the needs, values, and cultural conditions of their clients.[17]

Baby boomers expect quality, performance, relevance, and practical help, especially when they are paying high fees for counseling.

COMPETENCE

Can you imagine trusting yourself to a surgeon who radiates uncertainty about what he or she is doing? If surgery is needed, every patient wants the services of a skilled practitioner whose training, experience, manner of speech, workplace, and reputation all point to the doctor's competence as an expert. Baby boomers expect the same in their business consultants, lawyers, religious leaders, and personal counselors. Helpers will not connect and make an impact when they flounder, have a superior or dogmatic attitude, fail to pay attention to counselee concerns, are unable to answer questions, or appear to be operating with a directionless, seat-of-the-pants approach to counseling.

Consumer-conscious counselees seek counselors who are knowledgeable—but willing to listen and to learn—confident, attentive, likable, understanding, energetic, and confident both in themselves and in the value of counseling. The effective helper is less a changer of people than a guide and a creator of circumstances that will enable the counselee to solve problems and make changes. But the competent counselor does not leave counselees to find their own directions. The best counselors are familiar with interventions that can stimulate change. According to one respected textbook on helping, "If you are not clear about what brings about change, your ability to promote it is very limited."[18]

Within recent years a significant lay counseling movement has arisen and shown that peers often can be effective people helpers.[19] But there are times when the expertise of a more experienced, highly trained professional is needed. Baby boomers expect their counselors—lay, pastoral, or professional—to know what they are doing and to demonstrate this by subsequent changes in their counselees.

SELF-AWARENESS

Christians know that we are all created by God, that we all fell into sin, and that we are people whom God loved enough to send his Son, Jesus Christ, to take the punishment for our sins on the cross. Those who accept God's gift of forgiveness become his children, able to have abundant life on earth and certain of eternal life in heaven (John 3:16; 10:10).

This basic doctrine is at the core of the Christian counselor's life, but often these beliefs do not make a great difference in our lives or in the lives of our counselees. The doctrine does not get translated into practice, perhaps in part because we fail to see the obstacles in our own lives. Some counselors are not aware of their own unique strengths and weaknesses, have not disentangled from persisting sins that can drag them down, are unaware of personality uniquenesses that could hinder their helping, or are caught in unhealthy, toxic forms of belief[20] that could interfere with their lives and their counseling.

"The ability to be involved in an effective interpersonal interaction is influenced by our feelings and attitudes about ourselves," according to one established textbook of counseling. "If we lack awareness about ourselves, we may be unable to establish the type of counseling relationship that is best for the client."[21] Insecure counselors may put themselves down, give an appearance of cockiness, or seek to avoid any interactions that would bring criticism. Assertive, action-oriented, intellectual counselors may squelch the expression of feelings in their counselees and show impatience if the therapeutic process is too slow. Counselors with unresolved intimacy needs may be distant or inclined to shy away from closeness to a counselee or, in contrast, may allow personal feelings of attraction to turn the counseling into a more personal relationship. If we feel threatened or intimidated by a counselee, we may respond defensively but with subtle attitudes and behaviors that we do not even recognize.

Because of these influences on counseling, most training programs require students to get some counseling themselves so they have better self-understanding and can learn to free themselves from personal issues that might interfere with the helping relationship.

As we have seen, baby boomers appreciate honesty and resist any thing or person who is inauthentic. Because of this, baby boomer counselees respond positively when counselors occasionally talk about themselves, admit struggles, or acknowledge mistakes. But your counselees will resist if you talk too much about yourself. Their confidence in your ability to help will be shaken if you give the impression that your own life is out of control. Helpers can avoid this by knowing themselves and having their own noncounselee confidants and professional accountability partners.

COMMITMENT

As a group, baby boomers are not very trusting. They tend to challenge authority, including the counselor's authority, and they are likely to test any relationship to see if there is genuine commitment. Are you willing to work with your baby boomer clients and stay with them, even when there is pain and difficulties? Often this question needs to be answered in the mind of each client before he or she will trust you with intimate details of personal problems.

Helpers express their commitment when they are available and on time for appointments, attentive during counseling sessions, not distracted by telephone calls or other interruptions, able to keep confidences, intent on protecting the counselee's privacy, and determined to apply their skills and knowledge to counselee problems.

If you want to build good relationships with counselees and to connect with baby boomers, show through your behavior and your words that you genuinely care. If you do not sincerely care, your real attitude is likely to be detected, and you are unlikely to have an impact on the baby boomer generation.

MISSING THE MARK

The paragraphs of this chapter might be summarized in four words that describe personal characteristics. These cannot exist in any counselor, preacher, teacher, business person, employer, politician, advertiser, entertainer, or other person who wants to connect with the baby boom generation.

Authoritarian. This implies that "I have the answers and I am right." Baby boomers have grown up resisting this kind of superior, holier-than-thou attitude. They resisted it in the sixties, and they resist it now.

Hypercritical. Baby boomers have learned to be critical of others, but they do not like to be condemned for their own lifestyles, attitudes, and values—especially when the criticism comes from someone who uses a put-down manner. This does not mean that baby boomers are closed to correction. They will hear criticisms of themselves, but only if this comes from somebody who genuinely shows care and respect for their generation and who appears to have their best interests at heart.

Inauthentic. Someone has called this the age of authenticity. Baby boomers easily spot phoniness; they hate and resist it. They respond instead to others who are trustworthy, compassionate, supportive, and sincere.

Floundering. A generation that still seeks for values does not appreciate people who do not know where they stand or what they believe, who radiate uncertainty or incompetence, or who appear to be rudderless. Baby boomers may not agree with what you believe, but often they respect the fact that you have reached conclusions and are guided by clear principles.

It is possible to connect with baby boomers, but this takes understanding, determination, and effort. For counselors, it also takes a willingness to consider innovative approaches to people helping. We discuss this in the next chapter.

NOTES

1. We have been unable to document this story. *Walt Disney: An American Original* by Bob Thomas (New York: Pocket Books, 1976) states, "Walt considered himself religious, yet he never went to church. The heavy dose of religiosity in his childhood discouraged him; he especially disliked sanctimonious preachers. But he admired and respected every religion. . . ."

2. Landon Y. Jones, *Great Expectations: America and the Baby Boom Generation* (New York: Coward, McCann and Geoghegan, 1980),1.

3. This, of course, is in the United States alone, not counting baby boomers in Canada, Australia, and New Zealand.

4. Stanton L. Jones and Richard E. Butman, *Modern Psychotherapies: A Comprehensive Christian Appraisal* (Downers Grove, Ill.: InterVarsity, 1991), 261. Jones and Butman give an excellent summary and critique of Rogers and a variety of other therapists.

5. Gerard Egan, *The Skilled Helper: Model, Skills, and Methods for Effective Helping*, 4th ed. (Pacific Grove, Calif.: Brooks/Cole, 1990).

6. Arnold A. Lazarus, *The Practice of Multimodal Therapy* (New York: McGraw-Hill, 1981), 104.

7. L. M. Brammer, E. L. Shostrom, and P. J. Abrego, *Therapeutic Psychology: Fundamentals of Counseling and Psychotherapy*, 5th ed. (Englewood Cliffs, N.J.: Prentice Hall, 1989).

8. Ron Wilson, "The Rich Young Rulers," *World Vision* (October/November 1991), 19. Italics are in the original.

9. This quotation and some of the material in the following paragraphs are taken from a chapter titled "Special Populations at Risk," by Edwin L. Herr, *Counseling in a Dynamic Society: Opportunities and Challenges* (Alexandria, Va.: American Association for Counseling and Development, 1989). The quotation is from page 191.

10. This is a conclusion of Paula Rinehart, "The Pivotal Generation: Who Will Tap the Latent Potential of the Baby Boomers?" *Christianity Today* 33 (1989): 23, although the author gives no data to back her statement.

11. For an example of one baby boomer who is family-oriented and committed to a career, but not caught in the Me Generation mentality, see Resa W. King, "Not Exactly the 'Me' Generation," *Business Week* (May 20, 1991), 109.

12. Allan Bloom, *The Closing of the American Mind: How Higher Education Has Failed Democracy and Impoverished the Souls of Today's Students* (New York: Simon and Schuster, 1987).

13. David Brock, "His Panache Blooms Eternal," *Insight* (May 11, 1987), 13–14.

14. Bloom, *The Closing*, 166.

15. Richard Simon, "From the Editor," *Family Therapy Networker* 14 (September/October 1990): 2.

16. Relationship building is discussed in several basic textbooks on counseling. See, for example, Gerard Egan, *The Skilled Helper*; William H. Cormier and L. Sherilyn Cormier, *Interviewing Strategies for Helpers*, 3rd ed. (Pacific Grove, Calif.: Brooks/Cole, 1991); Barbara Okun, *Effective Helping: Interviewing and Counseling Strategies*, 3rd ed. (Monterey, Calif.: Brooks/Cole, 1987); and C. H. Patterson, *The Therapeutic Relationship: Foundations for an Eclectic Psychotherapy* (Monterey, Calif.: Brooks/Cole, 1985).

17. Esther Wattenberg, "The Fate of Baby Boomers and Their Children," *Social Work* (January/February 1986), 20–27.

18. Marianne Schneider Corey and Gerald Corey, *Becoming a Helper* (Pacific Grove, Calif.: Brooks/Cole, 1989), 43.

19. Siang-Yang Tan, *Lay Counseling: Equipping Christians for a Helping Ministry* (Grand Rapids: Zondervan, 1991).

20. Stephen Arterburn and Jack Felton, *Toxic Faith: Understanding and Overcoming Religious Addiction* (Nashville: Oliver-Nelson, 1991).

21. Cormier and Cormier, *Interviewing Strategies*, 12.

Chapter 8

Counseling Approaches with Baby Boomers

L LOYD WAS BORN LONG BEFORE the baby boom generation. Now into his seventies, he likes to reminisce about the old days: the Great Depression, his experiences in World War II, Korea, Truman and MacArthur, Nixon, the first men on the moon, and what the church used to be like.

No issue fires Lloyd's enthusiasm more than the younger generation. He has not read much about baby boomers, but he knows about people who are never satisfied, always on the move, messed up and drugged up, and without any awareness of the hard times that shaped the old-timers who are now senior citizens.

Lloyd's soapbox eloquence is humorous at times, but his heart harbors deep compassion for friends and family members who have suffered through baby boomer problems. One of his grandchildren had an abortion and another struggles with drugs. His nephew has had trouble finding stable employment, even though he has a college degree and is willing and anxious to work. "It's just plain too bad," Lloyd told us recently. "I don't know what to make of it. Things seem to be getting worse. I'm glad I'm not raising kids today."

Lloyd's comments remind us that we live in a world of incessant change. Baby boomers and their offspring face unique problems, and our caregiving may require unique methods of intervention. Throughout his lifetime, Lloyd has seen significant changes in social attitudes and values, but he stands as a reminder that traditional values and biblical truths remain as the firm, time-tested foundation on which all of us can and must build our lives.

The following pages serve as a reminder of where the field of counseling has come during the baby boomer era, and it points to methods that are most likely to be effective with baby boomer counselees both now and in the future.

DIVERSITY IN COUNSELING

Every counseling student soon discovers that literally hundreds of theories and counseling methodologies have emerged within this century. Almost all—including some that are uniquely Christian—have been proposed seriously and presented with enthusiastic claims of success.[1]

Near the end of the first baby boom decade, one widely consulted book described thirty-six systems of therapy.[2] Less than thirty years later, Corsini identified sixty-four major approaches to therapy and estimated that about 250 different counseling models were being used, each of which had claims for being effective.[3] Initially, the theoretical diversity in psychotherapy may have arisen because founders of the different schools based conclusions on their own personalities and on the types of patients whom they saw. In time, "with little more than faith and the sheer force of opinion to back their untested propositions and doctrinaire assertions" and by "worshipping their flimsy hypotheses into truth and then selecting 'research' to bolster their already well developed personal convictions, these schools became implacable and categorically indestructible."[4] During this period, Christian counseling also grew at a rapid rate, and eventually a small diversity of Christian approaches appeared. Several were proposed as being *the* biblical approach to counseling, even though there were significant differences between them.

All of this provides fuel for the fires of counseling critics who seek to undermine the work of Christian therapists by pointing to the confusion in our field. Even worse, theoretical diversity can create perplexity in the counselor who wants to be helpful but who has no desire to get bogged down in theoretical debates or caught in the verbal crossfire of theorists who laud their own positions and criticize the rest.

In the midst of this debate, the needs of individual counselees seem to have been lost. If a therapist uses familiar but never-changing methods and theories, counselees may get what the therapist is inclined to give, even if this is not what the client needs or wants.

This theoretical diversity has led most researchers and practitioners to conclude that no one treatment approach or theory can apply to everyone. No longer do we ask which theory is best. They all have weaknesses, and most have strengths. Instead, it is better to ask which methods, which theoretical approaches, which setting, and which kind of counselor can be most helpful for each counselee and for each type of problem.

A moment's reflection will show that Jesus dealt with people in different ways, and counselors must do the same. No single evangelistic approach works equally well with everyone. We do not all benefit from the same type of preaching or respond equally to the same forms of worship. Individuals learn in different ways and respond differently to recruitment campaigns or to appeals for funds. The Holy Spirit works in unique ways in different lives. Counselors, too, must tailor their approaches to meet the needs of each counselee.

ECLECTICISM AND INTEGRATIVE THERAPIES

Convinced that no one theory of change can help everyone and that no theory is superior over all others, most counselors have shifted toward eclecticism. According to one definition, eclecticism involves the "selection and orderly combination of comparable features from diverse sources, sometimes from otherwise incompatible theories and systems" in order to "find valid elements in all doctrines and theories and to combine them into a harmonious whole."[5]

Several years ago a survey of professional theorists found fewer than 2 percent who adhered to the approaches of one exclusive school of therapy.[6] Almost all agreed that no one theory is adequate to explain all problem behavior or to provide adequate methods for intervention. According to the research, most therapists build their work on two or more theories and seek ways to be a rapprochement between the different approaches.

During the past several decades, a variety of eclectic therapies have been developed, many of which are carefully crafted,[7] although others appear to be little more than a haphazard hodgepodge of methods and theoretical ideas. When counselors rely on subjectivity and clinical intuition to select helping approaches that are then called "eclectic," counseling can be directionless, undisciplined, and ultimately of limited value to baby boomer counselees.

In an effort to avoid the weaknesses of theoretical schools and undisciplined eclecticism, recent writers have proposed *integrative therapies*. These appear to differ little from carefully formulated eclectic theories; both resist the tossed-salad approaches that some forms of counseling use—indiscriminately mixing bits and pieces from various books, past experiences, and pet ideas. No consumer-conscious baby boomer is likely to tolerate such ineptness.

In contrast, carefully designed integrative approaches have come from several sources,[8] including the work of Christian psychologist Darrell Smith. In an exhaustive and exemplary presentation from an evangelical Christian perspective, Smith defines integrative therapy as "a comprehensive, multidimensional approach to counseling and psychotherapy that unifies biblical truths with complementary psychological concepts, principles, and methods derived from a variety of theoretical orientations. While disciplined and systematic, it is open to all sources of truth regarding human personality and behavior and is loyal to the tenets of evangelical Christianity."[9] To counsel effectively with members of the diverse baby boom generation, we need theories and techniques based on solid commitment to Christ, built on biblical authority, informed by established principles of therapy and behavior change, adaptable to counselee personalities and needs, integrated into practice, and open to continued refinement and growth. If this kind of therapy is to be effective with baby boomers, several core elements must be included.

THE CORE OF BABY BOOMER COUNSELING

Like each counselee, each counselor brings his or her own beliefs, values, personality, talents, perceptions, and experiences to counseling. To insure that these contribute to counseling and do not distract, try to keep the following in mind.

1. *Each baby boomer counselee is a unique individual.* Skilled counselors know that every counselee must be treated as a unique person, regardless of age, but baby boomers especially appreciate counselors who are aware of individual differences and counselee uniquenesses.

Following two sessions with a marriage counselor, a baby boomer couple decided not to return because "he wasn't in touch with us or with our problems." Apparently, there was similarity between this couple and another of the counselor's clients, and the therapist tended to assume that both husbands were alike—both pessimists and both the major source of conflict in their respective marriages. By overlooking counselee uniqueness, the counselor drove away some baby boomers who otherwise might have benefited from his help.

Baby boomers are a busy generation, with multiple activities and sometimes complex lifestyles. In counseling, they need a listener who will seek to understand their individualities and try to be in touch with their stresses and unique problems.

2. *The context of the problem is significant.* Nobody lives in a vacuum. Each of us is shaped by the forces in our backgrounds and influenced by the social situations in which we live and

work. To be effective, counseling often must seek to overcome the effects of painful past experiences and must help individuals cope with stressful situations in the present. Without an understanding of these past and/or present pressures, we are unlikely to be effective in counseling.

Earlier we mentioned psychiatrist Douglas LaBier who works with vocationally successful but emotionally troubled young adults in fast-track Washington careers. Often these baby boomers seek help because they have difficulty coping with their careers, their employers, and the realities of their work settings. According to the psychiatrist, however, many of his clients struggle because they work in pathological settings populated by self-centered people who make unreasonable demands. To assist counselees so they can adjust to such settings is not to give real help. Ultimately it is not healthy for any of us to adjust to unhealthy, toxic social systems.

Instead, suggests LaBier, the best help comes if we can try to change the toxic systems that produce dysfunctional employees. In an innovative but perhaps idealistic statement, LaBier writes that contrary to "the individually-based views of the mental health mainstream and the current pop psychology ideologies, some problems can only be solved through action on the level of the organization, institution, or society: at the level of policy or politics."[10] Sometimes institutions and their leaders are in need of help more than their suffering victims who come to us for counseling.

Probably most counselors are unable or unwilling to direct their efforts to bringing change in pathological work settings, families, or other social systems. But at least we can seek to understand how these social influences have molded baby boomers and how they create stress in the lives of many baby boomer counselees.

3. *Baby boomer counselees often want participation in the counseling process.*   This is not a passive generation, willing to take the medicine that the doctor dispenses. This is the generation that shops for values, restaurants, and churches. Apart from the poor who have limited alternatives, baby boomers tend to get second opinions before they have surgery, compare prices before they make a major purchase, evaluate different educational

opportunities for themselves or their children before enrolling in classes, and challenge anyone who makes authoritative statements (like this one).

Many of these people lack the time or the inclination to participate in counseling that is dispensed by a therapist who gives no explanation for what he or she is doing. In their sessions, clients may not openly question your methods or competence, but they are likely to be doing so whenever they come to your office or write a check to pay for your services. Most are likely to appreciate periodic explanations of what you are doing and your reasons for suggesting the approach that you take.

Even more, counselees are likely to appreciate the opportunity to help make decisions about the methods that might be used. There can be value in viewing counseling as a team effort. The counselor is an expert on human behavior and problem resolution, but the counselee knows most about his or her problem experiences and past efforts to resolve issues. Together both sides can work to find solutions in which the counselee feels some ownership and for which he or she takes responsibility.

4. *Counselors of baby boomers should consider using innovative approaches to counseling.* In the early days of psychoanalysis, Freud met with his patients for fifty minutes every day, five days a week, and sometimes for several years. Even in Vienna, where Freud worked and developed his theories, only the rich could afford such therapeutic luxury.

In contrast, modern baby boomers lack the money, time, or inclination to spend long hours of free association, dream analysis, working through transference, and other in-depth forms of therapy. This is the action generation, raised on television sitcoms where problems are solved in less than thirty or sixty minutes. These are people who use microwaves and FAX machines, prefer forty-five day weight loss programs, and believe advertisers who describe ways to learn a new language in two or three months. For many of these people (and their insurance companies who hold the purse strings), traditional, long-term therapy is not an option.

What are some options? The following is suggestive of other approaches that can be used with baby boomers, often in conjunction with more traditional counseling.[11]

SELF-MANAGEMENT. When they reach middle age, many baby boomers discover (like generations who have gone before) that weight is easier to gain and harder to lose as we get older. In a weight-conscious society like ours, diets are common and weight loss programs are so prevalent that recent government action has sought to control the fradulent advertising claims of potentially harmful weight-management clinics.

Even when they consult a physician, dietician, or other competent advisor, weight-conscious people realize that all diets involve at least some self-management. If there is no self-control over calorie intake and/or no disciplined exercise, there is not likely to be lasting weight loss.

It could be argued that all successful therapy is in one way like dieting; it involves at least some self-management. Before they consult a counselor, it is probable that most people have tried to solve their problems on their own, without help. Many succeed, but others turn to friends, pastors, or counselors for assistance with problem management. In such situations, the people with the problems must agree to cooperate with their counselors and to make behavioral changes if the counseling is to be effective.

Self-management approaches to counseling are attractive to baby boomers who like to be independent and active in much of what they do. Together, the counselor and counselee can arrive at some goals for the counseling, discuss possible self-management strategies, select one or more approaches that seem most likely to be effective, rehearse these (if necessary) in the counselor's presence, try out the strategies as part of the homework to be done between sessions, and then return for a reevaluation of the process.

Self-management approaches are more likely to work if there is consistent self-evaluation, self-reinforcement (in which counselees reward themselves whenever they reach a goal), and environmental support from and accountability to others. Dieters, for example, are more likely to lose weight if they keep a graph of their weight every morning (self-monitoring), do something (other than eating a cookie) to reward themselves whenever another pound is lost, and give a regular accounting to another caring person. The program is most likely to succeed if the helper is a good model (fat therapists are poor diet counselors), if the counselee is motivated to change, and if there can be special encouragement during times when the counselee is discouraged.

SHORT-TERM APPROACHES.   At times we all encounter crises; disruptive, sometimes unanticipated, life events that disturb and disorganize our lives, overwhelm our emotions, and often leave us disoriented and confused about how to cope. While crisis events may be similar—the unexpected death of a loved one, the loss of a job, the experience of an accident, or the trauma of a heart attack—people respond in different ways, depending on their past learning and experiences, lifestyles, beliefs, and perceptions. Most can be helped through the crisis by supportive, caring friends, and by crisis-conscious caregivers who might include police officers, paramedics, hospital personnel, pastors, counselors, or compassionate strangers who appear on the crisis scene and give immediate needed help—and then disappear.

Crisis counseling seeks to give support, opportunity for expression of feelings, clarification of issues, and help with adaptive problem solving. According to counselor Barbara Okun, crisis intervention involves

> clarification and accurate assessment of the source of stress and the meaning of the stress to the helpee, and it entails active, directive cognitive restructuring. Crisis intervention helps clients develop adaptive problem-solving mechanisms so that they can return to the level at which they were functioning before the crisis. Crisis intervention is reality oriented, clarifying cognitive perceptions, confronting denial and distortions, and providing emotional support rather than false reassurance. [In addition, crisis counseling seeks to use] existing helpee relationship networks to provide support and help determine and implement effective coping strategies.[12]

Most counselors would agree that crisis intervention is a time-limited, situation-specific type of counseling. Usually the counseling begins shortly after the crisis and continues until the counselee is able to continue with life apart from the counselor.

In some form, crisis counseling has probably existed throughout history. Closely aligned to crisis management but more recent are the emphases on short-term counseling and brief therapy.[13] As defined in an early treatment of this subject, brief therapy involves four steps:

1. The counselee describes the problem in specific terms such as its nature, duration, frequency, and effects. The counselor seeks to understand as clearly as possible, seeking to determine whether or not the persisting problem serves some useful purpose to the counselee. Some people complain about being sick, for example, but the sickness brings benefits such as increased attention from others and release from some work responsibilities.

2. The counselor investigates previous attempts at solving the problem. What has been done? What has worked? What has not worked? What might be preventing successful resolution of the problem?

3. There is an effort to get a clear indication of what the counselee would like to have change. How will the counselor and counselee know when the problem has been solved or the goals attained?

4. A plan to produce change is formulated and implemented. Then the counselee is guided and encouraged as he or she tries out and evaluates the plans.[14]

Short-term therapies, like self-management techniques, tend to be highly cognitive and focused on active involvement from the counselee. These approaches are of more limited effectiveness with counselees who are deeply disturbed or with people whose problems are largely biological. But for individuals in the baby boom generation, cognitive, participatory approaches are likely to be more attractive and most effective.[15]

LAY COUNSELING. When people need help with a problem, few are likely to start with a professional counselor. Most of us probably talk first with a spouse, friend, relative, or some other nonprofessional. Baby boomers, who as a group appear to be less inhibited about mentioning their struggles to one another, are likely to get most of their counseling from friends. In the informal settings of church foyers, restaurants, health clubs, or bars, issues are discussed and problems sometimes are solved even though they are never brought to a more skilled counselor.

The widely recognized importance of lay counseling has led to a growing movement designed to train and equip nonprofessional people helpers. Books and training programs have appeared with increasing frequency during the past decade, and researchers have begun the careful evaluation of lay interventions.[16]

At times professionals have been critical of this new movement. Often this reflects a legitimate concern lest unskilled helpers do more harm than good. Of course lay counseling fails at times, and nonprofessionals make mistakes. (The same is true for professionals.) Regardless of what professionals may think, however, the lay counseling movement is likely to continue. Already it has taken its place alongside professional and pastoral counseling as a legitimate means through which many people—including Christians and baby boomers—can get counseling help.

OTHER INNOVATIONS.   In addition to (or instead of) more traditional therapy, there are a variety of other techniques that can be helpful to baby boomer counselees. These methods include mentoring,[17] giving spiritual direction,[18] involving people in discipleship programs, teaching stress inoculation,[19] assigning reading, encouraging participation in twelve-step programs and other support groups,[20] giving relaxation training, assigning homework including journaling, and stimulating counselee involvement in a good local church. When confronted with this variety of potential counseling interventions, you might find it helpful to consult Table 5 to guide your selection of methodologies.

In seeking to help baby boomers, counselors must continually be sensitive to cross-cultural issues in counseling. As we have seen, many baby boomers are African-American, Hispanic, unemployed, uneducated, struggling with women's issues, disinterested in religion, veterans of the Vietnam war, or in other ways representative of cultures, minority groups,

Table 5
Selecting Effective Counseling Strategies

In general, the most effective counseling intervention strategies:
1. are practical, feasible, and easy to use;
2. match the unique characteristics and preferences of the counselee;
3. are relevant for dealing with the counselee's problem(s);
4. are positive rather than punitive;
5. encourage the development of self-management skills;
6. instill hope and strengthen the counselee's expectation that he or she will get better and be able to handle future problem situations more effectively;
7. are supported by the counseling literature;
8. do not create additional problems for the counselee or for significant other people;
9. do not burden the counselee or significant others with too many things to do;
10. do not require more of the counselor than he or she is able to give or is responsible for giving;
11. do not build on previous unsuccessful solutions;
12. are derived from and/or consistent with biblical truth.

Adapted (except for point 12) from William H. Cormier and L. Sherilyn Cormier, *Interviewing Strategies for Helpers: Fundamental Skills and Cognitive Behavioral Interventions*, 3rd. ed. (Pacific Grove, Calif.: Brooks/Cole, 1991), 295.

---

or past experiences that may differ from those of the counselor. Add the above groups together and we probably have the largest segment of baby boomers. Many will not respond to traditional counseling methods that have been developed in urban, mostly white, largely male, university settings. No counselor is likely to be effective if he or she ignores these multicultural diversities.[21]

Elements in Baby Boomer Counseling

Like people of all ages, baby boomers are complex individuals, molded by a host of influences. To understand these influences and to give effective help, the counselor must focus on at least four elements: the counselee's physiology, thinking, feelings, and behavior. Each of these can contribute to the development of problems and to their solution. Each must be seen both from a human and scientific perspective and from the perspective of the counselee's relationship with the Creator who made us, understands us, and enables us to cope with the problems of life.

PHYSIOLOGY

Baby boomers are fitness conscious. This is the generation that has stimulated a fascination with jogging, aerobic and aro-aerobic exercise, health clubs, and a commitment to healthier eating. Many baby boomers know about adrenalin and stress, the harmful effects of fat and high cholesterol, the physiological implications of burnout and workaholic lifestyles, the dangers in sexual promiscuity including the spread of AIDS, and the link between body chemistry and mood states including depression. This knowledge does not always change behavior—many still drink, are still promiscuous, still push their bodies to the point of exhaustion—but there is widespread awareness that the body's condition has an important impact on our lifestyles, work effectiveness, emotional states, and personal problems. No competent counselor can ignore biological influences, both because astute baby boomers are aware of these issues and because increasing scientific evidence supports the role physiology plays in problem arousal and resolution. Failure to consider the psychological effects of disease, sleep deprivation, neurophysiological-biochemical influences, or other physiological effects can be a major oversight for the counselor and serve as a real injustice to the counselee.

As an example, consider the baby boomer who came to a counselor because of her high anxiety and two recent panic attacks. The condition was having serious consequences in her marriage, family, and job. She was aware of Philippians 4:6, had prayed that the anxiety would go away, and had tried to modify her lifestyle. After an initial interview, the counselor helped her develop a plan that would bring greater understanding of her problem, change some of her behavior, and alter many perspectives about her life situation, her relationships with God and others, and her views of herself.

In the weeks that followed, the counselee cooperated fully, sought to understand her circumstances, and made a number of changes. But the anxiety continued, and she still had an occasional attack. At this point, the counselor suggested that she consult with her physician. After some testing she was diagnosed as having a thyroid problem and appeared to be addicted to caffeine—both of which can trigger anxiety. When these physical issues were corrected, she was able to continue with therapy and soon resolved her anxiety problem.

THINKING

What people think (and say) often influences what they do. This is true of everyone, but some people, the thinking types, are fascinated with concepts, ideas, and words. They try to behave in logical, rational, deliberate, and systematic ways, even though they do not always succeed. Others are less interested in cognitive issues and less inclined to think things through logically before they take action.

Despite these individual differences, counselors recognize that illogical, irrational, self-defeatest types of thinking can create problems. The counselor has a responsibility to understand how each counselee thinks, to help people see their problems more rationally, and to encourage them to think differently about their problems and problem solutions. This approach is of special importance to counselees who prefer to see life and its problems from a rational perspective.

FEELING

While some people have a thinking approach to life, others are more inclined to go with their feelings. If something feels right, these people take action. In contrast to cognitive people, the feelers are more inclined to express their feelings and to be open when they are angry, anxious, bitter, hostile, excited, or afraid.

All human beings are emotional creatures, even though some are more expressive and aware of their feelings than others. As part of counseling it can be helpful to encourage people to describe, clarify, and understand their conflicting or immobilizing emotions. When these emotional distortions are cleared away, counselees often get a better feel for their problems and are better able to make changes. They know that it is hard to solve problems or to think clearly if one is angry, depressed, or in love.

ACTION

Many problems come because of what individuals do or fail to do. Therapy often involves helping people change behavior, forsake sinful activities, and learn new skills. This can be true of all counselees.

Just as there are thinking-oriented and feeling-oriented people, however, there are those whose lives are characterized by action, goal direction, and a determination to plunge into the thick of things, to get something done, and to make things happen. Action-oriented people may be loud and highly visible or quiet and subtle, but their goal is to be active and productive. In counseling, they often need help to modify or eliminate unproductive behavior and to be taught new ways of doing things.

THINKING—FEELING—ACTING

Counselors and educators tend to agree that effective caregiving must include a focus on how people think, feel, and act—all three.[22] One writer has suggested a T-F-A (thinking, feeling, acting) System of therapy that guides counselors and is useful as a model for evaluating other counseling approaches.[23]

All of us think, experience emotions, and take actions, but since most of us appear to focus on one of these three elements, counseling should adapt. As he or she observes and listens, a counselor can choose intervention strategies that are consistent with the counselee's apparent life orientation. Thinking-oriented people are guided by their thoughts and inclined to discuss their problems logically. They respond best to counseling that encourages changes in thinking and ways of viewing the world or personal problem situation. Feeling-oriented people, in contrast, are more inclined to talk about and to show their emotions. They benefit from expressing their feelings in therapy and respond well to sensitive counselors who are not afraid of feelings. Emotions cannot be turned on and off like a television set, however, so feeling-oriented people do need to change some of their thinking and actions if their feelings are to change. Action-oriented counselees will soon reveal that they are goal-directed and sometimes inclined to act first and think later. These people are best helped when counselors can guide them into actions that will be more productive and will change behavior for the better.

Christian counselors know that some counselees could more likely be classified as spiritually-oriented people. They try to view life from a supernatural perspective, seek to live in accordance with biblical truths or with the teachings of a spiritual leader, and are inclined to attribute life events to the influence of God, to the leading of the Holy Spirit, or to the destructive-deceptive influence of Satan and his demonic legions.

For some, this is an unhealthy perspective, filled with paranoid fears of demons, tied to dependence on some influential teacher, or used as an excuse for doing nothing. These are people who blame all their problems on the devil, meet every problem with an exorcism, or wait passively for God to do something to make things better.

For many others, however, this spiritual orientation is very healthy. It is characteristic of people who determine to think carefully, to deal with their feelings, and to take responsibility both for their past sins and failures and for their future behavior change. These people know that God is sovereign, that his Word can be trusted, that we are involved in spiritual battles, that Satanic forces cannot be ignored or left unchallenged, and that God can be relied on to give help, guidance, comfort, and insight in all of the issues, crises, or transitions of life. Like the rest of humanity, some of these spiritually sensitive people are more thinking-, feeling-, or action-oriented, but all know that God is ultimately in control.

This spiritual orientation suggests an addition to the T-F-A System, and we might instead propose a T-F-A-S (thinking-feeling-action-spirituality) System. With an awareness of the physiological bases of behavior and use of some variation of the T-F-A-S System, counselors are better able to adapt their approaches to each counselee's style and personality. This allows a more individually tailored approach to counseling. Within this approach, caregivers can consider each counselee's developmental history, environmental and situational concerns, inner conflicts or tensions, personal values, and religious beliefs.

CONCLUSIONS

Near the end of his first letter to the Thessalonians, Paul instructed believers to "warn those who are idle, encourage the timid, help the weak, be patient with everyone" (1 Thessalonians 5:14). In summary, this is the work of the Christian counselor.

At present a comprehensive model of Christian counseling does not exist.[24] Each counselor is charged with the responsibility of addressing a myriad of issues that are unique to each counselee and set within our foundations of truth: God's Word, God's attributes, and the guidance of the Holy Spirit. With baby boomer counselees, our work will involve an understanding of this multifaceted generation, a commitment to show the counselor characteristics that are conducive to bringing therapeutic change, and a reliance on the Spirit's guidance as we seek to make wise and effective counseling interventions.

The task is large, but it is not impossible. And for counselors, few activities can be more rewarding than making a difference in the lives of those baby boomers who seek our help.

NOTES

1. For an excellent summary and critique of counseling theories, both Christian and secular, see Stanton L. Jones and Richard E. Butman, *Modern Psychotherapies: A Comprehensive Christian Appraisal* (Downers Grove, Ill.: InterVarsity, 1991). Also of value is Roger F. Hurding, *The Tree of Healing* (Grand Rapids: Zondervan, 1985). For a brief overview see Gary R. Collins, ed., *Helping People Grow: Practical Approaches to Christian Counseling* (Santa Ana, Calif.: Vision House, 1980).

2. R. A. Harper, *Psychoanalysis and Psychotherapy: 36 Systems* (Englewood Cliffs, N.J.: Prentice Hall, 1959).

3. R. Corsini, *Current Psychotherapies*, 4th ed. (Itasca, Ill.: F. E. Peacock, 1988).

4. A. O. Di Loreto, *Comparative Psychotherapy* (Chicago: Aldine-Atherton, 1971), 7.

5. Horace B. English and Ava Champney English, *A Comprehensive Dictionary of Psychological and Psychoanalytical Terms* (New York: Longmans Green, 1958), 168.

6. D. Smith, "Trends in Counseling and Psychotherapy," *American Psychologist* 37 (1982): 802–9 .

7. See, for example, J. Norcross, *Handbook of Eclectic Psychotherapy* (New York: Brunner/Mazel, 1986).

8. See, for example, Jay L. LeBow, "Integrative Family Therapy: An Overview of Major Issues," *Psychotherapy* 24 (1987): 584–94, and Kevin R. Kelly, "Theoretical Integration Is the Future for Mental Health Counseling," *Journal of Mental Health Counseling* 13 (1991): 106–11.

9. Darrell Smith, *Integrative Therapy: A Comprehensive Approach to the Methods and Principles of Counseling and Psychotherapy* (Grand Rapids: Baker, 1990), 11.

10. Douglas LaBier, *Modern Madness: The Emotional Fallout of Success* (Reading, Mass.: Addison-Wesley, 1986), 216.

11. For a more detailed discussion of some of these issues see Gary R. Collins, *Innovative Approaches to Counseling* (Waco, Tex.: Word, 1986).

12. Barbara F. Okun, *Effective Helping and Interviewing Counseling Techniques* (Monterey, Calif.: Brooks/Cole, 1987), 226.

13. For an up-to-date discussion of this topic, written from a Christian perspective, see David Dillon, *Short-Term Counseling* (Dallas: Word, 1992).

14. P. Watzlawick, J. Weakland, and R. Fisch, *Change: Principles, Problem Formation and Problem Resolution* (New York: Norton, 1974).

15. Christian psychologist Mark R. McMinn gives an excellent introduction to cognitive therapies in his book *Cognitive Therapy Techniques in Christian Counseling* (Dallas: Word, 1991).

16. For an excellent overview of lay counseling, including initial research, and an extensive review of the professional literature in this area, see Siang-Yang Tan, *Lay Counseling: Equipping Christians for a Helping Ministry* (Grand Rapids: Zondervan, 1991). Other books, written more for lay audiences, include Carol Lesser Baldwin, *Friendship Counseling: Biblical Foundations for Helping Others* (Grand Rapids: Zondervan, 1988), Joan Sturkie and Gordon R. Bear, *Christian Peer Counseling: Love in Action* (Dallas: Word, 1989), and H. Norman Wright, *How to Get Along with Almost Everyone: A Complete Guide to Building Positive Relationships with Family, Friends, Co-Workers* (Dallas: Word, 1989).

17. Ted W. Engstrom, with Norman B. Rohrer, *The Fine Art of Mentoring* (Brentwood,Tenn.: Wolgemuth and Hyatt, 1989).

18. For a comparison of spiritual direction and more traditional counseling, see Marilyn A. Ganje-Fling and Patricia R. McCarthy, "A Comparative

Analysis of Spiritual Direction and Psychotherapy," *Psychology and Theology* 19 (Spring 1991): 103–17.

19. D. Meichenbaum, *Stress-Inoculation Training* (Elmsford, N.Y.: Pergamon, 1985).

20. Support groups are often known as "self-help groups." For an overview of the current status of such approaches to counseling, see T. Borkman, "Self-Help Groups at the Turning Point: Emerging Egalitarian Alliances with the Formal Health Care System?" *American Journal of Community Psychology* 18 (1990): 321–32.

21. For an introduction to these issues, see Lillian Comas-Diaz and Ezra E. H. Griffith, eds., *Clinical Guidelines in Cross-Cultural Mental Health* (New York: Wiley, 1988). For a Christian perspective, see David J. Hesselgrave, *Counseling Cross-Culturally: An Introduction to Theory and Practice for Christians* (Grand Rapids: Baker, 1984).

22. See, for example, G. Corey, *Theory and Practice of Counseling and Psychotherapy*, 4th. ed. (Pacific Grove, Calif.: Brooks/Cole, 1991), R. Corsini and D. Wedding, eds., *Current Psychotherapies*, 4th ed. (Itasca, Ill.: F. E. Peacock, 1989), and Egan, *The Skilled Helper*.

23. E. Hutchins, "Ranking Major Counseling Strategies with the T-F-A/ Matrix System," *The Personnel and Guidance Journal* 60 (1982): 427–31. See also D. Hutchins, "Improving the Counseling Relationship," *The Personnel and Guidance Journal* 62 (1984): 572–75. Some of the material in the next several paragraphs is adapted from Hutchins's writings.

24. Smith's model in *Integrative Therapy* is a good step in this direction.

Chapter 9

Marriage Counseling with Baby Boomers

A JULES FEIFFER CARTOON SHOWS A COUPLE talking about their relationship. "You have contempt for me," the woman complains. "You treat me as if I'm stupid. You have no interest in my opinions. When my friends are around you behave as if I'm invisible."

When the man protests that he loves her, the woman asks "Then why do you act as if you don't like me?"

"Who said I liked you?" the man responds, "I just love you."[1]

The insightful cartoonist has identified part of the confusion that many baby boomers encounter in their relationships. Sometimes couples take the time to know and to like each other before they *make love* sexually, but often they *love* first, *like* later, and leave relationship building to the end.[2] Is it surprising that baby boomer marriages are so often shakey and confusing?

Consider the following problems that were brought to one of the authors in a private practice while this chapter was being written. These concerns were expressed by baby boomers, most of whom are Christians.

> *"We're here because our marriage is failing. I just don't know him anymore. It seems like we are total strangers. And all we do when we're together is fight."*
>
> *"My wife had an affair. Just yesterday, I was able to convince her to leave him and come here to try and put our marriage back together. Please help."*
>
> *"We're here because we just can't cope anymore. We've got financial pressures, we both work, our kids are out of control. All we do is go, go, go."*
>
> *"He's been physically abusing me."*
>
> *"During the day I'm supposed to be this perfect, innocent, sweet Christian woman, but at night I am to be his little whore. I can't stand him, and I certainly don't want to make love to him. He's a jerk!"*
>
> *"I want help for my marriage, my family . . . and me. I've been accused of molesting my seven-year-old daughter, and the court has mandated professional counseling."*
>
> *"I want to bring my husband next time. We need some marital help. John is nice, but he's an alcoholic. I rarely see him—about one or two nights a week. We have no money. My youngest son is out of control. The school is calling; I can't control him at home. I'm working fifty-five to sixty hours a week just to get by. I'm about to lose it!"*
>
> *"Sex, sex, sex—that's all he is, wants, thinks and talks about. He doesn't love me. I think—no, I know—all he wants is someone to sleep with."*
>
> *"We're getting a divorce but thought we should come for counseling one last time before we do it."*
>
> *"I just want to stop sometimes, to enjoy life, my wife (whom I dearly love yet fail to show her at times), my children (they're growing up so fast), our beautiful home (I need to spend time there, too). Life used to be so simple, but now it just goes. It's just unbelievable how fast it goes. It scares me. Mom and Dad are getting older. I haven't taken time for my brothers and sisters. I feel so tired, so guilty, and sometimes so lonely. Where am I going? My how the time rushes by. I've been doing a little*

extra work trying to cover some extra bills. You know how that goes. . . ."

CHANGES AND MYTHS IN MODERN MARRIAGE

Marriage and family life have changed drastically during the baby boomer era. The changing roles of both men and women, the influence of the Pill, the influx of women into the workplace, the sexual revolution, the impact of computers and television, the myriad of new choices available to almost everyone—these are among the influences that baby boomer families have both experienced and helped to create. "Fewer and fewer American families conform to traditional stereotypes," writes demographer Peter Morrison. Families "are more diverse and less stable now than ever before. More children are born to unmarried mothers, and more childhood years are spent in fatherless families. Couples marry later and are quick to divorce. Fully 54 percent of wives with preschool-age children are now in the workforce."[3] Changes in the family have been so dramatic and family diversity is now so great that a recent college textbook begins with a revealing question: "Do we know a family when we see one?"[4]

Each one of us, including our counselees, has built images and ideas of what marriage and the family is and should be like. These different viewpoints are shaped by our past experiences, what we have seen on television, what we would dream for in the future and, for Christians, what we have heard in sermons or read in the Bible. Some see the family as a place of acceptance, a haven in the midst of a heartless world, a place where one feels comfortable and appreciated. Poet Robert Frost seemed to view the family as a last resort. Home, he wrote, "is the place where, when you have to go there, they have to take you in." Some people view families as places of violence, abuse, and other forms of mistreatment. Others think of the family as an encumbrance, of marriage as a boring and stultifying experience, of child rearing as a succession of problems and expenses, and of family relationships as obstacles that inhibit one's personal fulfillment and development. Most counselors soon learn that a casual statement such as, "I'll be going home for the holidays," can mean different things for different people.

According to one recent analysis,[5] many of our perceptions about family life have come from some widely accepted but largely inaccurate myths about marriage and the family. These myths influence our behavior, affect our marriages, and often are carried into counseling without anyone ever acknowledging their existence.

Myth #1: Families and marriages in the past were more stable, better adjusted, and happier than they are today. Most of us have a tendency to idealize the past. We think fondly of the old-fashioned Christmas, and some are nostalgic about the good times they had when they were children. We assume that past family life was filled with good manners, effective communication, mutual commitment, clearly defined roles, and happy evenings together around a crackling fire. We fail to realize that desertion by spouses, child beating, sexual unfaithfulness, marital failure, and harassment in the home were common in the past (even though they were more often hidden) just as they are common now. Even if this myth of happier families in the past contained some truth, we live with the pressures of the present. Dreaming about the good old days does little to help baby boomers cope with the changing realities and stresses of their contemporary families.

Myth #2: There are firm boundaries between the family and the rest of life. This has been called "the myth of separate worlds." It assumes that the family is a freestanding, independent, self-sufficient entity that is not much affected by social pressures, the economy, politics, relatives, the places where family members work, the values portrayed by the media, or the policies of government. Perhaps nobody would claim to believe such a myth, but books on marriage and family, including Christian books, often assume that the family can be treated and married couples can be counseled as if they were isolated from the societies and neighborhoods where they live. No family is an island, and no counselor can expect to be helpful if he or she is unaware of the changing society that has a daily impact on family relationships and togetherness.

Myth #3: There is a typical American family or a typical Christian family. This "myth of the monolithic family form" assumes that we know what the family is supposed to look like.

Often this typical family picture is drawn from our images of families in the past or from books, observations of our own parents, sermons, popular lectures, or even the speeches of politicians. Many tend to assume, for example, that the typical family is middle class, monogamous, with a father who works to provide for the family and a mother who stays at home, children who go to neighborhood schools, grandparents who are nearby and supportive, with each family living in a single-family house.

Less than 10 percent of families in America fit this image. Single-parent families, blended families, households maintained by unmarried adults who live together, several generation families, multiracial families, alcoholic families—each is common, and such diversity seems likely to increase. More recently we have heard about the postmodern family in which each family member has his or her own definition of truth and family therapists assume that no absolutes exist on which to build family stability.[6]

Even among Christians there are different opinions about what constitutes a biblical family. The counselor needs to know what he or she believes and how baby boomer perceptions of marriage and the family may be different from those of the therapist.

Myth #4: All families have similar experiences. This is the assumption that all family members have common needs, common interests, and common backgrounds. Many of the problems that couples bring to counseling are because the husband, wife, or other family members have very different expectations for their families and bring different experiences to their family problems. Perhaps we see this most clearly when three generations discuss some potentially controversial issue such as rock music or politics. Different experiences and different perspectives often lead to different conclusions about what is wrong and how problems can be solved.

Myth #5: Most baby boomers have little commitment to marriage, marital harmony, sexual fidelity, and effective parenting. Hopefully the preceding chapters have shown that this myth is far from the truth. The divorce boom of the late sixties and early seventies appears to be on the decline. With increased interest in their families, baby boomers are giving greater attention to marriage, relationship building, parenting skills, and what has come to be known as *cocooning*. According to *Time* reporter Janice Castro, many Americans (baby boomers included) are embracing simpler pleasures and homier values in place of materialism. "They've been thinking hard about what really matters in their lives, and they've decided to make some changes. What matters is having time for family and friends, rest and recreation, good deeds and spirituality."[7] In a recent Time/CNN poll 69 percent of those questioned said they would like to "slow down and live a more relaxed life," and 98 percent indicated that it was more important these days to spend time with the family. Convincing survey data shows that a majority of the people polled desire more traditional values and ideals concerning marriage.[8]

This return to the family and renewed commitment to marriage makes sense, especially when one considers research on marital stability. One reviewer read 130 articles comparing marital status, self-reports of happiness, and issues such as alcoholism, suicide, schizophrenia, and other psychiatric problems. The research showed that married men and women are generally happier and less stressed than people who are unmarried.[9] There is evidence that a marital partner who provides companionship and psychic aid buffers one's mate against physical and emotional pathology. In most marriages, it seems, the role of buffer shifts from one spouse to the other, depending on the circumstances.

While some might argue that marital stability is a myth from the past, God's design for marriage still stands strong.

GOD'S DESIGN FOR MARRIAGE

The Scriptures clearly define God's blueprint for marriage. The key elements are set forth in several well-known passages. In Genesis 2:24, for example, we read that a man will "leave his father and mother and be united to his wife, and they will become one flesh." Marriage is to involve a departure from parents, a public and legal coming together of a husband and wife, a uniting or bonding, and a shared intimacy of their entire beings. Ephesians 5:23 portrays the marital relationship as a reflection of Christ and his relationship with the church. And Matthew 19:1–12 reminds us of God's intent for marriage to be permanent.

God created man and woman in his image to complement one another. Marriage was designed by God to be fulfilling, enriching, and Christ honoring. But for many, including baby boomers who come to us for counseling, marriage has fallen far short of the divine ideal.

Discord in Baby Boomer Marriages

The estimates vary slightly, depending on the research, but some estimates suggest that as many as two-thirds of new marriages end in divorce. A host of researchers, writers, sociologists, and others have attempted to find reasons for the instability of modern marriage. As we all know, there are no simple explanations, but several issues are of special importance for those who counsel baby boomer couples.

Individual Gratification

Baby boomers can see little reason to remain in any relationship if needs are not being met, if one feels victimized by the selfish demands of a partner, or if more fulfilling alternatives seem to be available elsewhere. This attitude leads many to shift from church to church, from job to job, and sometimes from marriage to marriage. According to one recent study, "both men and women are more willing to leave an unhappy marriage if they feel that they have some control over their lives" and are able to get along without one's spouse.[10]

Ginny, age twenty-eight and the mother of two, is an example. "My husband is so selfish," she told a counselor. "All he does is think of himself. He expects me to work, care for the children, clean the house, wash his clothes, iron for him, and be ready and willing anytime he wants it! I'm sick of it! I wish for once he'd think of me and help me. He has his nights out with the boys, doesn't call, and does very little around the house except complain. I've had enough of this, and with the help of my family and friends, I'm to the point where I can make it on my own."

The increased tolerance of baby boomers for differing lifestyles undoubtedly contributes to the tendency of some to move out of a difficult marriage. Many do not believe in long-term commitments or in the permanency of marriage.

UNREALISTIC EXPECTATIONS

Baby boomers have always played for the big prize. Life was supposed to be that way: "You can reach for the stars and get what you want." Even as adults, many have not bought into the limitations of life. They expect boom not bust. Many buy into get-rich-quick schemes, high-powered success seminars, and participation in lotteries and sweepstakes. Often their views of marriage are no exception. Despite the struggles of their married friends, many assume that "our love will be different," and they enter marriage expecting continual bliss and sexual excitement.

One major textbook on marital therapy cites unrealistic expectations as a major contributor to marital unhappiness.[11] Some couples, for example, enter marriage assuming that "my spouse will always try to please, rarely be angry, and always be open and honest." When reality challenges these expectations, there is disappointment and often strife. As romantic dreams and hopes are dashed in a sea of dismay, there is less willingness to stay with the ship of marriage and more willingness to bail out.

Premarital counseling, marital enrichment programs,[12] relevant sermons, and couple counseling can all help married baby boomers to have realistic expectations for their marriages, without taking away anyone's expectation, hope, and enthusiasm for marriage.

ATTITUDES ABOUT DIVORCE

In the Old Testament we read that God hates divorce (Malachi 2:16), although there are some conditions in which divorce is acceptable, despite its devastating impact (Matthew 19:1–12). But divorce rates continue to be high in the four baby boomer countries, in part because legal and social conditions have removed many of the obstacles and sanctions against marital breakups.[13] The introduction of no-fault divorce and the liberal attitudes in many churches have contributed to the ease with which marriages can be terminated. According to one Census Bureau report of women, "first marriages are taking place later, more adult women will never marry at all, divorce has likely peaked, remarriage after divorce is becoming less frequent, and among current cohorts of women, those representing the first ten years of the baby boom are expected to have the highest incidence of divorce."[14]

Country singer Michael Martin Murphy once wrote a popular song about marriage and commitment titled "What's Forever For?" Isn't love for a lifetime? the lyrics asked. Don't most marriages involve a commitment to remain together "until death do us part"? A recent professional journal reported that unhappy marriages tend to stabilize when a couple persists in believing that marriage should be a lifelong commitment.[15]

COMMUNICATION

Every counselor knows that communication breakdown is a key to marital discord. "We just can't communicate anymore," said one recent counselee in words that most counselors have heard. "I don't know if we really know each other anymore." Learning to communicate verbally and nonverbally, and learning to maintain and enhance this communication, are important for maintaining marital stability.

Baby boomers have grown up in an era of increasingly sophisticated technology that has caused our times to be known as the information age. High-tech computers enable us to access and process masses of information, but even information processing experts can find it difficult to talk, hear, listen, and understand the communication that comes from their own loved ones.

Up to 90 percent of couples who come for counseling indicate that communication breakdowns are at the basis of their marital problems.[16] Stimulating and strengthening interpersonal communication between spouses is a high priority challenge for marriage counselors.

INFIDELITY

The Bible states clearly that adultery is sin (Exodus 20:14; Matthew 5:27–28), but vows of fidelity have been broken since early biblical times. Within recent years, and among baby boomers, infidelity appears to have soared to unprecedented heights. A recent national survey concluded that about one-third of all married Americans (31 percent) have had or are now having an affair and that 62 percent of these people believe there is nothing morally wrong with the affairs they are having.[17] Others cite figures that are higher. One estimate suggests that 50 to 65 percent of husbands and 45 to 55 percent of wives have experienced extramarital affairs by the time they reach age forty.[18] Some plan to be unfaithful, but most of those involved in affairs say the infidelity started as a result of a chance encounter, rather than by design. Evidence suggests that Christians are more likely to remain faithful to their spouses, but only the naive among us would conclude that the epidemic of infidelity is limited to nonbelievers.

All of us live in a stress-saturated society, and many baby boomers are part of "saturated families," that are filled to overflowing with demands, pressures, and things to do.[19] Many have marriages that are plagued with financial pressures, infertility, problems with children, domestic violence, substance abuse, sexual dysfunction, or persisting personality clashes. Sometimes the partners separate without ever seeking help from a pastor, professional therapist, or other counselor.

EFFECTS OF STRESS ON BABY BOOMER MARRIAGES

Marriage problems are rarely simple. Often a number of stresses accumulate, and each complicates and provokes the others. In time the pressures mount like a swirling whirlwind, and when the couple comes for counseling they often feel helpless, defeated, and distant from one another.

HELPLESSNESS

Shattered expectations about marriage, continual bickering, arguments, loss of hope, talk of separation and divorce—all of these can sap the strength of a married couple and make their lives miserable. Often there is loneliness, desperation, anxiety, and a sense of helplessness. Sometimes one of the partners will get frantic in an effort to save the marriage while the other slips further into a state of apathy and hopelessness. Even when the couple sincerely wants to revive their faltering marriage, there often is a resigned sense of helplessness and futility.

DEFEAT

It is difficult to be hopeful when one feels helpless and out of control.

"We've tried that a thousand times," one baby boomer told her counselor. "I literally don't think there's anything left. For years we have simply existed. He does his thing, and I do mine."

The statistics on separation and divorce hide the prevalence of marriages in which a husband and wife "simply exist." Sometimes these are Christian couples who resist divorce but who have little interaction, no genuinely fulfilling sexual contacts with one another, and no hope that things will get better.

What prevents these defeated marriages from ending? A national survey of families and households found a variety of issues that hold unsatisfactory marriages together.[20] Some—especially Catholics and conservative Protestants—stay in the marriage because their religion disapproves of divorce. Others stay because of their belief in the permanence of marriage, fear of the economic consequences of divorce, concern for the children, or unwillingness to face the social disapproval that would come from family or friends. The longer a couple has been married, the less likely they are to divorce, even if the marriage has gone sour. As they get older, husbands and wives often find other sources of fulfillment, so they are more willing to tolerate the seemingly hopeless marital situation at home.

DISTANCING

As they grow apart, husbands and wives feel increasing distance from one another. They may live in the same house, eating and even sleeping together, but they pull apart emotionally, psychologically, and spiritually. Over time, they lose their sense of intimacy, feel alienated from one another, and psychologically are already separated. Divorce is the ultimate stage of distancing, the emotional separation that culminates in physical and legal uncoupling.

As the distancing process continues, one or both of the partners may feel abandoned, betrayed, lonely, inadequate, depressed, sad, or grief-stricken. The pain is intensified by confusion about issues such as legal definitions of property and assets, child support enforcement, custody and visitation rights, or ways of relating to former in-laws and current extended family members. Although prevalent, divorce is painful and never is a happy solution to marital problems.

COUNSELING AND BABY BOOMER MARRIAGES

Counseling with one person can be a challenging task. Working with a married couple or with a whole family can be even more difficult, especially if the counselees feel overwhelmed by stress, helplessness, defeat, and alienation.

Baby boomers are often adept at dealing with people in business or social situations, but frequently this interpersonal skill does not extend to intimate relationships like marriage.[21] Often couples lack the ability to make joint decisions, decipher nonverbal messages from one's mate, build acceptance and trust, give affirmation, reach mutual decisions, or resolve conflicts without destroying each other or the relationship.

Counselors can observe partner interactions and coach the couple as they develop new skills for relating. We can help them to listen, to communicate clearly, to develop realistic expectations, to change their perspectives, to break old patterns of behavior, and to find new ways of talking and behaving. Baby boomers value commitment, cooperation, trust, and loyalty, even though they often do not know how to practice such values in their lives and marriages. At times there will be a need to determine how the couple's attitudes and beliefs developed before you can work on helping them change.

In his book on Christian marriage counseling,[22] Everett Worthington presents an approach that is relatively brief, involves seeing the couple together, and centers on three stages: assessment, intervention, and termination.

At the beginning, the counselor seeks to understand the problem from the perspectives of the husband and wife and asks them to commit to at least three *assessment* sessions. Counselor warmth and empathy are desirable but not necessary, according to Worthington. Of greater importance is the counselor's ability to convey that he or she understands. Few counselors are likely to follow Worthington's example of providing the couple with a written "assessment and recommendations" report during the third session, but such a practice clarifies misunderstandings, gives structure to the counseling, prevents the counselor from premature intervention, and stimulates hope that the marriage can get better. It is not surprising that assessment has been called "the cornerstone of treatment."[23]

If a couple decides to go on to stage two, a time frame is discussed. In most cases this involves eight to sixteen counseling sessions. Two goals are central to the Worthington approach: to break up old patterns of noncontact so that new patterns of intimacy can be built, and to break up old communication patterns so that new ways of communication can be established. Often this *intervention* stage involves creating and trying out new action plans. At times the new behaviors will be tried in the counselor's presence; often they will be practiced at home between sessions.

Frequently there will be failure with resulting discouragement, but at such times the counselor suggests that they try again with another plan. Worthington believes all counseling interventions will have at least one and often several S-E-R cycles (a surge of enthusiasm, euphoria that sometimes causes couples to stop counseling prematurely, followed by relapse). "Only by your prayers, perseverance with interventions, patience and powers of persuasion coupled with God's grace will the couple realize gains through counseling. Even then, progress is not like climbing a mountain. It is more like riding a wild roller coaster with its slow climbs followed by sometimes dizzying plunges and then other laborious climbs."[24]

The third phase, *termination*, may involve three or four sessions with increasing space between meetings. The couple and their counselor discuss gains that have been made, reasons for periodic failures, and ways to continue improvement without the counselor's help. This is the stage of solidifying, maintaining, and generalizing change before the counseling relationship ends. Sometimes a written report helps the couple remember what they have learned and determine how they can continue building their relationship.

Not all counselors will agree with this cognitive-behavioral approach to marriage counseling, but pragmatically minded, involvement-oriented, time-pressured baby boomers are likely to respond positively to approaches that focus on results rather than on theory. Others have noted that cognitive-behavioral approaches are highly consistent with biblical teaching.[25]

Whatever approach you use, several prominent issues are likely to be significant in your marriage counseling.

COMMITMENT

During the first counseling session with a baby boomer couple, the wife stated that she was not sure she loved her husband anymore. "I don't feel anything for him," she said. "I can't see any sense in staying together."

This statement, similar to many that most counselors have heard in their work, shifts attention away from repairing and rebuilding a broken marriage to the basic issue of commitment.

Building and strengthening commitment in the relationship is central to effective marital counseling. By its very nature marriage represents a covenant before God and one's fellow human beings. It is meant to be a reflection of God's unconditional commitment to us (Ephesians 5:25–33).

When they stand together at a wedding ceremony, a man and woman make a public, legal, and often spiritual commitment to stay with each other in the marriage regardless of unforeseen future stresses and other difficulties. Genuine commitment is more than a one-time statement of purpose, however. It is an ongoing process that involves intentions, thoughts, and actions. The committed couple seeks to coordinate their lives into a mutually caring relationship that is intended to be as permanent as the relationships we have with our children or parents.

This can be a revolutionary notion to baby boomers who have been raised in an age of individualism when relationships are often short-lived. When marital permanence is not valued, divorce is more likely[26] and genuine intimacy is not possible. "We are not likely to reveal our innermost thoughts to people who can't make a promise that they will 'stick around' and that they will be there when we need them."[27] Perhaps it is of interest to note one sociological study of twelve thousand couples, including many baby boomers. Researchers found almost none who had lived together for ten years or more without being married.[28] When there is no commitment to marriage, there is much less security or likelihood that a couple will remain together.

Because commitment is such a basic foundation for marital stability, counselors should seek to assess counselee attitudes toward commitment, challenge unhealthy attitudes, and strengthen beliefs about marital permanence.

INTIMACY

As they left the parking lot following their wedding, a couple was reminded, "Enjoy the honeymoon. It won't last forever!"

Early in their marriage, both partners do tend to be be more unselfish than egocentric. Often they assume that their marriage will be wonderful, and the honeymoon may reinforce the emotional and sexual closeness that both feel. Inevitably, however, partners begin to assert their own values, desires, and interests. Eventually there is conflict, and unless this self-centered process is curtailed, the relationship can dissolve in a sea of mutual distrust and turmoil.

Intimacy has been defined as a relationship that involves "an emotional bond with proven mutual commitment and trust between two people, [a bond] that provides personal and relationship security and rewards." Although the development of intimacy is ongoing, intimacy can also be viewed as an end result that extends far beyond sexuality. It is possible for a couple to be sexually involved but to have no real emotional intimacy, even as one can be intimate with another human being, such as a close friend, without any sexual involvement.[29]

Intimacy is a bonding that allows partners to feel safe, valued, and accepted, even when they take risks that could leave them vulnerable. In many baby boomer marriages this kind of security is unknown. There is no concept of a couple coming together with their strengths and weaknesses, to complement and build up one another.

Marriage counselors can stimulate intimacy by encouraging open communication, helping couples see the need to be interdependent, stimulating mutual trust, building realistic perceptions of each other and of marriage, encouraging activities that bond a couple together, guiding husbands and wives as they develop more positive self-esteem so that they are better able to be vulnerable. Christian counselors recognize that only Christ can break down walls of partition and bring genuine peace and intimacy. Prayer, for example, is a powerful way of building and maintaining relationships. And since consistent conflict can undermine intimacy, couples should be helped to discuss and to find ways to resolve their differences.

CONFLICT RESOLUTION

Is marital conflict inevitable?

Is it true that "perfect agreement on everything, like perfect intimacy, is to be found only in romantic novels and heaven"?[30]

When a couple never experiences any disagreement, does this mean that they are blissfully happy?

Most baby boomers would agree with their counselors that conflict and disagreement in marriage are almost universal. In any relationship that endures over time and that matures, disagreement will be inevitable. In contrast to distressed couples, who report an average of 3.4 conflicts over a five-day period, happily married couples, on the average, have 1 conflict during a five-day period.[31] Happily married couples learn to face their disagreements as they arise and to deal with them in ways that are not vindictive or destructive to the relationship. Conflict is most likely to be damaging when frustrations are unstated for long periods of time (instead of being dealt with as they arise), when one or both partners is rigid and unwilling to change, or when there is misunderstanding, insecurity, and a lack of conflict-coping skills.

When two people marry, they bring two sets of beliefs, emotions, values, opinions, preferences, past experiences, parental models, self-perceptions, and interpersonal skills. In addition, each brings expectations, based in part on the media and baby boomer views of the family.[32] Initially, the couple tends to overlook differences, but as time passes and they know one another better, then frustrations, disappointments, and resentments tend to emerge. Misunderstandings and conflicts combine to ignite anger and resentment. The person who previously has been a lover, ally, and companion begins to be seen as an antagonist.[33]

Individuals and couples have different ways of dealing with conflict. Table 6, adapted from a textbook on interpersonal conflict,[34] shows that conflict management styles reflect one's concern for others and concern for oneself. When there is a high concern for oneself and not much concern for the other person, disagreements are handled through competition. In contrast, when a person has little assertiveness or concern for oneself and little desire to cooperate with the other person, there is a tendency to avoid difficult issues. In helping couples resolve conflict, try to determine their ways of handling differences. Recognize that the husband and wife may use different conflict management styles. This can complicate your work.

In their practical volume on conflict resolution, Lowry and Meyers give biblical and psychological principles for helping people resolve conflicts.[35] Among the recommendations: try to uncover the real issues that are creating the conflict, separate issues from personality attacks—and focus on the former, look for common interests and goals, stimulate clear understanding and communication between the conflicting parties, help the couple develop options for resolving their differences, guide as they try out and evaluate different options. A goal in

Table 6
Styles of Handling Conflict

C **O** **N** **C** **E** **R** **N**	High Assertiveness or Aggressiveness	Competition	Collaboration
F **O** **R**			Compromise
S **E** **L** **F**	Low Assertiveness	Avoidance	Accommodation (Giving in)
		Low cooperation	High cooperation

CONCERN FOR OTHERS

Adapted from Joyce H. Wilmot and William W. Wilmot, *Interpersonal Conflict* (Dubuque, Iowa: Brown, 1978), p. 19.

---

conflict resolution is to find some way in which each party can benefit in a win-win situation.[36] This will involve flexibility and a determination to reach a solution. The result is a better relationship. In contrast when one party wins and the other loses, there can be long-term resentment and persisting tension.

The Christian counselor cannot ignore the importance of forgiveness in conflict resolution. Based on their years of experience as professional Christian marriage counselors, Friesen and Friesen have concluded that "a lack of forgiveness creates walls of bitterness, resentment, anger, and depression. Forgiveness done in a loving, caring manner is based upon respect and unconditional love for the individual."[37] Such forgiveness is difficult and may take time.

True conflict resolution only occurs when there is forgiveness—the kind that is commanded by Christ and made possible through the power and leading of the Holy Spirit.

CONCLUSION

Baby boomer marriages and families have not been stable. This is well known and often mentioned in descriptions of the baby boom generation.

From this it does not follow that baby boom marriages are destined to be unhappy and unstable. Modern marriages are under pressures that earlier generations never knew; baby boomer couples have family challenges that our ancestors did not face. But marriage is an institution created by God and meant to survive. Many families have serious problems that may change only through prayer and the help of skilled Christian counselors. Even so, we need to remember that the country is filled with healthy, mature, and growing baby boomer families.

May their number increase!

NOTES

1. The cartoon is reproduced in Leonard Cargan's *Marriages and Families* (New York: HarperCollins, 1991), 107.

2. This issue is the theme of a recent book on marriage written by Susan S. Hendrick and Clyde Hendrick, *Liking, Loving, and Relating*, 2nd ed. (Pacific Grove, Calif.: Brooks/Cole, 1992).

3. Peter Morrison, *Changing Family Structure: Who Cares for America's Dependents?* (Santa Monica, Calif.: Rand Corporation, 1986), 2.

4. Suzanne K. Steinmetz, Sylvia Clavan, and Karen F. Stein, *Marriage and Family Realities: Historical and Contemporary Perspectives* (New York: Harper and Row, 1990).

5. Maxine Baca Zinn and C. Stanley Eitsen, *Diversity in Families* (New York: HarperCollins, 1990), 9–20. We have drawn on this book for some of our discussion of family myths.

6. Maureen O'Hara and Walter Truett Anderson, "Welcome to the Postmodern World," *Family Therapy Networker* 15 (September/October 1991): 18–25. See also William J. Doherty, "Family Therapy Goes Postmodern," *Family Therapy Networker* 15 (September/October 1991): 37–42.

7. Janice Castro, "The Simple Life," *Time* (April 8 , 1991), 58 .

8. Roper Center, "Conventional Women and Men in a World of Change," *Public Perspective* 1, no. 4 (1990): 24–28.

9. Robert H. Coombs, "Marital Status and Personal Well-Being: A Literature Review," *Family Relations* 40 (1991): 97–102. See also Norval D. Glenn and Charles N. Weaver, "The Changing Relationship of Marital Status to Reported Happiness," *Journal of Marriage and the Family* 50 (1988): 317–24.

10. Tim B. Heaton and Stan L. Albrecht, "Stable Unhappy Marriages," 53 (1991): 747–58.

11. P. H. Bornstein and M. T. Bornstein, *Marital Therapy: A Behavioral-Communicative Approach* (New York: Pergamon, 1986).

12. There is evidence that most who attend marriage enrichment weekends perceive the experience as either neutral or somewhat positive. People who have come with "grave marital distress prior to the weekend" are most likely to *either* be strongly helped or to be harmed by the marriage encounter weekend. Careful screening and follow-up would appear to be important if the enrichment programs are to be beneficial. See William J. Doherty, Mary Ellen Lester, and Geoffrey Leigh, "Marriage Encounter Weekends: Couples Who Win and Couples Who Lose," *Journal of Marital and Family Therapy* 12 (1986): 49–61.

13. A. Thorton, "Changing Attitudes Toward Separation and Divorce," *American Journal of Sociology* 90 (1985): 857–72.

14. Arthur J. Norton and Jeanne E. Moorman, "Current Trends in Marriage and Divorce Among American Women," *Journal of Marriage and the Family* 49 (1987): 3–14.

15. Heaton and Albrecht, "Stable Unhappy Marriages," 749.

16. Bornstein and Bornstein, *Marital Therapy*.

17. James Patterson and Peter Kim, *The Day America Told the Truth* (New York: Prentice Hall, 1991), 94–99.

18. V. Pestrak, D. Martin, and M. Martin, "Extramarital Sex: An Examination of the Literature," *International Journal of Family Therapy* 7 (2) (1985): 107–15.

19. Kenneth J. Gergen, "The Saturated Family," *Family Therapy Networker* 15 (September/October 1991): 26–35.

20. Heaton and Albrecht, "Stable Unhappy Marriages."

21. A. T. Beck, *Love Is Never Enough* (New York: Harper and Row, 1988).

22. Everett Worthington, Jr., *Marriage Counseling: A Christian Approach to Counseling Couples* (Downers Grove, Ill.: InterVarsity, 1989).

23. Ibid., 105.

24. Ibid.

25. See, for example, H. Norman Wright, *Marital Counseling: A Biblical, Behavioral, Cognitive Approach* (New York: Harper and Row, 1981), and DeLoss D. Friesen and Ruby M. Friesen, *Counseling and Marriage* (Waco, Tex.: Word, 1989). See also Mark R. McMinn, *Cognitive Therapy Techniques in Christian Counseling* (Dallas: Word, 1991).

26. This is the conclusion of Allan Bloom in his widely discussed book *The Closing of the American Mind* (New York: Simon and Schuster, 1987).

27. Karen Kayser Kersten and Lawrence K. Kersten, *Marriage and the Family: Studying Close Relationships* (New York: Harper and Row, 1988), 217–18.

28. Philip Blumstein and Pepper Schwartz, *American Couples* (New York: Morrow, 1983).

29. Kersten and Kersten, *Marriage and Family*, 7.

30. Carol Tavris, *Anger: The Misunderstood Emotion* (New York: Simon and Schuster, 1982).

31. G. R. Birchler, Robert L. Weiss, and J. P. Vincent, "Multimethod Analysis of Social Reinforcement Exchange in Maritally Distressed and Nondistressed Spouse and Stranger Dyads," *Journal of Personality and Social Psychology* 31 (1975): 349–60.

32. See chapter 4.

33. Beck, *Love Is Never Enough*, 5.

34. Joyce H. Wilmot and William W. Wilmot, *Interpersonal Conflict* (Dubuque, Iowa: Brown, 1978).

35. L. Randolph Lowry and Richard W. Meyers, *Conflict Management and Counseling* (Dallas: Word, 1991).

36. F. Jandt, *Win-Win Negotiating—Turning Conflict into Agreement* (New York: Wiley, 1985).

37. Friesen and Friesen, *Counseling and Marriage*, 137.

Chapter 10

Personal Counseling with Baby Boomers

Dan, age forty-one, is single again.

"I lost my wife and two daughters a couple of months ago when the divorce went through," he told his counselor.

"I'm in the midst of what I guess is a values search. I'm trying to figure out what's really important.

"Until recently it was bars and crazy times with my friends. . . . Nobody could tell me anything. I just wouldn't listen.

"Now when I go on a business trip, instead of booze, parties, and women, I look for a gym where I can work out. I'm trying to put my life together. It has helped me a lot."

Ann, who is twenty-eight, lives alone. She is angry, frustrated with life, bitter over the abuse she received as a child, unable to get more than menial jobs. Recently she attempted suicide and saw a counselor in the hospital.

Michael, thirty-nine, still is waiting for the big "deal" that he expects to come. Working fifty-plus hours as a psych assistant, he "wheels and deals" each evening. He has tried everything and not succeeded in much of anything. But this time he feels that he finally has found an opportunity that will be a winner.

Julie is a baby boomer struggling with life after her divorce. She has taken a new job and relocated to a new community, but being a single parent of three active kids is tough. Dating is a new experience for her, the kids miss their dad, and the people at her church have been so critical that she feels isolated when she most needs support and acceptance.

BOOKS AND ARTICLES ABOUT BABY BOOMERS sometimes imply that people in this generation are all alike. The preceding pages have emphasized, in contrast, that baby boomers are a group of individuals. They share many values, attitudes, and perspectives, but each person is unique. Each has a distinctive set of experiences, perspectives, and struggles that differs from all the rest. Some are caught in high-pressure, materialistic, self-centered lifestyles; more are ordinary people, moving through adulthood, raising their kids, and trying to make ends meet. Some baby boomers are mired in immobilizing problems while others cope very well. Some have attitudes or values that arouse criticism or media attention; others are conservative, hard-working, productive, and rarely mentioned in published or television descriptions of the baby boomer phenomenon.

Those who counsel baby boomers and their family members need to be aware of the diversity of this generation, the severity of some problems, the uniqueness of each counselee, and the fact that while some struggle and seek counseling help, others get along fine without the assistance of others.

BABY BOOMER BLUES

Depression in western society appears to be reaching epidemic proportions, especially among baby boomers. Hopelessness, giving up, passivity, low self-esteem, attempts at suicide—all rare in less technically advanced cultures—appear to be on the increase in countries like those where most baby boomers live.[1] Previous chapters have suggested reasons for this widespread despair, but several appear repeatedly in baby boomer counselees. Most seek help because they are still searching, lonely, anxious, depressed, involved in career dissatisfaction or transition, dealing with singleness, and aging.

STILL SEARCHING

Baby boomers have grown up in the midst of change, expansion, idealism, and soaring expectations. This was the generation that dared to question and jettison established values, including some that probably needed to be reexamined. Among these people there was little interest in discipline or long-range planning but lots of emphasis on immediate gratification and self-absorption. Unlike their parents whose lives were dominated by efforts to survive, this generation has expected more: "fulfillment, intimacy, pleasure—goals that are elusive to define or realize and thus fertile ground for disillusionment."[2] When hoped-for dreams never came true, many baby boomers worked harder, and some still continue to expect that the best is yet to be.

As they approach middle age, many baby boomers feel trapped by their lives. They are still searching for clear values and life purposes, but while they await clarification of their ultimate life directions, many feel stuck in boring jobs, stagnant dating relationships, meaningless marriages, unfulfilling lifestyles, dull churches, and/or binding inner insecurities. Most realize that abandoning obligations and running away is neither realistic nor responsible, so they remain in their circumstances, frustrated, fighting depression, and searching for a new life direction that will offer new hope.

LONELINESS

Jim Dethmer, associate pastor of the baby boomer–oriented Willow Creek Community Church in Illinois, notes that this is "a relationally vacuous generation struggling in their ability to form lasting relationships." They are five hundred times more likely then their parents to be single, and half of those who marry probably will divorce.[3] Many live in the suburbs, away from friends and family, tied to demanding jobs that sometimes require travel and moves, lacking the time needed to build friendships, and entertained by television that robs people of meaningful conversation. Often they do not know how to develop good interpersonal skills, to enjoy true friendships without competing, or to relax long enough to connect with other human beings and with God.

Roughly one-quarter of adults in our society live alone, and the numbers are estimated to reach 33 percent by the year 2000.[4] Many of these are baby boomers, many of whom are lonely. Others live and work in situations where they feel a crowded loneliness, surrounded by people but still feeling very much by themselves. Many would identify with the lyrics of a song that describes people living in one place, dreaming of another, unable to commit to either, and obsessed with the question of "How do I get to where I'm going?"

A call-in guest on a recent Christian talk show described her frustrations of being engaged to a man who "says he wants to get married but isn't ready to set a date, doesn't get along with his parents, and is still trying to get settled in his career. I don't want to push him," the caller continued, "but the uncertainty is very frustrating."

Such frustration often is tied to feelings of rootlessness and accompanied by a sense of alienation, social anxiety, low self-esteem, and dissatisfaction with family or home life. Although women more often admit to being lonely, objective studies show that feelings of loneliness are most common in men.[5] All of this helps explain the baby boomer interest in small groups and in building family stability. Churches are likely to grow if they encourage support networks that emphasize honesty, disclosure, and mutual caring. People who are lonely often stay by themselves, however, so they may need encouragement to join church activities or to talk with a counselor.

When they do come for counseling, several interventions can be helpful. *Cognitive-behavior therapy* helps people change their self-defeating thought patterns, faulty perceptions, irrational beliefs, and sense of helplessness. *Social skills training* is especially helpful for shy, inhibited, insecure, and other socially unskilled people who need help in relating to others.

Social support provides encouragement and stimulates opportunities for lonely people to get involved with others.[6] For
many baby boomers there is an additional need for help in *time
management* so relating to others can be fit into their busy
schedules. Other lonely people could benefit from *family counseling*, especially if counselees are living with relatives but
feeling persistent isolation and loneliness.[7]

STRESS AND ANXIETY

Most counselors are familiar with addiction to alcohol,
drugs, or other substances that are swallowed or injected into
the bloodstream, but we are less familiar with addiction to
chemicals that already exist inside the body. Christian psychologist Archibald Hart notes, for example, that we can
become addicted to our own adrenalin.[8]

Baby boomers who are under stress, hard-driving, ambitious, workaholic, highly competitive, constantly on the move,
or driven by their careers and lifestyles are also people whose
bodies consistently pump high amounts of adrenalin. This is a
hormone that gives us energy, keeps us going, and psychs us
up, especially in times of crisis when we need an extra physiological push. Like addicts who are aroused by illicit drugs,
people who are frantic, overworked, hurried, or stress-aroused
are buoyed by the adrenalin in their systems. Sometimes these
people take pride in their high-energy lifestyles, and they
rarely relax or come down from the adrenalin high. This description could apply to people of all ages, but it seems to be
most prevalent among baby boomers.

Hart gives several indicators of adrenalin addiction that
could apply to counselors as well as to our counselees. There
is high likelihood that one is hooked on adrenalin if he or she:
- would rather engage in activity (such as work) than sleep;
- feels very unhappy when the activity stops;
- only feels excited or encouraged when engaged in the activity; at other times feels "low";
- forgets other problems when involved in the activity;
- turns to the activity and feels better whenever feelings of
  depression appear;
- fantasizes about the activity when away from it;[9]

- thinks so much about the activity that sleep is difficult.

Addicted people have trouble relaxing. They fidget or feel guilty when they rest and often experience irritability, depression, and a strong compulsion to get busy doing something.

Adrenalin-addicted people are not the only ones who experience anxiety. In times of crisis or uncertainty, any of us can sense inner feelings of apprehension, uneasiness, concern, worry, and heightened awareness. These are times when our hearts beat faster, blood pressure and muscle tension increase, and the body is placed on the alert, ready to react. For most people the anxiety passes as circumstances change, but the perpetually anxious baby boomer, like the adrenalin-addicted individual, stays in a continued state of arousal. Eventually that wears down the body and sometimes leads to heart disease, ulcers, high blood pressure, stomach problems, jumpiness, interpersonal tension, and even spiritual decline.

Counselors can help baby boomers slow down and learn to relax.[10] This is not likely to be successful unless there are changes in the counselee's attitudes and self-perceptions. No amount of relaxation training is likely to be effective with baby boomers who are trying to prove themselves, who believe that self-worth is tied to career accomplishments, who consider inactivity to be a sign of laziness, or whose lives have little of interest apart from their work. If adrenalin-driven people do not slow down voluntarily, however, their bodies will slow them down through physical collapse.

Hart's observations on relaxation are of special significance to Christian baby boomers.

> Christians have not shown the world as clearly as we ought that the practice of genuine Christianity can more effectively reduce stress and help people live more fulfilling lives. We are often so frantic in living out our faith that we cause more stress than we cure. This should become a challenge for us, particularly as we develop our prayer lives and rediscover that there is a Christian meditation—too long neglected by twentieth-century Christians—that can produce profound peace and communion with God.[11]

DEPRESSION

"Have the baby boomers peaked? Peaked physically? Peaked economically? Peaked in their ability to set the cultural tone? Peaked in their capacity to enjoy themselves?" Baby boomer Laurence Shames raised these questions at the beginning of a reflective article about his own generation. "If we've learned anything, it's that most things aren't worth getting tired over."[12]

Shames suggests that one word has become the unofficial motto of the baby boomer generation: *MORE*. Throughout life these people have wanted more money, more excitement, more achievement. The drive for more has kept these people going, but the realities of burnout, financial setbacks, marriage failures, and personal disillusionment have left many baby boomers discouraged, pessimistic, and characterized by a what's-the-use, resigned attitude that already is leading to increased rates of suicide among baby boomers.[13]

It is well known that depression in our society is both prevalent and on the rise.[14] The causes of this common malady are complex and often physical, but frequently depression comes in response to loss. For many in the baby boomer generation, there has been a loss of their dreams, a loss of the expectation that life would give more, a loss of occupational or financial security, a loss of relationships due to separation or a death, a loss of a marriage, a loss of health as the generation ages, and for some, a loss of hope. In generations past, one could always find stability in the home, the church, or the security of one's government, but even this has gone as homes break up, church leaders fall, and politicians are generally distrusted. Baby boomers have no place to turn except inward, to themselves. But "in a self standing alone without the buffer of larger beliefs, helplessness and failure can all too easily become hopelessness and despair."[15]

To diagnose depression, one psychiatrist has suggested use of the mnemonic device "Depressed Sig E Caps." The word *depressed* refers to the primary symptom of sadness, hopelessness, or discouragement. The first letters in *Sig E Caps* point to eight other common symptoms: sleep disturbances, interest loss, guilt, energy decline, concentration difficulties, appetite loss, psychomotor changes, and suicide thoughts. A diagnosis of major depression requires the presence of a depressed mood or loss of interest in usual activities plus at least four of the other symptoms.[16]

Depressed people often respond well to antidepressant medication, but this does not take away the realities of baby boomer losses. Because of the influence of thinking on emotion, depressed baby boomers need help in understanding and evaluating the life events and thoughts that contribute to the depression. Losses, unfulfilled expectations, automatic self-talk, maladaptive behaviors, distorted self-perceptions, and definitions of success all need to be discussed and reevaluated.[17] Christians must recognize their uniqueness as followers of Jesus Christ and seek to live lives in accordance with the values of Scripture.

Writing from a secular perspective, Shames gives good advice to his baby boomer colleagues.

> By sheer numbers, we have been shaping the country as we've gone along—changing it from one big nursery to a hotbed of adolescent unrest to a scramble of young adults' ambitions. It's time to change it again. Here at midlife, the trick is to shore up the future by being reasonable about that future; by making an honest, non-hysterical assessment of what the prospects are. It's time to work toward an idea of the well-lived life that has less to do with more and more to do with better.[18]

Christians know that *better* only comes when one has a growing relationship with Jesus Christ.

CAREER CONFUSION AND TRANSITION

When we meet strangers in our society, we first exchange names and then ask, "What kind of work do you do?" Very often the name is forgotten, but the occupation of a new acquaintance becomes the first major topic of discussion. "In this mobile, depersonalized society, one's occupation is the basis of more prestige and identity than one's name," according to Charles Sell.[19] Many of us, especially those who are baby boomers, get self-satisfaction, self-worth, and self-identity from vocation. But careers often become idolized and the control-ling center of life.[20] Involvement in a fulfilling, well-paying, high-prestige career is a highly valued mark of success and *the* goal for millions of baby boomers.

Most of them do not make it.

Unlike previous generations, baby boomers are likely to have several careers and a variety of jobs during their lives. Often these will be boring, beneath the level of one's abilities and education, unfulfilling, and not secure, at least when eco-nomic times are tough. Conflicts between the demands of work and the needs of one's family can complicate difficult voca-tional situations and lead to tension in both places.[21] Christians who have a yearning to be in work that honors God and fur-thers his kingdom frequently find themselves trapped in jobs that appear to have no connection with anything of eternal sig-nificance. The potential for frustration is accentuated when the worker has no sense of dignity in the job, is overworked, un-derpaid, not challenged, and/or expected to make statements or decisions that are ethically questionable. Working under these conditions, many baby boomers long for change and dream of making a move, but they are trapped by the realities of an overpopulated job market and the need for keeping a steady job that pays the bills, regardless of its undesirability.

In a survey of two thousand people who call themselves Christians and attend church regularly, more than 90 percent reported that they had never heard a sermon, read a book, heard a tape, or attended a seminar that applied biblical principles to work.[22] As baby boomers return to church in greater numbers, Christian leaders can make a significant impact by addressing work-related issues in sermons, small group discussions, and similar settings. Publicly or in private counseling, try to communicate that success in life and value as a person is not dependent on success in a career. God is more concerned about who we are and what we are becom-ing than in what we do. Work in a Christian setting is more obviously related to God's kingdom, but he needs believers scattered in all segments of the labor force where they can do their jobs well and make a difference, even if their work seems meaningless.

This kind of cognitive reevaluation does not imply that change is never an option. Baby boomers should be encouraged to evaluate their careers periodically, to look at their strengths and weaknesses, to evaluate the wisdom of making a vocational change or of getting more training, and to determine how present work is affecting one's family, spiritual life, and psychological stability. With the guidance of the Holy Spirit and the wise counsel of caring human beings, each baby boomer should decide whether and when change is desirable.[23]

SINGLENESS

Do single fathers make good mothers? This intriguing question was the basis of a research study on the competence of single fathers who had custody of one or more children. Most of the surveyed fathers had no outside housekeeping help. They did their own grocery shopping, food preparation, house cleaning, and yard work, while they maintained their careers, chauffeured their kids to various activities, and sought to fill both father and mother roles.[24]

Perhaps these were unusual fathers (custody of children is more often given to mothers unless the fathers are clearly competent). Since the research was based on the respondents' self-reports, there was no way of knowing if what the fathers reported was an accurate picture of what they did. Nevertheless, the study confirmed what every single parent knows: it is not easy to raise children alone.

Statistics are always changing, of course, but estimates based on census data suggest that one-quarter of all children in the United States live with a single parent, that 60 percent of all black children live in a single-parent household, and that about half of all baby boomer children and grandchildren will spend at least part of their childhood years in single-parent families. The vast majority of these households are headed by women, most of whom earn significantly less than single-parent males. While a majority of households are still headed by a married couple, the baby boom generation has given rise to "the most profound change in family formation over the past three decades: the single-parent family.[25]

Some single-parent families are headed by a never-married parent, although a majority are the result of divorce. Regardless of the prior circumstances, single-parent baby boomers encounter a number of unique problems. These include financial struggles (especially for women), the constant pressure of too much to do, the strain of solo decision making, feelings of loneliness and isolation from same-age friends, difficulties in making child care arrangements, concern over the adjustment of children, feelings of incompetence and depression, the strains associated with dating, and the social stigma of being without a mate. Divorced parents, in addition, often feel guilt, self-blame, grief over lost relationships, tensions with ex-relatives, and conflicts that arise from custody and visitation issues.[26] Christians have the added pressure of dealing with church disapproval that often surrounds divorce. For career-conscious single parents, additional stresses come with efforts to maintain vocational competence and job satisfaction. This is a special challenge for women.[27]

The recent emphasis on single-parent families should not hide the fact that many baby boomers are single because they have never married. Counselors and researchers sometimes overlook this group because they are assumed to be in a minority or in a transient stage that will lead to marriage. But in addition to baby boomers who are single because they have chosen to delay marriage, many remain single throughout their entire lives—often by choice. These people often value their freedom and increased opportunity for personal and career development. Even so, evidence from several studies indicates that never-married adults, in general, are less stable psychologically and more prone to mental illness than those who are currently or formerly married.[28]

All of this has implications for the counselor. Most of us who work with baby boomers will focus much of our attention on the needs and unique problems of baby boomers who live without a marriage partner.

AGING

The year 2010 is not far away. It is then that the first of the baby boomers will reach retirement age. Twenty years later, in 2030, the United States will have over fifty million retirees, twice the number of people over sixty-five today. Forward-looking political leaders and social planners are already trying to evaluate the effect of this massive upsurge of baby boomer retirees on social security, health, social services, and government spending in the next century.

Until they reached middle age, few baby boomers thought much about growing old. If we live long enough, we all watch our parents get older,[29] but for most of us youthful idealism dulls our awareness of personal aging until we reach middle age. It is then that we become part of the sandwich generation (caught between aging parents and demanding children) and begin to realize that on this earth, life does not go on forever.

Counselors in the coming decades are likely to encounter increasing numbers of aging baby boomers who are struggling with bodies that are in decline, careers that may never be successful, marriages that have failed, children who have disappointed, and religious beliefs that leave church goers feeling spiritually empty. As they go through their forties and fifties, on into their sixties, baby boomers will need help to evaluate their lives, to accept the disappointments, and to go on to live the best possible later years.

BABY BOOMER STRENGTHS

Counselors and counseling books deal with problems. No chapter on counseling baby boomers would be possible without a major emphasis on the difficulties that people in this generation face.

We should remember, however, that baby boomers bring many strengths to the counseling relationship. These are survivors who expect to overcome problems. In contrast to their parents, baby boomers are less resistant to counseling, more willing to change, and motivated to have the counseling succeed. They expect competence in their counselors and are not reluctant to ask questions about methodologies and techniques. But they respond well to counselors who are open and not threatened by baby boomer desires to participate in the counseling process.

This generation's well-known commitment to fitness keeps baby boomer counselees physically active and more diet conscious. This, in turn, reduces the negative influence of stress. As they reach middle age, many are looking for clearer values, simpler lifestyles, more established roots,[30] greater security, and more stable relationships. Religion, once so widely rejected by baby boomers, is now of greater interest. This gives more freedom to Christian counselors and greater acceptance of their message that Christ must be a part of any lasting solution to contemporary problems.

COUNSELING GUIDELINES

All counseling begins with the building of a relationship, involves problem assessment and the development of counseling goals (at least in the counselor's mind), the selection and use of interventions, and the evaluation of these methods, leading eventually to termination of the counseling.

With individual baby boomers, there can be no formal list of topics to be discussed in counseling, but several issues should be kept in mind.

Modeling and Mentoring. This may never arise verbally in a counseling session, but each counselor is an example of what he or she believes and communicates. Baby boomers learn by watching, and they value authenticity. They are not impressed with counselors who say one thing but reflect something else in their lifestyles.

Stress Management. Baby boomers live stressful, overburdened lives, and some feel out of control. Counselors can help counselees evaluate their schedules and responsibilities and learn more effective ways to manage pressures.

Perceptual Change. Paranoid patients are not the only people who misperceive their life situations. At times all of us get things out of perspective and need to view problems and solutions in a new light. Counselees may need to be more realistic, more balanced in their thinking, and less inclined to view all of life in the light of one's present circumstances. Often we must help counselees see their lives from a biblical perspective. Even with our finite minds, Christians are aware that God often views things from a different perspective than we do, especially when we are in the midst of difficulties.

Emotional Baggage. Someone has suggested that all of us grow up wounded. Even people whose home lives have been secure and whose childhoods have been happy often reach adulthood with feelings of disappointment, insecurity, unresolved guilt, or confusion about the future.

During the late eighties and into the nineties, a plethora of books appeared describing dysfunctional families and the destructive past influences that can hinder effective living in adulthood. These book writers created the impression that all families are dysfunctional and that every individual is an "adult child" of some kind of debilitating past influence.

It is easy to play this blame game in our minds—attributing present problems to our backgrounds, families, genetics, unhealthy religious beliefs, or other painful prior experiences. There can be no doubt that early events do affect the present and make life difficult for many people. Counselees can bring psychological and spiritual baggage from their pasts—especially if these counselees have been abused, sexually mistreated, or subjected to the toxic effects of an alcohol-infested home. These painful experiences need to be discussed, often in the presence of a caring counselor, but the past must never be permitted to serve as an excuse for doing nothing about the future. Counselees often need help in facing their pasts, but then they need to put these influences behind so that life can be lived in the present and the future.

Values and Beliefs. Family counselors nationwide recently received a brochure announcing a forthcoming conference for professional therapists.

Not long ago, we were sure that family therapy would revolutionize psychology, and that our shining, new systems theory was the vanguard of Truth, Progress and Reason [the brochure began]. In those days, we believed not only in the objective nature of reality but in our capacity to find it, describe it and put it to use in our own field. [But the world has changed, according to the conference planners.] We have all seen too many cherished certainties shattered by the whirling transformations of our times. It almost seems as if the very word "truth" can no longer be uttered. . . . This dissolution of certainties is changing the nature of clinical practice.

In response, the brochure suggested, we must look to the role of individual creativity and personal values to build our therapies for the future.[31]

Christian counselors would agree that many "cherished certainties" and traditional values are being challenged in our society, but we would not agree that we must turn into ourselves and seek to find moral values in each person's "individual creativity." If subjective standards are the only basis for right and wrong, we in fact have no basis for morality. If the only certainties in life are based on personal perspectives, we have no certainties.

The conference brochure shows how the baby boomer search for values has penetrated the counseling professions and left counselors and counselees both searching for something in which to believe and on which to stake their lives and values. In contrast, the Christian counselor derives his or her standards from the Bible. We respect the right of any person to disagree with our conclusions, and we avoid coercion or manipulation, but in an age of ethical and moral confusion, we have a responsibility to help baby boomer counselees find values that are consistent with biblical truth. The alternative is the drifting uncertainty that the conference brochure described.

SELF-CONTROL

For many baby boomers, life is out of control. They have lost control of their habits, lusts, careers, addictive behaviors, temptations, marriages, children, workaholic lifestyles, and other segments of life.

Christian baby boomers may be aware that self-control is a characteristic of true spirituality, one of the fruits of the Spirit, evidence of the Holy Spirit's work and presence (Galatians 5:22–23). But even committed believers can have difficulty controlling their habits and lifestyles. Lack of discipline, deliberate sin, the impact of peer pressure, the lingering effects of unhealthy or harmful past experiences, continued involvement in destructive relationships or work situations, distorted self-perceptions—these are among the influences that can prevent self-control, even in people who pray for divine help and who sincerely want to change. At times maybe all of us need a counselor who can help us understand the reasons for a lack of control and help us gain or regain control of those life areas that are persistently troubling.

SKILLS ACQUISITION

Often baby boomers reach adulthood but still lack basic social or interpersonal skills, money management skills, the ability to manage time, skills that enable one to get and retain a job, parenting skills, principles of effective communication, the ability to maintain a stable marriage, or other life management capabilities. Every college teacher has encountered students who have high intelligence and the ability to succeed but who fail because they lack basic self-discipline and study skills. When they reach adulthood many people have problems, not because of some conflict buried in their psyches or because of a past trauma, instead, they need a person to teach them how to live and to function more efficiently. In these situations, the counselor takes the role of a teacher—a teacher of skills.

CAREER COUNSELING

The grandparents and many parents of baby boomers selected a line of work when they were young that lasted for life. Some spent thirty or forty years in the same company or same daily routines and never dreamed of leaving, even if the work was boring.

This type of lifelong loyalty to one field of work is rare among baby boomers and likely to become rarer. This generation seeks fulfillment in all of life, including work, and baby boomers are more likely to change their jobs for something better if this is at all possible.

At times people change because they have no alternative. In an age of technology, previously secure positions can become obsolete and phased out. New vocations are created, and mobility is common. In general, the fewer one's vocational skills and training, the less opportunities exist for finding or changing to more satisfying and well-paying work. Recently, however, with the great number of highly educated, motivated baby boomer workers and the more limited numbers of positions, unemployability is common in all segments of the population. Well-qualified people who want work are out of jobs and looking for employment. Often they change vocations in the process.

Career guidance is a specialized area of counseling expertise. Even without this special training, counselors can give initial guidance, encouragement, and perspectives as baby boomers face forced or voluntary unemployment, prepare to change positions, cope with difficult work situations, take the risks of midlife career changes, or seek further education to prepare for a different type of work.

CONCLUSIONS

Counseling usually involves helping people solve personal problems and cope with persisting stresses. Nevertheless, as we seek to understand and help baby boomers, we should not overlook the importance of helping people anticipate and prevent the development of future problems. This preventive therapy can occur in the counseling room, but it also can take place through sermons, classes, seminars, informal conversations, and other noncounseling interventions. Ultimately, preventing personal problems may be the most effective way to help.

NOTES

1. Martin E. P. Seligman, "Boomer Blues," *Psychology Today* (October 1988), 50–55. For a Christian perspective see Gary R. Collins, "We Have a Bigger Answer," *Decision* 31 (April 1990): 7–8.

2. The quotation is from Jack Sheen, a licensed psychologist in Baltimore whose practice consists almost exclusively of baby boomers. Cited by Paula Rinehart, "The Pivotal Generation," *Christianity Today* 33 (October 6, 1989): 23.

3. Ibid., 24.

4. Kerby Anderson, *Future Tense: Eight Coming Crises of the Baby Boom Generation* (Nashville: Thomas Nelson, 1991).

5. Ron D. Hays and M. Robin DiMatteo, "A Short-Form Measure of Loneliness," *Journal of Personality Assessment* 51 (1987): 69–81.

6. Benedict T. McWhirter, "Loneliness: A Review of Current Literature, With Implications for Counseling and Research," *Journal of Counseling and Development* 68 (March/April 1990): 417–22.

7. Tom Large, "Some Aspects of Loneliness in Families," *Family Process* 28 (1989): 25–35.

8. This is discussed in detail in Archibald D. Hart, *The Hidden Link Between Adrenalin and Stress* (Dallas: Word, 1988).

9. Ibid., 87.

10. In part three of his book, Hart describes practical ways for helping people to relax.

11. Hart, *Adrenalin and Stress*, 171.

12. Laurence Shames, "Has the Thirty- and Fortysomething Generation Passed Its Peak?" *Utne Reader* (January/February 1990), 78–82.

13. Judy Folkenberg, "Suicide: A Future Boom for Baby Boomers?" *Psychology Today* (September 1987), 22.

14. The prevalence of depression in the general population is 5–12 percent lifetime for men and 9–26 percent lifetime for women. The risk of developing depression has increased from 15–20 percent in the 1920s to 40–60 percent in cohorts born in the 1960s. These statistics are cited by Samuel Gershon, "Depression Overview: Symptoms and Treatment Strategies," *Journal of Clinical Psychiatry* 52 (October 1991): 437–38.

15. Seligman, "Boomer Blues," 55.

16. Gershon, "Depression Overview," 437.

17. Two excellent and practical Christian books can be of help to counselors who work with depressed baby boomers. See Archibald D. Hart, *Counseling the Depressed* (Waco, Tex.: Word, 1987), and Mark R. McMinn, *Cognitive Therapy Techniques in Christian Counseling* (Dallas: Word, 1991).

18. Shames, "The Thirty- and Fortysomething Generation," 82.

19. Charles M. Sell, *Transition: The Stages of Adult Life* (Chicago: Moody, 1985), 23.

20. Doug Sherman and William Hendricks, *Your Work Matters to God* (Colorado Springs: NavPress, 1987).

21. Richard T. Kinnier, Ellen C. Katz, and Martha A. Berry, "Successful Resolutions to the Career-Versus-Family Conflict," *Journal of Counseling and Development* 69 (May/June 1991): 439–44.

22. Sherman and Hendricks, *Your Work Matters*, 16.

23. For a biblical perspective on careers, see John A. Bernbaum and Simon M. Steer, *Why Work? Careers and Employment in Biblical Perspective* (Grand Rapids: Baker, 1986). A thorough discussion of vocational counseling is presented by Vernon G. Zunker, *Career Counseling: Applied Concepts of Life Planning*, 3rd ed. (Pacific Grove, Calif.: Brooks/Cole, 1990).

24. Barbara J. Risman, "Can Men 'Mother'? Life as a Single Father." In Barbara J. Risman and Pepper Schwartz, ed., *Gender in Intimate Relationships: A Microstructural Approach* (Belmont, Calif.: Wadsworth, 1989), 155–64.

25. The quotation and many of the statistics are taken from Esther Wattenberg, " The Fate of Baby Boomers and Their Children," *Social Work* (January/February 1986). See also Felicity Barringer, "Changes in Family Patterns: Solitude and Single Parents," *New York Times*, June 6, 1991.

26. Herbert Goldenberg and Irene Goldenberg, *Counseling Today's Families* (Pacific Grove, Calif.: Brooks/Cole, 1990).

27. Sharon K. Houseknecht and Suzanne Vaughn, "The Impact of Singlehood on the Career Patterns of Professional Women," *Journal of Marriage and the Family* 49 (May 1987): 353–66. See also Elinor Lottinville and Avraham Scherman, "Job Satisfaction of Married, Divorced, and Single Working Women in a Medical Setting," *The Career Development Quarterly* 37 (December 1988): 165–76.

28. Michael W. Johnson and Susan J. Eklund, "Life Adjustment of the Never Married: A Review With Implications for Counseling," *Journal of Counseling and Development* 63 (December 1984): 230–36.

29. Jeffrey A. Giordano, "Parents of Baby Boomers: A New Generation of Young-Old," *Family Relations* 37 (October 1988), 411–14.

30. Brad Edmondson, "Making Yourself at Home: The Baby Boom Generation Yearns to Settle Down," *Utne Reader* (May/June 1990), 74–82.

31. "Making It Up As We Go Along," program theme for the 15th Annual Family Therapy Network Symposium, March 13–14, 1992.

Chapter 11

Spiritual Counseling with Baby Boomers

Bᴀʙʏ ʙᴏᴏᴍᴇʀ ᴄᴏʟᴜᴍɴɪsᴛ Bᴏʙ Gʀᴇᴇɴᴇ does not hold much hope for the future of his generation. "Boy, if you thought the members of the so-called Baby Boom generation were hated already, wait until you see what's coming," Greene wrote in a recent column.

> The Baby Boom generation—the largest and most disliked in history—is on the verge of becoming really despised. In 30 or 40 years, the Baby Boomers are going to need personal bodyguards to keep younger Americans from kicking them around. Which is going to be quite a sight to see, since the Baby Boomers will be 70 or 80 years old by then. . . .
>
> Younger Americans will be looking upon the old Boomers as non-productive leeches who are screwing up the quality of life just by staying alive. . . . Not only that, but even in our wheelchairs and walkers we'll be called Baby Boomers.[1]

Columnist Greene probably is overly pessimistic about the future of baby boomers, but his comments point to changes

187

that are taking place and will take place as the generation gets older. The people who battled "the establishment" in the sixties and seventies have now become part of the mainstream and are facing challenges from their own children. Already we see evidence of baby boomers grappling with the realities of middle age. As they get older, many seek spiritual values for themselves and religious foundations for their children. It is not surprising that families, in large numbers, are looking for help and answers in religion. Their ranks are filling the churches, and their spiritual questions and concerns are popping up in the offices of Christian counselors, including counseling pastors.

RELIGIOUS SEARCHING AND EXPECTATIONS

Robert Page pastored a multigenerational church in North Dakota that recently commemorated its one-hundredth anniversary. Described as a "beautiful, sturdy structure" that has served its worshipers well through many seasons of ministry, the old church is having to make some changes. "Precious senior adults" still gather faithfully for midweek prayer meeting and ask God to increase their numbers, but the baby boomers and baby busters are nowhere in sight. They spend Wednesday evening bringing their kids to exciting, high-energy youth programs, and they reserve their Sunday nights for "cocooning with their families from life's mind-boggling pace or sharing in prayer and Bible study within the intimate setting of a small group."[2]

The members of that century-old church, like people in churches across the land, know that we live and worship in the midst of change. The methodologies of the 70s rarely meet the needs of society in the 90s. Churches will die and miss tremendous opportunities for ministry if they tenaciously cling to the past and ignore the questions and expectations of searching, returning, aging baby boomers and their families

The Searching.   Listening is the basis of good counseling. All of us know that. For this reason, each baby boomer counselee must be heard as an individual with unique needs, frustrations, desires, and spiritual expectations. Churches that reach and attract baby boomers are churches that listen and try to understand what the generation is seeking. Based on telephone marketing surveys, one growing church in Texas has concluded that baby boomers dislike boring sermons, unfriendly people, poor quality child care, and too much talk about money. The result is a church that lets people "sample before they buy in," never get asked for money, always receive a friendly greeting, and put their children in one of the best church day-care centers in the state.[3] It is not surprising that one church growth specialist concludes that baby boomers already are changing the ways in which pastors do their work in American churches.[4]

As you listen to baby boomers, you are likely to discover those who look for practical principles for raising children, building marriages, and handling stress. Many want religious experiences that help them make sense of life with all its turmoil and uncertainty. Often they seek clear values for themselves and their children. They want support and fulfilling relationships with other caring people. At times almost all want guidance as they make decisions and face the choice points of life. Some want a faith that can help them overcome addiction, loneliness, dysfunctional family backgrounds, or lives that are marked by failure. As they grow older and watch their parents age, baby boomers are beginning to raise questions about the ultimate destiny of human beings. They realize that there is more to life than possessions and promotions or fun and fulfillment. In time, all of our bodies break down and die. Then what?

Dallas Willard's much acclaimed book on spiritual disciplines captures the essence of what many baby boomers seek. Psychological, social, and political revolutions have not been able to "transform the heart of darkness that lies deep in the breast of every human being," Willard writes. "Amid a flood of self-fulfillment there is an epidemic of depression, suicide, personal emptiness, and escapism through drugs and alcohol, cultic obsession, consumerism, and sex and violence—all combined with an inability to sustain deep and enduring personal relationships. So obviously the problem is a spiritual one. And so must be the cure."[5] Many who come for counseling are looking for that kind of cure.

But spiritual seekers want more than cures for the problems of life. As we have noted previously, baby boomers want lively, contemporary music and interesting, relevant sermons. They have little interest in denominational issues, ponderous preaching, politics from the pulpit, judgmental statements, pre-packaged programs, or churches where the people never laugh, share, or care. Most do not want to be passive specta-tors in the worship service; they want active participation and uplifting religious experiences. Lives that are dominated by busyness and pressure want religious teaching and personal involvement that make the trip to church worth the effort. Counselors who keep these desires in mind are likely to com-municate better with baby boomers who seek help on spiritual issues.

A Caution.   Although relevant churches and Christian counselors listen to baby boomers and seek to be sensitive to their spiritual struggles and searches, this attitude must be tempered by an important consideration: the Christian faith is not a market-driven religion, based on personal preferences of the parishioners or on the findings of professional pollsters.

In their efforts to be accommodating, many clergy and coun-selors have cut out much of the Gospel. *Sin* has become a taboo word, *repentance* or *commitment* are rarely mentioned, the call of Jesus to "take up a cross" and follow him is overlooked, God's nature and sovereignty are downplayed, counseling ses-sions are indistinguishable from secular approaches to therapy, and church services become shows with lots of fanfare but little substance, Scripture-based teaching, challenge, or calls for life-changing decisions. It would be irresponsible to imply that all or even most baby boomer churches present such an emascu-lated Christianity. But this is true of some, and the temptation always exists.

Jesus warned that following him would not be easy. True believers could expect to be hated and persecuted, he warned. His followers are like sheep among wolves.[6] Many who seek answers to their spiritual questions can be expected to turn away, as did the rich young man,[7] unwilling to part with past lifestyles and to make major life changes. Others will embrace their new religious experiences enthusiastically but soon drift away when faced with trouble, persecution, the worries of life, or the deceitfulness of attractive wealth.[8]

Baby boomers, like people of every other generation, go to church for a variety of reasons and have differing motives for staying. In themselves, there is nothing wrong with wanting good friendships, uplifting religious experiences, interesting teaching, helpful counseling, and a place where moral values can be instilled in one's impressionable youngsters. But if people are not challenged and lives are not changed, then something is very wrong, and the spiritual seeker will ultimately be frustrated,[9] disappointed, and eventually inclined to look elsewhere for spiritual experiences and answers to religious questions.

Religious Questions

If you could ask God three questions, what would they be?

The Gallup pollsters presented a list of potential questions to a group of respondents and found the answers presented in Table 7. This list includes some of the basic philosophical and theological questions that have been debated for centuries, but the questions are no less relevant today.

Table 7
Asking God Questions

Suppose you could ask God any three questions on this list. What would they be?

Will there ever be lasting peace?	37%
How can I be a better person?	33%
What does the future hold for me and my family?	31%
Will there ever be a cure for all diseases?	28%
Why is there suffering in the world?	29%
Is there life after death?	26%
What is heaven like?	22%
Will man ever love his fellow man?	21%
Why is there evil in the world?	16%
When will the world end?	16%
Why was man created?	10%

George Gallup, Jr., and Sarah Jones, *100 Questions and Answers: Religion in America* (Princeton, N.J.: Princeton Religion Research Center, 1989), 172.

Several years ago, Charles Swindoll published what he called the "four spiritual flaws" in the thinking of many believers: (1) all problems are solved when one becomes a Christian, (2) all the problems one ever faces are addressed in the Bible, (3) if anyone has problems he or she is unspiritual, and (4) being exposed to sound biblical teaching automatically solves problems.[10] These are widely held myths, but none is true. Problems do not disappear when one becomes a believer and neither do clear answers always materialize, even among those with good Bible knowledge.

There is a difference between turning to God for help and clarification versus the expectation that God will meet every need and give answers to all our questions. Even Jesus did not know when the world would end, and there are ultimate questions that our finite minds cannot comprehend—at least while we live on this earth.[11]

Baby boomers want a balance between clear logical thinking about theological issues and a personal experience with God. In a cover story on prayer, *Newsweek* concluded that "in allegedly rootless, materialistic, self-centered America, there is also a hunger for a personal experience of God that prayer seeks to satisfy." This hunger for God is a lifelong spiritual quest, the magazine observed. Baby boomers are described as being "just as devout as the oldsters," concerned about ultimate issues, and seeking to know God.[12]

Christian counselors must recognize, however, that the baby boomer's search for spiritual answers and experiences is not limited to traditional Christianity and neither is there much interest in finding the one true church. New Age ideas and other forms of religiosity have attracted considerable interest among baby boomers, many of whom see no reason to limit the spiritual search to one single faith. "I'm a Christian New-Ager," said one of our students, who believes that she can be more spiritual if she combines elements from different religious ideologies.[13] Counselors are likely to encounter this diversity, coupled with the prevailing view that each individual ultimately is the source of his or her own authority on spiritual issues. For many baby boomers and busters, personal convictions carry far more weight than biblical truths or ecclesiastical dogma.

BABY BOOMER SPIRITUALITY

Not long ago, the respected Musical Heritage Society announced its featured selections for Christmas.[14] One compact disc, *A Festival of Christmas Carols*, included "Hark the Herald Angels Sing," "What Child is This?" and "Away in a Manger." A second was Malcolm Daglish's *Hymnology of Earth* with selections titled "Great Trees," "Psalm of Solstice," and " The Dark Around Us." The theme of the Daglish music is religious, according to a reviewer. It creates "a general feeling of devotion, based on the mysteries of the natural rhythms of the Earth."

The contrast between these two compact discs portrays a polarity of thinking that permeates much of our society, reflects an emerging contrast between two views of spirituality, and has great relevance for spiritual counseling.

Australian writer Rowland Croucher recently defined spirituality from a Christian perspective. "Christian Spirituality is about the movements of God's Spirit in one's life, in the community of faith, and in the cosmos," Croucher wrote. "It is concerned with how all realities relate, enlivened, enlightened, and empowered by the Spirit of Jesus. . . . *Spiritual formation is the dynamic process whereby the Word of God is applied by the Spirit of God to the heart and mind of the child of God so that she or he becomes more like the Son of God.*"[15]

For centuries, Christians have defined *spirituality* in terms of one's relationship with God, but this has begun to change. For some, *spirituality* is a synonym for *religion*. For many others the term has broader connotations, referring to human potential, ultimate purposes, well-being, higher entities, wholeness, or openness to the infinite. Today, discussions of spirituality often have abandoned or deemphasized the concept of God, redefined the meaning of God, or urged us to look within ourselves if we want to find God.

New Age Spirituality. The New Age Movement (NAM) is not easily defined, and descriptions of New Age spirituality are even more elusive. Despite wide diversity, most New Age advocates would agree that theirs is an introspective spirituality. For many, spirituality involves "tapping into the unlimited power within us." Looking outward to Christ, seeking guidance in the Scriptures, getting involved in church services, or believing in the Christ who came to a manger, are all rejected as being narrow, insensitive, "arrogant and uncompassionate in a world of pluralism, a world in which there are many worthwhile religious ways."[16]

The new spirituality is subjective, encouraging people to "get in contact with the Higher Self within us," or to look into ourselves to find God. Many would add that we are all gods or in the process of becoming gods, and some suggest that the ultimate goal of spirituality is to experience unity with one another and with the universe.

Psychiatrist M. Scott Peck divides spirituality into four levels. Lower levels view God as an external, transcendent Being, but the most mature top level spirituality is a "mystical communal stage of spiritual development," a stage "of unity, of an underlying connectedness between things: between men and women, between us and the other creatures and even inanimate matter as well, fitting together according to an ordinarily invisible fabric underlying the cosmos."[17]

This may sound like pantheistic gobbledygook, but it is not far removed from the thinking of many baby boomers. From this perspective, true spirituality seeks to find the energy and unrealized potential within ourselves and within nature. It is a spirituality that is slipping unnoticed into many churches and into mainstream psychotherapy.

Christian Spirituality. When he was asked about the growing ministry of Jesus, John the Baptist made a brief statement that gives the essence of spirituality for the follower of Christ: "He must become greater; I must become less" (John 3:30 NIV).

Christians cannot conceive of true spirituality without the guidance of the Holy Spirit of God and the truth of the Word of God. Christian spirituality does not ignore human potential, interpersonal relationships, meditation, or even personal success or concern for the environment. But neither does Christian spirituality ignore the realities of sin, the significance of self-denial and self-control, or the centrality of obedience to God the Father and the formative influence of Jesus Christ who is both our redeemer and our model. Christian spirituality is a process of becoming increasingly Christlike—a process that goes beyond mere self-reflection to find hope, forgiveness, redemption, and ultimate meaning in the living Christ. Christian spiritual growth involves introspection and self-examination but goes much further to include reading and obeying the Scriptures, attendance at worship services, self-sacrificing service, personal discipline, and a firm commitment to Christ. Is it surprising that millions turn away, as did the rich young ruler? New Age spirituality is easier, less demanding, and much more vague.

Recent research suggests that Christian spiritual direction and contemporary psychotherapy have many common features, despite their often dissimilar goals.[18] Until recently, therapists ignored spiritual issues, but as these slip increasingly into counseling, it is sobering that so many of our non-Christian colleagues are taken with New Age and other counterfeits of true biblical spirituality. And it is equally distressing to note that baby boomers often see no conflict between their Christian faith and their involvement with New Age thinking.

When he visited ancient Athens, the apostle Paul was greatly distressed to find a city filled with idols, false religion, and ungodly religious practices. But Paul did not wring his hands in despair. Instead, he familiarized himself with the philosophies, the literature, and the erroneous thinking of the society where he was living. And he used his knowledge to debate, challenge, and counteract the godless spirituality of his time (Acts 17:16–17).

The new popular emphasis on spirituality gives Christian counselors both an opportunity and a challenge. When error abounds, the contrast with simple truth often can be seen with greater clarity, especially when that truth is presented lucidly and with sensitivity. Like Paul in Athens, church leaders and Christian counselors in the 1990s can become familiar with counterfeit spirituality (in its many forms) and can boldly present clear alternatives, both to our colleagues and to our baby boomer counselees.

BABY BOOMER BAGGAGE

When they use the word *baggage*, counselors refer to past events, attitudes, traumas, and memories that people still carry in their minds. As a heavy suitcase can impede our progress through airports or bus stations, psychological baggage from the past can interfere with one's movement through life. The popular recovery movement in counseling, with its many twelve-step programs, is an effort to help people cast off the baggage of childhood trauma, past abuse, dysfunctional family backgrounds, entrenched misperceptions, or unhealthy self-talk.

Many baby boomers have reached adulthood with religious baggage that interferes with their clear understanding of the Gospel. Some have grown up in religious homes where parents failed to practice what they claimed to believe, refused to listen to their children's questions or doubts, instilled a fear of God rather than a love for him, or rigidly adhered to lists of "do's and don't's" that distracted from a true understanding of God's divine nature.[19] According to psychologist Donald E. Sloat, many of these baby boomers became addicted to unhealthy religion. He calls them "adult children of evangelicals."[20] From a different perspective, Texas pastor Gerald Mann observes that these "baby boomers have a mind-set of what a church is and we have to overcome their biases."[21]

Overcoming bias is not easy, and neither do people easily drop the attitudes, suspicions, misperceptions, and feelings of anger and distrust of religion that many carry like heavy luggage. Often these people hunger for a closeness with God and yearn for an authentic spirituality, but they tend to be cautious about religious people and religion—especially traditional religion.

How do we break down these resistances?

Once again, Paul's experiences in Athens can be instructive. He interacted with people in the places of worship and in the marketplace. He learned about their poetry, their religious perspectives, their ways of thinking. There is no evidence that he came charging into Athens, ready to challenge erroneous ideas and condemn hypocrisy. Instead, he observed, listened, got to know the people, let them see what he was like, and earned the right to be heard.

Anyone who has taught in a foreign country knows the importance of learning about the culture, trying to understand,

and showing a gracious spirit before presenting one's message. Often we have to be seen and watched before we can be heard. Counselors call this "rapport building." It is crucial with baby boomers and is one reason why baby boomer–sensitive churches give visitors the freedom to observe and wait before they are asked to make any commitments. The effective counselor listens, without condemnation, until he or she builds a trusting relationship. Christian caregivers never condone sinful behavior or agree with a counselee's faulty religious thinking, but there is a willingness to show respect, even for people with whom we disagree. In time, the counselor must seek to challenge faulty thinking and to carve away some of the unhealthy religious baggage from the past.

Sharon Hildebrandt is an evangelical Christian who counsels with baby boomers and others who have abandoned the church, claim they have been hurt by past religious involvements, and state that they never will go back.[22] Based on her counseling and surveys, Hildebrandt has listed the most frequent complaints:

- Sick congregations that are dominated by powerful leaders who shun accountability, reject contact with other churches or denominations, and claim to be the only valid interpreter "not only of what's happening in his life, but in your life as well."
- The use of guilt, shame, and displays of emotion that appear designed to manipulate churchgoers and to build bonds of unity and dependence on the leader.
- Constant reminders to distrust outsiders and nonbelievers, even while there are appeals to bring new people into the church.
- Churches that have little interest in problems of daily life, such as alcoholism, eating disorders, divorce, financial pressures, or the stresses of family life.
- Systems that create "workaholics for God," with staff members or volunteers chained to their duties by guilt or feelings of loyalty to the pastor.
- An obsession with sexual topics, often accompanied by morally questionable practices in some of the leaders who so strongly condemn immorality.

In a sobering and insightful book dealing with religious addiction and "toxic faith," Stephen Arterburn and Jack Felton describe the nature of religious baggage, explain how unhealthy religion develops, and list some characteristics of healthy faith. In their program for treating the victims of pathological religion, Arterburn and Felton suggest the following objectives.[23]

1. *Breaking through denial.* "The number one objective in the recovery of religious addicts is to break through the denial that addiction exists."[24] Many realize that help is needed but are reluctant to let go of their unhealthy, but secure, faulty thinking about religion and other issues.

2. *Surrendering to God.* Some victims of toxic faith want to draw close to God, but many others have no interest in spiritual growth. Most are afraid that confession and surrender will pull them back into devastating pathological religious settings. Even so, Christian counselors know that until an individual yields to God, there will be no power available to bring and maintain change.

It usually takes time for the counselee to reach the point of willingly surrendering to God, and there may be subsequent relapses. Surrendering is a process. The counselor can encourage this process and pray for his or her counselees, but these people cannot (and should not) be coerced into submitting to God.

3. *Changing toxic thinking.* Much of the counselor's work will involve confronting the counselee's disoriented thinking and replacing erroneous thoughts with thoughts that are based on reality. For example, people with religious baggage often have distorted ideas about the attributes of God, human responsibility, forgiveness, God's will, evangelism, spirituality, the nature of the church, giving, and a variety of other issues. Many of these people have learned to squelch questions or doubts about religion, condemn themselves, follow rigid rules, or deny their feelings. Issues like these need to be discussed with a counselor who is biblically informed, able to understand the counselee's pain and confusion, noncondemning, and willing to enter into discussions of difficult religious questions without feeling threatened.

4. *Giving information.* Counseling involves much more than the giving of information, but often the counselee has been vic-

timized by a lifetime of propaganda, ignorance, and erroneous data. Many counselees find help, therefore, if they can be pointed to accurate information, clear biblical teaching, and religious truths that are relevant to their lives.

Some have never thought about the nature of healthy religion. The characteristics cited in Table 8 could help counselors and their counselees understand the nature.of faith that is not toxic.

Table 8
Some Characteristics of Healthy Religion

The individual who has a healthy and maturing faith has:
    Clear beliefs, held firmly but not rigidly.
    Behavior and attitudes that are consistent with one's beliefs.
    Religious practices (e.g., prayer, worship) that are consistent with one's beliefs.
    Balance between reason and emotion.
    A realistic and essentially positive self-concept.
    Interdependence with other believers.
    Nonjudgmental, nondefensive, respectful interactions with people who believe differently.
    Willingness to take responsibility for one's actions.
    Willingness and ability to forgive.
    Willingness and ability to postpone immediate gratification so that greater satisfaction can come in the future.
    Ability to look at oneself, one's problems, and one's religious community objectively.
    Love that is seen in close relationships but that extends to acts of service, compassion, social justice, and evangelism.

---

5. *Working in a support group.* It is very difficult, perhaps impossible, for an individual to cast off unhealthy religion without help. Saul of Tarsus is a good example. Following his conversion on the road to Damascus, he was blind and led to a spiritual leader named Ananias, who was used by God to start the three-year learning process that would enable Saul to get

rid of his faulty religious ideas and to replace them with a maturing Christian faith.[25] According to Arterburn and Felton, spiritual recovery is best accomplished in support groups where individuals find encouragement, support, accountability, acceptance, and periodic firm but loving confrontation.

6. *Helping with family and social relationships.* Toxic religion often starts in families. It may arise from the behaviors and attitudes of family members who, themselves, embrace pathological religion. Counselees need help in relating to their families, even when family members are critical and unwilling to change their own religious thinking.

Treatment also helps counselees develop healthy social relationships. Recovering people need supportive friendships with people who are found in churches, gyms, college courses, and at work—but rarely in bars or night clubs.

7. *Working on the body.* Every counselor knows but sometimes forgets that good diet, weight control, regular exercise, sufficient rest, and periodic relaxation can all contribute to recovery. Counselees who take care of their bodies are better able to handle the stresses of life, including the religious stresses.

SPIRITUAL COUNSELING

In one sense, all Christian counseling is spiritual. It is a process in which followers of Jesus Christ seek to be guided by the Holy Spirit as they apply their God-given abilities, skills, training, knowledge, and insights to the task of helping others move toward personal wholeness, interpersonal competence, mental stability, and spiritual maturity.[26] At times the counseling will focus on issues of toxic faith and spiritual maturity, but it is impossible to isolate the spiritual from all other issues and areas of life.

Before we can help baby boomers with their spiritual struggles and questions, counselors must evaluate their own spiritual lives. We will be minimally effective as spiritual counselors unless we make prayer a priority in our own busy schedules, spend time concentrating on the nature of God, make it a practice to read and meditate on the Scripture, and involve ourselves in corporate worship and service. Reading books, taking courses, and learning about spiritual issues can all be valuable, but the best spiritual counselors seek to walk with God, be yielded to Christ, obey his Word, and be guided by the Holy Spirit.

Spiritually informed and sensitive counselors can help baby boomers evaluate their spiritual expectations, deal with their misconceptions about religion, confess their sins and find forgiveness, learn the meaning of mature religion, find fulfilling involvement with other growing believers, learn how to live lives that honor God, find effective ways to grow spiritually, develop biblically based behaviors concerning giving and serving, and find answers to their spiritual questions. Trained Christian counselors may have perspectives and therapeutic techniques that differ from those of untrained counselors, but when we deal with spiritual issues, the professional Christian therapist is close to what churches know as disciplers or spiritual mentors and guides.

Despite the increasing interest in spirituality among baby boomers, life is often too busy to spend time with God. Baby boomers and their counselors might find help in a prayer published while this book was being written.[27] The following words are worth reading slowly.

> Lord of the still small voice:
> > It is no wonder that so often I can't hear you
> > > for the roar of the crowd that is in my world,
> > > for the rush of the schedule,
> > > for the sounds of a never-silent age
> > > that is full up with music boxes blaring.
> > I'm weary of all the noise and the hustle,
> > > yet I can't stop;
> > > No—that isn't right; rather, I won't stop
> > > to discover the renewal of being
> > > quiet in your presence.
> > Yet how can I imagine
> > > that if in your incarnation you had to get away
> > > to be with your Father in peace,
> > > that I shouldn't need to get apart with you
> > > before I come apart without you. . . .

Lord of all. . . .
Protect the time you allot to me
    that no intrusion would come to assassinate
    the precious moments of stillness with you. . . .
Provide that retreat I so desperately need
    in days of stillness,
    in hours of quiet,
    in minutes of rest and peace,
    even in seconds when your presence is so real
    that it transforms my soul.
So meet me; by your grace.   Amen

NOTES

1. Bob Greene, "Oh, Baby, Just Wait Another 40 Years," *Chicago Tribune,* January 12, 1992.

2. Robert Page, "The Glorious Challenge of Pastoring a Multigenerational Church," *The Evangelical Beacon* (April 1991), 12–14.

3. Cited by Kenneth L. Woodward, "A Time to Seek," *Newsweek* (December 17, 1990), 56.

4. Elmer Towns, *How to Reach the Baby Boomer* (Lynchburg, Va.: Church Growth Institute, 1990).

5. Dallas Willard, *The Spirit of the Disciplines: Understanding How God Changes Lives* (San Francisco: Harper and Row, 1988), viii.

6. Matthew 10:16; John 15:18–20.

7. Matthew 19:16–22.

8. Matthew 13:18–22.

9. This is the theme of a brief article by Rodney Clap, "Bull Market for Religion," *Christianity Today* (April 3, 1987), 15.

10. Charles R. Swindoll, *Three Steps Forward and Two Steps Back* (Minneapolis, Minn.: World Wide, 1980).

11. Matthew 24:36; Romans 11:33.

12. Kenneth L. Woodward, "Talking to God," *Newsweek* (January 6, 1992), 38–44.

13. According to a survey reported by Woodward in his article "A Time to Seek," 60 percent of baby boomers "reject the notion that one should be limited to a single faith."

14. Most of the paragraphs in this section are adapted from an article by Gary R. Collins, "Spirituality and Mental Health," *Christian Mental Health for the Professional Therapist* (Fall 1991), 1–3.

15. Rowland Croucher, "Spiritual Formation," *Grid* (World Vision of Australia, Winter 1991), 1–2. Italics added.

16. Donald G. Bloesch, "Lost in the Mystical Myths," *Christianity Today* 35 (August 16, 1991): 22–24.

17. M. Scott Peck, *The Different Drum: Community Making and Peace* (New York: Simon and Schuster, 1987), 192.

18. Marilyn A. Ganje-Fling and Patricia R. McCarthy, "A Comparative Analysis of Spiritual Direction and Psychotherapy," *Journal of Psychology and Theology* 19 (1991): 103–17.

19. Donald E. Sloat, *The Dangers of Growing Up in a Christian Home* (Nashville: Thomas Nelson, 1986).

20. Donald E. Sloat, *Growing Up Holy and Wholly: Understanding and Hope for Adult Children of Evangelicals* (Brentwood, Tenn.: Wolgemuth and Hyatt, 1990).

21. The quotation is taken from the article by Woodward, "A Time to Seek," 56.

22. Quoted by Terry Mattingly, "Some Believe They Are Addicted to Religion," *Chicago Tribune*, April 26, 1991.

23. Stephen Arterburn and Jack Felton, *Toxic Faith: Understanding and Overcoming Religious Addiction* (Nashville: Oliver-Nelson, 1991). The following paragraphs are adapted from chapter 9, "Treatment and Recovery."

24. Arterburn and Felton, *Toxic Faith*, 266.

25. The conversion and early spiritual growth of Saul is recorded in Acts 9:1–22.

26. See chapter one, "What is Christian Counseling," in Gary R. Collins, ed., *Case Studies in Christian Counseling* (Dallas: Word, 1991), 11–17.

27. Rowland Croucher and Grace Thomlinson, eds., *High Mountains Deep Valleys* (Sutherland, NSW, Australia: Albatross, 1991), 32–33. Reprinted with permission.

PART THREE

Reaching Beyond
Baby Boomers

Chapter 12

Helping Baby Busters and the Children of Baby Boomers

Dᴜʀɪɴɢ ᴛʜᴇ ʏᴇᴀʀs ᴡʜᴇɴ ᴛʜᴇ ꜰɪʀsᴛ baby boomers were growing up, a parallel growth was taking place in the field of counseling. Freud's theories and methods were being challenged. A host of new group therapies were appearing, especially during the sixties. Behaviorism and behavior therapy reached their peak of influence and then began to fade. As we moved into the eighties, cognitive therapy emerged as a more popular approach to counseling, and short-term therapies began to replace many of the more traditional long-term methods.

In the midst of these changes, something called "systems theory" became widely accepted, especially among family therapists. There are numerous forms of systems theory and systems approaches to counseling, but some basics are widely accepted. Each family (like each church, company, academic institution, or other organization) is assumed to be a social unit, known as a system. Each system includes subsystems composed of individuals and subgroups of individuals.

All systems and subsystems are surrounded by boundaries. There are two types of these. System boundaries are like the borders between countries; subsystem boundaries are like the borders between states. In a family, for example, system boundaries would separate one family from another. Subsystem boundaries separate individual family members (or small groups within a family, such as a husband and wife or a group of the children) from each other. To function well, each of us must have good personal and family boundaries. People in the system must respect the boundaries of others, but we also must have flexibility and permeability of boundaries. Rigid boundaries distance people from one another. Fuzzy boundaries can create confusion, instability, misunderstanding, and inappropriate behavior.

In traditional forms of counseling, most therapists try to understand and help the individual who has the problem. Systems theory assumes, however, that problems go beyond the individual. One person may come for counseling, but he or she is a part of several systems and subsystems that may have created or be contributing to the counselee's difficulties. We do not assume that the counselee is a helpless victim of someone else's folly, that he or she did nothing to bring on the problem and has no responsibility to make changes. But systems therapists do agree that counseling must consider the individual's social systems as well as the individual's own thinking, behavior, and feelings.

How does all of this relate to baby boomers and to their problems? Let us consider a fictional family in which Jack and Jill are a college-educated baby boomer couple in their late thirties. Both have been involved in building careers, but they are tired of the corporate lifestyle and are interested in downshifting. Their two children, John and Jane, are in junior high school, apparently picking up values that concern their parents. Jane has not been doing well in school, and John, who has had one minor brush with the police, is disruptive in class. Jack's parents are reaching retirement age and looking to their baby boom children for guidance in planning for the later years. Jeff, John's younger brother, is a baby buster who still lives at home and cannot seem to settle on a career or a direction in life. He likes the security of living with his parents, but he does not want to be treated like a child. That would cross his boundaries and invade his personal space.

In our example, the family is a system that consists of seven people: two baby boomers, two baby boomer children, two parents of baby boomers and one baby buster. Each is an individual with boundaries that separate family members from each other. Each has unique problems, challenges, goals, and perceptions. They all live in the same community, but each is also part of a subculture consisting of their friends, work associates, and daily environments. Each person also influences and is influenced by the family of which they are all members.

Suppose that Jack and Jill come for career counseling, marriage guidance, or help in raising their children. Counseling can influence the couple, but it will also have an impact on the other family members, some of whom might react negatively to the changes in Jack and Jill. As you counsel, you might discover that the behavior of the children is contributing to the parental stresses and that the parents are thinking of changing their lifestyles, in part, because they are hoping that this will reduce some of the pressures on their family.

The school may send Jane for counseling about her poor grades, or you may see John because of his disruptive behavior, but you know that the children's problems may stem, in part, from the struggles of their parents. And if either of the children changes, the rest of the family will be affected.

We could reach similar conclusions about the older parents and about the baby buster brother. Each person's behavior influences and in turn is influenced by the others.

All of this suggests that those who counsel, work with, or minister to baby boomers must also be aware of the needs and influences of those who are both older and younger than the baby boom generation. In part 1 of this book, we sought to paint a verbal portrait of baby boomers and of the baby busters who follow. In part 2, we dealt with the most significant therapeutic issues that counselors must face in their work with baby boomers. In this part of the book, we will discuss ways of helping and working with the children of baby boomers, with baby busters, and with the parents of baby boomers, many of whom are now approaching or entering the retirement years.

BABY BOOMER CHILDREN

Counselors sometimes regard the obligation to see children as "an unfortunate occupational hazard that can distract us from the real work" of helping adults deal with their personal and family problems.[1] Few counselors are trained to work with children or adolescents. Many of us do not really understand or know how to communicate with them, especially since they rarely respond well to our adult-oriented counseling methods. But we cannot hope to work effectively with baby boomers if we ignore their children.

In one study of highly educated baby boomers (who, of course, would not represent the entire baby boom generation) nearly one half of the respondents agreed that parents should not sacrifice in order to give their children the best. Among this group . . .

> parenthood had been devalued. America was no longer a society dominated by children or even by families. As families continued to break down, more and more children were caught up in divorce and grew up with a different idea—if any idea at all—of how the traditional family operated. Many of these children are emotionally and psychologically wounded. A decade earlier, the psychiatric field of childhood depression did not exist. Now it is a growth industry. Children as young as six and seven are trying to kill themselves in numbers previously unthinkable. Yet these are the same people who will carry us through the twenty-first century.[2]

Space permits only brief discussion of the problems faced by baby boomer children and of the ways by which counselors might intervene.[3] In working with these young people, however, you might discover that many are very insightful, not only about their own problems, but also about the struggles that are faced by their baby boomer parents.

DIVORCE

Before 1960 about one child in nine saw his or her parents get a divorce. Twenty years later the number had jumped to one child in three.[4] And how do these children respond when their baby boomer parents divorce?

Psychologist Judith S. Wallerstein jolted a lot of readers when she published a book documenting the pain that many of these children experience.[5] "The children are enormously angry at being lost in the shuffle. They feel they are paying for their parents' mistakes." Many of these young people suffer anxiety, discouragement, insecurity, and guilt that may last for years after their parents separate. According to another researcher, "divorce-related issues were never far from their minds, and a substantial number of them were experiencing problems in their development that children whose parents had never divorced did not have to face."[6]

Living in a one-parent family, for example, can lead to great childhood insecurity, even when the parent is deeply devoted to his or her children. Frequently, single parents work long hours to care for family needs, money is in short supply, and overburdened parents often lack the time or the energy to spend in quality interactions with their children. As a result there can be loneliness, isolation, or depression in the children, and all of these can be worse if there are persisting tensions between the divorced or divorcing parents.

The child's ability to cope largely depends on his or her personality and level of psychological development. A parental divorce is always stressful for children, even for grown children whose older parents separate, but counseling could be easier when a child is old enough to understand the causes of divorce and the effects this is likely to have in the future. Effective counselors, like good parents, must try to be aware of each child's personality makeup, ways of communicating, and ability to think and understand.

Children are not simply pawns in the marital embroilments of their parents. The same children who are affected by parental divorce also have great ability to influence, change, and often complicate the environments in which they live.[7] They are important parts of the system, and they must be taken seriously.

PARENTAL INEPTITUDE

Even when they stay together, baby boomer parents can influence their children adversely by making excessive demands, by being too busy to parent, by their ambivalent attitudes toward the parenting role, or by lacking good parenting skills.

Parental Demands. Several years ago a group of baby boom parents were asked to list the qualities they most wanted in their children. *Intelligence* topped the list, followed by *personality, creativity,* and *imagination.* Values such as honesty, trust, or love did not make the list, but there was concern about giving children stimulation, enrichment, and a head start.[8]

In making demands on their children, parents tend to err in one of two major directions. Some push their children too hard, pressuring them to perform in school or athletics and not giving them much opportunity to relax and enjoy the pleasures of childhood. In contrast, other parents do not push their kids enough but allow them to do what they like with little accountability and few expectations. The first error can lead to feelings of inadequacy, failure, discouragement, and thoughts of rebellion. The second leaves children feeling confused, wondering if their parents do not really care, and sometimes testing the parents in an unconscious push for structure and limits.

Parental Busyness. Old Testament parents were instructed to love and to obey God, to talk at home about his commandments, and to impress these on their children and grandchildren (Deuteronomy 6:4–7,12). New Testament parents were told to train and instruct their children without exasperating them (Ephesians 6:4). Throughout history, fathers and mothers—whatever their religion—have nurtured and guided their children to adulthood.

Could it be true, however, that "baby boomers have become the first generation of parents to be widely unavailable to their children"?[9] Nobody can say with certainty if we are the busiest generation in history, but millions of us appear to be running all the time, on a treadmill that sometimes seems to be going nowhere fast.[10] Our widespread hyperactivity leaves many parents with no time for their children. Busy with their careers or with the need to work long hours in order to provide basic family necessities, many parents do not have time for long conversations and leisurely activities with their kids. As a result, many baby boomer children feel isolated from their parents, largely alone in a rapidly changing world, without good role models, and raised by day-care workers, by older siblings, or often by the images on a television screen. According to one recent report, the television baby sitter "is overwhelmingly our children's primary source of information, culture, and morality." [11]

One teenager recently described her generation as the children of "in-between parents," who squeeze time with their children in between all the other things they have to do. Many have accepted the myth that quality of time is more important than quantity. But quality time does not come unless parents are available and willing to work at building relationships with their kids. "You can't suddenly buzz in with your twelve-year-old and turn on quality time in the few minutes you have before dinner, or after dinner before you have to go out for a meeting," writes one observer. [12] Parents have to work at building quality relationships, and that kind of work takes time.

Some baby boomer parents have recognized the dangers of their busy and hyperactive lifestyles. This has led to the downshifting and slower pace of life that we discussed in earlier chapters. But many parents do not have the luxury of cutting back from their work in order to spend more time with their kids. While the children suffer because their mothers and fathers are kept so busy, the baby boomer parents feel guilty and helpless to change.

Parental Ambivalence.   In past generations, child rearing was an important part of family life. Contraception often was ineffective and abortion was not common, so children came with greater frequency than they do today. Despite the challenges and disappointments of parenthood, raising children was considered important and worth the sacrifices involved.

Much of this has changed in the baby boomer era. When Ann Landers asked her readers if they would choose again to be parents, 70 percent of the fifty thousand who replied said that they would not have children if they could be given the opportunity to live their lives over. Baby boomers are the first generation with the ability to regulate their fertility effectively, so we have a greater proportion of "wanted" children. But the child-oriented society that existed throughout much of our history has given way to "an era of public attitudes toward children that vary between benign neglect and outward hostility."[13]

A comic strip titled "The Buckets" appears in newspapers throughout the country. Undoubtedly the intent is to be humorous, but the cartoonist constantly puts down children and conveys a repeated caustic message that kids are messy, noisy, out of control, and annoying. Elsewhere in the media and in the psychological literature, we read about the trauma and stress in children, get the message that parents do not know how to raise their children without messing them up, and are led to believe that the schools are even more incompetent.

Of course there are problems with our children, serious problems,[14] and baby boomer parents often are overwhelmed by their child-rearing responsibilities. Many respond with ambivalence and go on with their lives, largely oblivious to the needs and pressures in their kids. Other parents are overwhelmed and largely immobilized in their parenting roles. Still others, perhaps the majority, want to be good parents, but they are not sure how to do so.

Parental Skills. How does one raise children in this age of rapid change, media influence, and shifting values? How does a parent relate to the needs and demands of adolescents, many of whom show a lack of respect, stability, purpose, and self-esteem?

Baby boomer parents have recently been presented with a plethora of books, articles, seminars, and radio programs, all seeking to give help with child rearing. No longer do we have one advice-giving leader like the controversial Dr. Spock, but sometimes it seems that we have too many advice givers, and this results in confusion.

DEPRESSION

There was a time, not many years ago, when parents assumed that children rarely got depressed, hardly ever contemplated suicide, and usually grew out of problems when they did appear. No longer are we that naive. Depression in children and adolescents has become a major problem,[15] suicide thoughts and attempts are high, especially in late adolescence,[16] and there is evidence that depression accompanies a number of youthful problems including high anxiety, substance abuse, eating disorders, learning difficulties, aggressive behavior, and other conduct disorders.[17] Some therapists, especially those who recognize the importance of family systems, suggest that childhood and adolescent depression often appear as a result of tension and dysfunction within the family.[18] It is not surprising that disrupted and unstable baby boomer families often produce disturbed and depressed baby boomer kids.

Treating these kids and their families sometimes takes the fine touch of a specialist, especially if the problems are long standing, mixed with other types of disorders, physiologically based, or an indication of marital and other stresses in the home.

One approach that often brings permanent change is the use of *reframing* in which the young person is encouraged to explore new ways of thinking, feeling, viewing the situation, and acting. Because of their limited maturity and inexperience, depressed children and adolescents sometimes see their problems and family situations as being far worse than they really are. By learning to see issues in a different light, the young person is given more hope and the depression, anxieties, or other disorders become less intense and sometimes disappear.

COUNSELING AND OTHER INTERVENTIONS

Do early traumatic and other painful experiences damage a young person for life? The answer, it appears, is "sometimes yes but often no."

Since the time of Plato, continuing through Freud, and into the present, many have accepted the idea that the personality is formed within the first few years and that early experiences have an indelible impact on later development and adjustment. Widely accepted by parents, pastors, therapists, and writers of books on dysfunctional families, this view is not supported by scientific studies, according to one recent report.[19] Early emotional deprivation and trauma can and often do have a significant impact on adult personality and stability. That has been demonstrated. But research does not support the idea that our personalities, abilities to handle stress, or journeys through life are inflexibly determined by what we have experienced during some critical period in childhood. One's current experiences can count for much more. Stated in a more practical way: most people can change, even if they have grown up in the midst of difficult circumstances. This is cause for hope among baby boomers and their children.

How does all of this relate to helping baby boomer children?

Christian counselors should remember that children are a gift from God (Psalm 127:3–4). Jesus overruled the disciples when they tried to keep the children away. "Do not hinder them," he stated as he reached out and took them in his arms (Mark 10:13–16). Young people should be treated with respect, as Jesus treated them with kindness and affirmation (Luke 17:2), but we need not handle them like fine china that will shatter into serious or irreparable psychological damage if they are disciplined by loving parents (Ephesians 6:4).

There are numerous ways by which counselors and other helpers can be of assistance to baby boomer children.

CREATE A STABLE ENVIRONMENT

In an era marked by the rapid change that we have mentioned so often in these pages, many young people have come to accept the reality of impermanence—in their values, their families, their careers, their friendships, and even in their relationships with God. Some live constantly with instability, pressures, and danger. They need to retreat, periodically, to find acceptance, stability, and opportunity to relax in the confines of a safe and nondisruptive environment.

Al grew up in a home where his baby boomer parents had emphasized Christian values, attended church regularly, and never withheld the love and attention that their children needed. When Al reached puberty, however, his parents met some neighbors whose values were very different. Soon the parents stopped attending church, began drinking with their new friends, spent increasing time away from home, and left Al and his sister feeling very insecure, confused, and alone. In a family that had never talked much about feelings, Al kept his anger and hurt inside, but there was one place where he felt secure—in the church youth group. There he found friendship, acceptance, and adults who may not have known about his struggles, but who espoused the values that had come first from his parents and long had given him security.

Some churches are not like the congregation that helped Al through his difficult teen years. Their leaders create tension, make incessant demands, and perpetually instill guilt in their attendees. But when the church is a caring body of believers, it also serves as a therapeutic community that gives many baby boomer children, and their parents, a solid rock of certainty and stability in the midst of a stormy world of change.

REMEMBER THE INDIVIDUAL

Counselors who work with whole families and who emphasize systems theory sometimes lose sight of the individual family members. It is true that a child's problems often may indicate that the whole family is having difficulties, but there is increasing evidence that resolving family issues does not always clear up a child's distresses. Problems with peer pressure, impulse control, low frustration tolerance, or poor self-esteem, for example, often respond best to approaches that involve seeing children or adolescents individually.

If we are to communicate effectively with young individuals, we must try to be aware of the child's age, personality, verbal skills, and ability to understand and/or express inner feelings about problems. Small children, for example, rarely respond well to straight talk or to *Why* questions (such as "Why are you so sad?" or "Why can't you get along in school?") These children have not learned to talk about their feelings or about the turmoil inside, but they do express themselves through behavior (including misbehavior), through drawing pictures, or through games. Depending on the age, many will enjoy playing with dolls, making up stories, or expressing themselves in other ways that can be revealing. One professional uses a scribble game in which the counselor and child take turns scribbling on a page and then looking for pictures and filling in the spaces between the lines. Together they make up stories that both reveal what the child is thinking and allow the counselor to weave in some story endings that can reassure and/or teach ways to cope.

Of course with adolescents the approach is different. They appreciate the opportunity to be with an understanding adult who does not push, who is compassionate and available, who has some understanding of adolescence and of contemporary teenage pressures, who serves as a good model of adult stability, and who gives a place of safety where confidential talk is possible.

Some might argue that these are *secular* psychology methods that cannot qualify as Christian counseling. The ministry of Jesus shows, however, that he met people where they were, listened with compassion, and guided each person individually. He did not always cite Bible verses, even though he consistently lived in accordance with divine principles. With the little children, he took them in his arms and showed them love and security.

HELPING CHILDREN BY HELPING THEIR PARENTS

Sometimes parents insist that their children are deeply disturbed or in need of counseling, but it soon becomes apparent that the real problem is with the parents themselves. Their attitudes and behaviors create and maintain the problems in their children. Often these mothers and fathers need encouragement, support, information, parenting models, opportunity to discuss their frustrations, and practical help in parenting skills.

As we have noted, baby boomers like to be involved in decision making, including decisions about how they can better manage their children. Many are open to reading about parenting or to trying new child-rearing methods. Some research[20] has shown, for example, that highly controlling, rigid parents often have problems with their children who, in turn, tend to be more disobedient, aggressive, and delinquent. Other parents, no less inclined to maintain clear standards, nevertheless seek to be close to their children and to show support rather than control. These parents tend to have children who are well adjusted, more independent, less inclined to get into trouble, and in better rapport with their families. As an example of parental management training, counselors could teach baby boomer parents how to be less controlling and more supportive.

Table 9 gives a biblical model of parenting, based on God's ways of dealing with his children. This could be shared with parents and followed with discussions about how these principles could be applied to specific issues in the home.

Table 9
A Biblical View of Parenting

God shows his love in the following ways, each of which can be an example for Christian parents.

God:

cares for his children (Luke 15:11–32; I Peter 5:7).

responds to the needs of his children (John 3:16; 14:18; Philippians 4:19; Titus 3:3–7).

gives to his children, as he gave his Son (Luke 11:13; John 3:16; 1 Peter 1:3–4).

respects his children, caring for them and for his whole creation (2 Corinthians 5:17–20; Colossians 1:12;1 Peter 2:9–10).

knows his children intimately (Psalm 139; Matthew 6:25–34; John 1:14; Ephesians 1:4–5, 11–12; Philippians 2:5–8; Hebrews 2:17–18).

forgives his children (Luke 19:41–42; Ephesians 4:32; Hebrews 4:15, 8:12; 1 John 1:9).

disciplines his children as an expression of his love (Proverbs 3:11–12; John 15:2; Hebrews 12:5–8).

comforts his children (Isaiah 49:13; 2 Corinthians 1:3–5; Philippians 2:1).

listens (Exodus 2:24–25; 1 John 5:14–15).

Adapted from M. Chartier, "Parenting: A Theological Model," Journal of Psychology and Theology 6 (1978): 54–61.

Some parents, of course, have neither the time, the desire, the flexibility in their schedules, nor the personal stability to learn better parenting skills. For these parents, help in solving their own problems may be the most effective way to bring greater stability in their children.

EMPOWERMENT

Counseling often is viewed as a therapeutic process, designed to bring healing, guidance, support, restoration, and direction to people who are struggling with the problems of life. The term *empowerment* goes beyond problem solving and focuses, in addition, on the process of instilling confidence and giving people the skills and self-assurance that enable them to become more competent and capable individuals.

In an insightful discussion of empowerment and Christian parenting, Jack and Judith Balswick note that empowerment is not designed to give anyone the power to dominate others. "Jesus rejected the use of power to control others, and affirmed instead the use of power to serve others, to lift up the fallen, to forgive the guilty, to encourage responsibility and maturity in the weak, and to empower the powerless." Jesus' relationship with the disciples is an example of empowering men to serve and to grow after he was gone. "Parents who are empowerers will help their children become competent and capable persons who will, in turn, empower others."[21]

When their children are small, parents tell each child what to do. Later parents teach, then they participate with the child in making decisions, and eventually they allow and encourage their maturing children to take responsibility for their own actions.

How do baby boomer parents get their children to this stage of maturity? The Minneapolis-based Search Institute recently gave a partial answer based on a survey of forty-six thousand public school students in grades six through twelve. Almost all of these were children of baby boomers.

According to the research findings, children are most likely to grow into healthy maturity when they have positive guidance from both their families and their communities. The best families provide rules, discipline, encouragement, and caring. Effective parents are interested in their children's education, encourage them to take schoolwork seriously, teach the importance of sexual restraint, and model the importance of helping others. The community supplements this by providing educational experiences, community rules, friends, recreational opportunities, and spiritual nurture that comes from churches. In their homes and communities, maturing students learn to be concerned about world hunger and poverty, develop positive expectations for the future, and develop assertive, decision-making, friend-making, and planning skills. All of this sounds ideal, but the closer baby boomers and their children can come to reaching these goals, the more likely they are to move safely into mature adulthood.[22]

HELPING BABY BUSTERS

The authors of this book are biased in favor of baby busters. As mentioned earlier, we work with them often and consistently find them to be challenging and willing to learn. They do not always come for counseling, and many of them never appear in church, but there are ways by which they can be helped.

1. *Listen in an effort to understand.*   Every counselor knows that we do not communicate if we do not first seek to understand. Reading books like this can help, but the best way to know what baby busters are thinking is to talk with them, to listen, to watch their lifestyles. They are willing to share, especially with older people who are willing to hear without condemning.

2. *Be a model.*   This has to be spontaneous. We do not turn on some kind of modeling role for younger people to observe when we know they are watching. They are adept at spotting phonies, but they are genuinely moved when they see authentic Christianity, good marital communication, balanced lifestyles, or examples of older people who handle crises with dignity, especially when they are not aware of being watched.

Many baby busters are looking for examples of stability—individuals, churches, organizations, and teachers who can provide consistency in an age of turmoil. In their search for values, young adults can be greatly affected by the examples they see in older adults who live successfully and with clear standards in the midst of constant change. It is sad that a generation that has few heroes also has difficulty finding models that they can admire and emulate.

3. *Help them to deal with their anxieties and to make decisions.* As we noted in chapter 6, many of these young people have reasons to be insecure about the future. Raised in a world where almost everything seems to be in flux, many do feel overwhelmed by the need to make career choices, to build intimate relationships, to commit to marriage, to make long-term decisions about the future. As they get older, most realize that they cannot keep all of their options open forever, but in times of personal transitions and cultural transformations, many young adults feel overwhelmed and uncertain how to act.

Reassurance can help, and people struggling with a decision often find value in exploring their options with a knowledgeable and more experienced listener-encourager. Baby busters need to see that while some decisions will be life changing, others can allow us to make life course adjustments later. In baby boomer countries, many people (especially those who are better educated) change careers several times throughout life, so making an early choice does not necessarily doom one to being stuck for life in the wrong vocation. Baby busters need to know this, but so do their parents who sometimes keep pushing their grown children to make decisions. When this happens, there often is additional stress on the young adults in their families.

Many baby busters have grown up without basic living skills, such as how to relate to others, how to deal with stress, how to manage time, how to handle finances, how to cope with discouragement, how to find one's spiritual gifts, or how to find a career. Most are willing to learn how to improve their skills in these and related areas of life—especially if the learning can be practical, not time-consuming, and relevant to young adults.

4. *Challenge them to make a difference.* "Some Americans are more indifferent than others, and the most indifferent are those

in the baby bust generation." This was the conclusion of a recent research study which found that young Americans "know less and care less about the news than any generation of Americans in the past fifty years. . . . They don't follow the news, even on TV."[23] As a result, some have been calling baby busters "The Age of Indifference."

Probably it is true that many in this generation are lethargic, but they also are willing to be prodded into action, especially if they are urged to get involved in short-term, results-oriented projects that they can help to plan and evaluate. One survey found, for example, that 43 percent of baby busters were environmentally conscious and willing to be involved with projects to save the planet.[24] These young people respond well to summer mission trips, week-long construction projects overseas, food distribution in the inner city, and similar action-oriented projects.

Baby boomers have often been called the Me Generation, and some of that attitude has filtered down to baby busters. But like many of their older brothers and sisters, baby busters are showing increasing signs of being a We Generation that is genuinely concerned about social needs and reaching out to others. These can be sensitive, caring people who frequently are turned on by opportunities to do something that can genuinely benefit society. But like all who are in or following the baby boom generation, these young adults want to be involved in their own projects; they resist the imposition of somebody else's agenda, even if the cause is worthy.

5. *Continually evaluate educational, counseling, and church-related approaches to baby busters.* This generation is accustomed to good visual aids, contemporary music, and teaching that is relevant, practical, and meaningful. Leith Anderson notes that this is a Disneyland generation, attracted to a theme park that is stable, strong, of the highest quality, consistent, exciting, and interesting.

Counselors and churches are not in the business of competing with Donald Duck or Big Bird. Christians must hold firmly to age-old and time-tested biblical values, but we also must seek methods that are flexible, creative, challenging, highly relevant, and alert to the needs of baby busters, baby boomers, and baby boomer children.

Few challenges are more stimulating and more rewarding.

NOTES

1. Ron Taffel, "How to Talk with Kids," *Family Therapy Networker* (July/August 1991), 38–45, 68–70.

2. Landon Y. Jones, *Great Expectations: America and the Baby Boom Generation* (New York: Coward, McCann and Geoghegan, 1980), 216–7.

3. For a more complete discussion of counseling young people, refer to the book by Dr. Grant Martin that appears later in the Contemporary Christian Counseling series.

4. Neil Kalter, *Growing Up With Divorce: Helping Your Child Avoid Immediate and Later Emotional Problems* (New York: The Free Press, 1990), 1.

5. Judith S. Wallerstein and Sandra Blakeslee, *Second Chances: Men, Women and Children a Decade After Divorce* (New York: Ticknor and Fields, 1989).

6. Kalter, *Growing Up With Divorce*, viii.

7. For further discussion of these issues see Lawrence Diller, "Not Seen and Not Heard: Family Therapists Often Neglect Their Youngest Clients," *The Family Therapy Networker* 15 (July/August 1991): 18–27, 66.

8. Rona Maynard, "Are Baby Boom Mothers Pushing Their Kids Too Hard?" *Chatelaine* (March 1984).

9. Jones, *Great Expectations*, 206.

10. This is the theme of an insightful book by Melvyn Kinder, *Going Nowhere Fast: Step Off Life's Treadmills and Find Peace of Mind* (New York: Prentice Hall, 1990).

11. James Patterson and Peter Kim, *The Day America Told the Truth* (New York: Prentice Hall, 1991), 219.

12. Patricia Hersch, "The Resounding Silence," *The Family Therapy Networker* 14 (July/August 1990): 19–29.

13. Jones, *Great Expectations*, 213.

14. See, for example, James Dobson and Gary L. Bauer, *Children at Risk: The Battle for the Hearts and Minds of Our Kids* (Dallas: Word, 1990).

15. M. M. Lefkowitz and E. P. Tesiny, "Depression in Children: Parent, Teacher, and Child Perspectives," *Journal of Abnormal Child Psychology* 8 (1985): 221–35, and John F. Van Wicklin, "Adolescent Depression: A Systematic Overview," *Journal of Psychology and Christianity* 9 (1990): 5–14.

16. Robert A. King, "Child and Adolescent Suicide," *Psychiatry* 2 (Philadelphia: Lippincott, 1990): chap. 44.

17. David A. Cole and Sarah Carpentieri, "Social Status and the Comorbidity of Child Depression and Conduct Disorder," *Journal of Consulting and Clinical Psychology* 58 (1990): 748–57. See Kathleen McCoy, *Coping with Teenage Depression: A Parent's Guide* (New York: New American Library,

1982) and several articles in the special issue on "Adolescent Depression," *Journal of Psychology and Christianity* 9 (1990).

18. Michael D. Lastoria, "A Family Systems Approach to Adolescent Depression," *Journal of Psychology and Christianity* 9 (1990): 44–54.

19. Warner Bridger, "Early Childhood and Its Effects," *The Harvard Mental Health Letter* 8 (August 1991): 4–6.

20. See, for example, Denise B. Kandel, "Parenting Styles, Drug Use, and Children's Adjustment in Families of Young Adults," *Journal of Marriage and Family* 52 (February 1990): 183–96, and Paul R. Amato, "Dimensions of the Family Environment as Perceived by Children: A Multidimensional Scaling Analysis," *Journal of Marriage and Family Therapy* 22 (August 1990): 613–20.

21. Jack Balswick and Judith Balswick, "A Maturity-Empowering Model of Christian Parenting," *Journal of Psychology and Theology* 17 (1989): 36–43.

22. "Backbone: Essential for Survival on the Troubled Journey," *Search Institute Source* 7 (April 1991). For more information write Search Institute, 122 West Franklin, Suite 525, Minneapolis, MN 55404.

23. Cited by Paterson and Kim, *The Day America*, 218.

24. From a Time/CNN poll reported by Gross and Scott, "Proceeding with Caution," 61.

Chapter 13

Helping the Parents of Baby Boomers

THE GRANDMOTHER HAD A DILEMMA.

After her baby boomer son divorced and remarried, he had kept in close contact with his first wife (who had custody of the children), and they worked together for the best interests of their son and daughter, ages seven and five.

Then one day, the son got a promotion that would require him to move away from the area, and shortly thereafter the grandmother learned that her grandchildren and their mother were also planning to move. The grandmother was faced with living in one part of the country, with her son living in another part, and the grandchildren in a third community—all separated by many miles. What would happen to the children whose parents were spread apart by such a great distance, the grandmother wondered. And as a long-distance grandmother, what could she do to help?

This lady is one of the "new elders" that we described in Table 1. These are the parents of baby boomers, most in their fifties and sixties, still in generally good health, alert and active. Many are more prosperous than their baby boom children, they have more discretionary income than any other age group,[1] and retirement gives them time for long awaited travel and leisure activities.

This is the generation that watched, often with shock and amazement, as their baby boomer children overflowed school classrooms in the fifties, vehemently fought the establishment in the sixties, embraced a whole new set of values in the seventies, formed the self-centered Me Generation in the eighties, and are adjusting to middle age in the nineties. Parents who were raised on traditional values still stand in amazement as they encounter explicit sex and horrifying violence on television, widespread acceptance of alternate sexual lifestyles, frequent divorce, and torn-apart families like the one that the grandmother faced.

Her counselor gave suggestions about parenting across the miles[2] and being a good grandmother to children who live far away. But the counselor noted, too, that "there are few things worse than seeing our adult children in predicaments we can't control, unless it's seeing our grandchildren" in difficult situations.[3] Individuals and families in our changing and mobile society face tough decisions that often involve and greatly affect the parents of baby boomers.

Stresses in the Parents of Baby Boomers

Many readers must have been jolted when the *Newsweek* editors published a cover showing two women, one middle aged and the other elderly, along with these arresting words: "The Average American Woman Spends 17 Years Raising Children and 18 Years Helping Aging Parents." Roughly three-fourths of those who care for the elderly are women, according to the magazine.[4] More than half of these women work outside the home, nearly 40 percent are still raising children of their own, and about one-third of the caregivers manage to care for their aging parents long distance, assessing changing needs by phone, often with assistance from neighbors. Less than 10 percent of younger caregivers have quit their jobs to give more time to caregiving obligations, but many have had to rearrange schedules, reduce hours, and take time away from work without pay so they could provide the care that is needed. A recent report found that one-third of all caregivers are over sixty-five themselves, caring for older parents or for a spouse. As the years pass that burden will shift to the baby boom generation.[5] Already, the psychological and financial costs of caregiving tend to be high and most fall (or soon will fall) squarely on baby boomers.

All four of the baby boom countries[6] tend to be *geronto-phobic* (afraid of aging) and characterized by a prejudice against the elderly, sometimes known as *ageism*. It is well known that older people often experience golden years after the mortgage is paid, the children are grown, and the pressures of regular employment are gone. Frequently, individuals over age fifty-five are free to be *opals* (older people with active lifestyles) or *rappies* (retired affluent professionals). Many have excellent health, good pensions, numerous social activities, and fulfilling lives. They visit periodically with their baby boomer children and grandchildren, but the generations pretty much go in different directions with little serious thought about the future.

This idyllic image can be shattered by two bullets of reality. First, many parents of baby boomers never experience the so-called golden years. These are people who reach their early sixties and discover that the long-anticipated dream of retirement is either a nightmare or a fading shadow of hoped-for things that will never be.

Dave, age sixty-one , took an early retirement after working all of his life in the same boring job with the same company. Lacking both education and ambition, Dave and his wife have always struggled to make ends meet, and they are learning that retirement is no different. They cannot afford to go on trips, and they would laugh at the suggestion that retired people are *opals* or *rappies*. Two of their four grown children still live at home because it is cheaper, and Dave spends his days watching television or taking naps. He has no hobbies, few friends, and little to occupy his time. For him, life is bland, and there is not much hope for the future. His baby boomer children urge him to get out and make friends, but Dave is shy, unmotivated, and not much interested in anything.

A second challenge to undermine the golden years is seen in Flora and Art. These baby boomer parents started their family shortly after Art came home from military service following the Second World War. Over forty years later, the children and grandchildren are scattered geographically, but there have been frequent family reunions, and since retirement, Art and Flora have traveled, taken several cruises, enrolled in courses at the local community college, and spent most winters in the south.

All of this came to an abrupt halt when Art had his stroke. Suddenly the parents could not retain their autonomy and mobility. Flora took on heavy responsibilities as a caregiver, and the whole family system changed. Art was no longer the strong, vivacious father and grandfather that everyone knew. He and Flora needed help with balancing their checkbook, paying their taxes, getting to and from the doctor, and taking care of household chores. The parents, who had always been independent and available to their children, suddenly became dependent and needing children whose lifestyles, careers, and parenting responsibilities were not easily adjusted—especially without warning. The readjustment was even more difficult because nobody had given much previous thought to the day when the sparkle would disappear from the *opal* parents.

Until recently, baby boomers have not had to think much about problems in the lives of their parents. But as the parents get older, both they and their baby boomer children are facing new stresses. These serve as constant reminders of what baby boomers themselves will face within only a few years.

CONTROL AND RESPONSIBILITY

Education and counseling both aim to help people take and maintain control over their daily lives. We teach young people to assume responsibility for their actions and for their finances, and we seek to guide young Christians as they discipline themselves to grow spiritually.

All of this becomes more difficult when people reach the later years. Mrs. S., for example, is in her late sixties, mentally alert, and generally in good health, except for failing eyesight that has forced her to stop driving. This was no problem when her husband was in good health, but when he got sick, the couple felt trapped in their condominium, unable to get out, and dependent on their busy adult children for rides to the grocery store or to doctor appointments.

This loss of control and independence is one of the most difficult issues that aging people face.[7] Unlike young children who grow increasingly independent, older adults often grow progressively dependent. Decision making is difficult when one needs help with housecleaning, transportation, or getting money from the bank. The older parents feel distressed about having to burden their adult children, but the baby boomers feel pressure as well. Having always viewed their parents as a source of strength and support, it is difficult to reverse roles and see parents as vulnerable, in need, potentially weak, and sometimes demanding. The most sensitive baby boomers want to help their parents maintain the best possible quality of life, but in the process they do not want to undermine the stability and quality of their own lives and family times. When misunderstandings arise there can be feelings of rejection, hurt, guilt, and anger on both sides.[8] Too often these feelings spill over and trigger the elder abuse that appears to be growing in society.

To prevent such abuse and to help baby boomers and their aging parents, counselors and other caregivers need to teach people how to maintain as much self-responsibility and self-control as possible without being insensitive to each other's changing needs. Stated in more technical terms, the parents of baby boomers and their baby boomer children, need to be empowered to cope with the changes that come with aging and to function with maximum self-confidence and mutual sensitivity.[9] At times this will involve helping families make needed but sometimes emotionally difficult life-changing decisions about issues such as housing, use of time, money management, and health care.

FORGIVENESS

As we journey through life, most of us make decisions or statements that we regret later. What we say or how we act may create deep divisions, resentments, disappointments, insecurities, and tensions that can remain hidden, sometimes festering for years. When everyone is younger, parents and children often ignore these inner sources of tension, hoping to deal with them later. As the years pass, however, family members recognize that opportunities for reconciliation are slipping away. When parents become more dependent on their grown children and family stresses increase, some of the old intergenerational conflicts, wounds, and resentments reappear.

Perhaps we all have friends like the baby boomer who recently spoke about the sudden death of his father. "I didn't expect him to die so soon," the younger man said. "There were things I wanted to say to him, things I wanted to apologize about, events from the past that I wanted to explain and to say 'I'm sorry!' But it was too late."

On the night before the funeral, the son asked to be alone for a while in the room with his father's coffin. It was there that the son made his tearful confession. He still regrets that he was too uncomfortable, maybe too proud, to make peace with his father before the older man died.

But this goes both ways. As they get older many parents also recognize the need to ask forgiveness and to work at reconciling strained or broken relationships with their children— before it is too late.

This is never easy, but its importance cannot be overemphasized. When family members hang on to their resentments and refuse to forgive, there can be no spiritual growth or emotional freedom. The resentments may be ignored or pushed from conscious awareness, but they still tend to control one's attitudes and actions, and they can undermine a person's health and sense of well being. "Very simply, to forgive your parents (or your adult children) allows you to change your relationship from one of resentment and distrust to one of love," writes Harold H. Bloomfield in his best-selling book *Making Peace With Your Parents*.[10] This means letting go of long held resentments, taking new risks, and sometimes forcing painful confrontations.[11] Each of us must forgive and let others forgive us if we are to experience true and lasting emotional freedom and peace of mind.

Counselors can often encourage this kind of forgiveness, but despite our best efforts, genuine reconciliation does not occur without the power of Christ. He who forgives freely (I John 1:9) is the only one who can give us the courage and the ability to let go of hurts or resentments, to forgive without needing to get revenge, and to begin the process of reconciliation.

ANXIETY AND LIFE PURPOSE

Several years ago, two researchers published a book describing their theory of *disengagement*. This is a view that "aging is an inevitable mutual withdrawal or disengagement, resulting in decreased interaction between the aging person and others in the social systems he [or she] belongs to. The process may be initiated by the individual or by others in the situation. The aging person may withdraw more markedly from some classes of people while remaining relatively close to others."[12] As the individual goes through the process of withdrawing from others, and society withdraws from the individual, the person begins to see himself or herself from a new perspective. Sometimes there are feelings of relief as old responsibilities and demands are let go and the individual is able to relax.

Frequently, however, something opposite occurs. The older person feels squeezed out of meaningful activity, pushed to a periphery of society, and left like a dusty antique on a back shelf of life. Insecurity, feelings of meaninglessness, and discouragement often follow, and on occasion these lead to illness and physical decline. Some people show an attachment anxiety that shows itself in clinging either to long-held relationships or to old roles and lifestyles. A few hide their anxiety by exaggerated expressions of independence, retaliation, or I-couldn't-care-less attitudes.

The most healthy older people concentrate on what Erikson called *generativity*—doing whatever is possible to pass one's observations and wisdom to the following generations. In later years this is followed by *ego integrity*—feeling a sense of fulfillment over one's life activities and accomplishments.[13] Sadly, many people are more inclined to stagnate as they approach the later years or to slide into despair. Like Dave, whom we mentioned on pages 228–229, these baby boomer parents seem to have given up on life—often to the consternation of their mates and children.

Leading the older person in a life review[14] is one effective way to help. At every age, people pause to take stock of their lives, but this has special meaning to the elderly. They like to reminisce, to talk about the past, and to reflect on what they might do in the years that are left. Sometimes the process is made more interesting if the individual is encouraged to pull out old photographs, school yearbooks, or other life memorabilia. Often, older people find it fulfilling to reflect on good memories and past accomplishments, to remember crises that were weathered, and to think about lives that have been influenced.

For many, however, life has been marked more with pain than with pleasant nostalgia. These people feel their lives have been filled with failure. Some who have spent years planning for the future now realize that their long-cherished goals will never be accomplished. Their children apparently will never become what the parents had hoped. Many feel guilt over the people they have wronged, regret over the opportunities they have missed, sadness over the relationships they have allowed to disintegrate, or discouragement over the contrast between the way things are and the way they were in the past.

How do we help such people? We can try to give comfort, encourage further expression of feelings, or move the individual's thinking to some other subject.[15] But the Christian counselor can do more. He or she remembers that with God it is never too late to find forgiveness, to start over, and to make a difference, even in the twilight of life. Some reach retirement feeling that they have failed miserably, but they go on to find meaningful ways of growing spiritually and serving God, despite declining health or reduced mobility. More than anyone else, the Christian can help baby boomer parents find new hope and a fresh perspective on life and death in the later years.

Spiritual Issues Facing Parents of Baby Boomers

When does old age begin?

Someone has suggested that old age is a combination of years plus attitude. Because of differences in perspective, some people are old at age sixty while others are ninety-five but still young in their attitudes and outlook. The parents of baby boomers are sometimes called the "young old" or even people in "late middle age," but within this group there are great differences. These depend in part on the way each person looks at life, but they also reflect variations in health, financial security, self-esteem, feelings of usefulness, and ability to maintain independence.

As they move into retirement, most people begin to think at least a little about the changes that are taking place in their lives and in their bodies. Often these changes revolve around one little word: *loss.* In growing older, people lose their youthful appearance, robust health, control of circumstances, old friendships, and opportunities to make a useful contribution to society. At first these are hardly noticed. One or two friends have heart attacks or retire early. We become aware of a loss of energy or perhaps a slip in visual acuity. A former classmate might become a widow, die, or be replaced at work by someone younger. At first these are isolated incidents, but as the years pass the losses accumulate and come in more rapid succession. And with the awareness of these losses, there may be lowered self-esteem and a heightened recognition that one's body and one's life are running down.

At present, most parents of baby boomers are in the early stages of this process, but sooner or later the majority will ponder questions of mortality and values, destiny, legacy, and sometimes ministry.

QUESTIONS OF MORALITY AND VALUES

Parents have always struggled with the contrast between their own values and the values of their children. Consider Old Testament history as an example. A succession of kings and other leaders were replaced by sons and daughters who often disagreed with the standards and beliefs of their parents. These variations often led to significant conflict.

The present-day value differences between baby boomers and their parents have been especially startling. Many of these parents watched their children accept and participate in a sexual revolution, a decline in the Protestant work ethic, the disintegration of family loyalty, and widespread disinterest in religion. Many parents still find rock music offensive, cannot understand the lack of commitment in their baby boomer children, disagree with the concepts of two-parent wage earners or day-care centers, feel uncomfortable with the casual lifestyles of young adults, and have difficulty with the baby boomer tendency to accept all people and points of view even when these are irrational or immoral—at least as perceived by the parents. In discussing consumer spending, one observer noted that baby boomer parents sometimes are surprised by the willingness of their adult children to go into debt. "Whereas their parents and grandparents were cautious and reserved about spending money, even when they had it, the boomers are exceedingly comfortable spending money, even when they *don't* have it. And it's likely that the boomers will take their spending style with them into their older years."[16] Some of these differences could create tension as the baby boomer parents become older, less able to control their checkbooks or circumstances, and more dependent on their children.

It is difficult for any of us to sacrifice our long-held values, especially as we get older. Our beliefs and values are a part of what gives us stability and makes each of us unique. As Waters and Goodman suggest, wearing someone else's values is like wearing someone else's shoes. "We can do it for a while, but we will begin to feel phony, uncomfortable with ourselves, and ultimately less worthwhile as a result."[17]

Many older people continue to wear values that their baby boomer children and grandchildren consider ill-fitting and out of style. At times, however, parents of adult children may act in ways that violate their values because such actions are seen as ways of preventing tension in the family. An older adult who values service to others, for example, may stop helping because his children think the neighbors are taking advantage of this generosity. Later, whenever he sees a neighbor, the man feels ashamed and less worthwhile because he has violated his standards by not giving help. The woman who values commitment to marriage may have great difficulty visiting in the home of her daughter who has just remarried following her second divorce. Parents who have

long valued hard work, independence, and promptness, may
struggle with the need to be dependent, sometimes on children who are less inclined to work hard and who do not
worry much about being on time.

Counselors and other church leaders can help baby boomer
family members assess their values and value differences,
evaluate their attitudes, resolve intergenerational value conflicts, and make choices about their behavior as it relates to
values.

QUESTIONS OF LEGACY

"Will those who come behind us find us faithful?" Christian musician Steve Green posed this sobering question in the
lyrics of a song that indirectly raises questions about the legacy
that each of us will leave after we are gone. When we are
young, few of us give any thought to issues such as these, but
older people are more inclined to ponder what they will leave
behind. Will they have left a better world than they inherited?
Will God ever say "Well done, good and faithful servant?" Will
they be admired when they die, or are they more likely to be
criticized and soon forgotten by their children and subsequent
generations?

In one hundred years, if the earth is still spinning and Christ
has not returned, most of us will be long forgotten in this
world, and with few exceptions, each person's life work will
be remembered only by God. For the Christian, however,
God's evaluation is the only one that really matters. This can
leave many of us feeling discouraged, thinking that we have
not been very faithful or productive.

Perhaps nobody has had the opportunities and gifts that
were given to King Solomon. He had received much and had
shared some of his God-given wisdom, especially in the book
of Proverbs. But as he grew older and became progressively
unfaithful to God, Solomon reached the conclusion that everything in life is meaningless (Ecclesiastes 1:2).[18] By the time of
his death, the wise old king did not have much of a legacy to
leave behind.

Many today are like him—people who realize that they have
never utilized their God-given gifts and instead have wasted

much of their lives. Often this leads to depression in the later years; despair over the seeming futility and failures of life. In extreme cases it can lead to the high rates of suicide that characterize the elderly.[19]

But to quote a cliché used by some baby boomers, "It isn't over 'til it's over." Feelings of frustration about failures and missed opportunities in the past can trigger increased activity in some people—last-ditch attempts to establish one's place in history, at least in family history. As long as we have life and breath, there still is time for any of us to make at least some difference.[20]

QUESTIONS OF DESTINY

For many older people, a major question at the end of life is not "What will I leave behind?" but "What will happen to me when I die?"

It would be incorrect to conclude that older people sit in their rocking chairs worrying all day about death. Even the oldest among the elderly, people who at present are grandparents of baby boomers, often give little thought to their own deaths. The parents of baby boomers are even more able to ignore death and dying issues because most of their contemporaries are still alive and relatively healthy.

As the years pass and there are more and more deaths among friends and family members, denial is more difficult, and frequent reminders of death can contribute to depression in the elderly.[21] With or without this depression, talk about death is more open as people get older. Many are less concerned about their own demise than about how they will die—whether the end will be painful, lonely, confused, part of a long illness, or sudden and unexpected.

Some research suggests that the fear of death is lower both among people who have strong religious beliefs and among those who reject such beliefs. Fear is higher among people who are undecided.[22] Christians realize, however, that belief in Christ and knowledge of the Scriptures can bring great comfort in the face of death, especially for those who are older and "ready to go," knowing that to be absent from the body is to be present with the Lord. No believer has to worry about some great unknown abyss when we have the promise that Jesus has gone on ahead to prepare a place for us (John 14:1–3). Heaven does not have a very positive image among some earth dwellers, but Christians can be confident that it will be a good place. The God who loved us enough to redeem us is unlikely to create a heaven that will be eternally boring, consisting of nothing more than endless days of sitting on clouds, strumming old-fashioned music on harps.[23]

QUESTIONS OF MINISTRY

What do the parents of baby boomers do after they retire, when they have taken their long awaited dream trips, and when all of the projects around the house have been completed? In our society, a person's self-esteem, feelings of usefulness, friendships, and status are often related to one's work. Even when a successful career ends with retirement accompanied with accolades for a job well done, many people sense a tremendous loss. In a society that expects people to be useful, the retired person often feels no longer needed. In a generation that values hard work, the parents of baby boomers sometimes feel guilt and sadness about leaving their places of employment at a time when they are physically and mentally capable of continuing. If the work stoppage comes because of a layoff or some other interruption, the sense of loss is even greater. After an initial period of adjustment, boredom often sets in, sometimes accompanied by anxiety, discouragement, problems with lowered self-esteem, and increased conflict with one's spouse or children.

The parents of baby boomers, especially those who are young retirees, want to be involved in useful activities. Many are still physically vigorous, intellectually alert, interested in adventure, and willing to enroll in continuing education courses. Christians often desire increased involvement in the church.

Some parts of the culture, including some churches, are not open to the involvement of seniors. But churches "that treat older Americans as people who are simply winding down after an exhausting life, waiting to experience heaven, will find that their population of seniors will diminish steadily."[24] When he first got involved in a ministry with older people, one church leader found that everybody was talking about ministry *to* the aging. Later it shifted to ministry *with* the aging, but the most recent talk concerns ministry *from* the aging. "They probably can teach us more about our faith than anybody. Who else has been in relationship with God longer?"[25]

Baby boomers and their parents need to understand the need for ministry and service to others. And this needs to be encouraged, especially in the later years when opportunities for gainful employment are fewer but the desire and time for volunteer activities are greater.

GIVING HELP TO PARENTS OF BABY BOOMERS

As we seek to help the parents of baby boomers, churches and Christian counselors have two challenges. We must help the baby boomers to care for their parents, and we must assist the parents as they care for themselves.

Several years ago, an official of the American Association of Retired Persons first used the phrase *sandwich generation* to describe adults who are caught between two or more generations and carrying some responsibility for both. These are people, like many baby boomers, who care about their older and younger relatives and who do not want to ignore or hurt either. For some families this is not a problem. As we have seen, they are able to honor and meet the needs of their parents without exasperating their children.

There are times, however, when busy baby boomers find themselves pulled by the conflicting needs and opinions of the older and younger generations. This tug-of-war tends to increase in the lives of baby boomers as their parents get older and their children move through the difficult teenage years. "It's okay if you want me to spend Easter alone," a widowed mother told her baby boomer son who was planning a trip to Disney World with his children. Her guilt-inducing comment put a damper on his whole trip and led to feelings of anger and resentment throughout the family. Mix this with confusion about ways to handle conflicting demands from both sides, and we see a picture of turmoil that can churn within many middle-age adults—especially when both sides have legitimate needs and the baby boomer is at a time in life when work pressure and career opportunities are greatest.

Books and articles can often assist baby boomers as they care for their older parents.[26] Some of these resources give practical information and helpful guidelines to assist people in the sandwich generation who want to make wise decisions. Among the suggestions for baby boomer adults:

- try to stimulate understanding and cooperation between the older and younger generations;
- whenever possible, do not make decisions without consulting the people involved;
- do not take over responsibilities that parents can handle for themselves;
- determine at times to say nothing and at times to stand firm;
- try to see situations from the perspectives of others; and
- make prayer a high priority.[27]

In addition to receiving help from their children, the parents of baby boomers can be assisted through their communities, their churches, their support groups, and their counselors.

HELP IN THE COMMUNITY

At the ripe old age of fifty, Americans are eligible to join the largest nonreligious organization in the United States: the American Association of Retired Persons. At age fifty-five some restaurants give senior citizen discounts and banks give their customers special "silver memberships." When they reach the early sixties, almost everyone is eligible for the senior citizen benefits that merchants and governments make available for older people—many of whom are far from old when they reach the age to receive these community perks.

If we are younger or our parents are in good health, most of us do not think much about community assistance programs for older adults. But when an individual or one's spouse has need of community help or financial benefits, programs that we rarely considered before—such as Medicaid, Medicare, social security payments, meals on wheels, tax benefits for seniors, adult day-care centers—all become of new relevance and importance. Some of these programs are underfunded and in danger of not meeting the needs for which they were intended. But there is one reason to expect that programs for the aging, especially government programs, will continue: older people are the largest voting block among the electorate, and when compared with every generation that follows, the elderly are most inclined to get out to vote on election day. These voters will not tolerate politicians who ignore the needs and wishes of their elderly constituents. As citizens, the rest of us can participate in the governmental process and can seek to understand what community resources are available to assist older people.

HELPING AND THE CHURCH

A denomination president recently described his visit to a church in the southwest. Most people in the community were retired, and the church had a congregation where the average age was well over sixty. The parishioners were retired from their vocations, the visitor noted, but "they were not retired from vital Christianity. This was not a group of 'doormat' Christians who had shifted into 'spiritual neutral' during their golden years. Quite to the contrary. These older Christians are spiritually alive and vital. And they are people of vision. They are planning strategy to actively reach their community with the love of Jesus Christ." [28]

Clearly this is an unusual church, probably filled with unusual people. Their congregation has no young baby boomers to give leadership to church activities, but the members undoubtedly are quite happy to plan their own programs, to serve, to reach their community, and to minister to one another as they grow spiritually. In congregations with large numbers of less enthusiastic older people, the churches often are dead. And when churches are filled with large numbers of younger people, the elderly often are shunted aside, even though they have great potential and availability for service and often have a sincere desire to grow and develop spiritually.

No church would develop a youth program that treats five-, fifteen-, and twenty-five year-olds in the same way, but sometimes we assume that people who are sixty-five are no different than those who are twenty-five years older. The parents of baby boomers surely have needs that are different from the baby boomer grandparents. To help these older adults, we can learn from successful programs that have been developed elsewhere,[29] but it also is important to talk with the baby boomer parents themselves. Like their baby boomer children, these older adults are likely to be more involved when they can take an active role in planning and leading church programs that are designed for their own age group.

HELP FROM SOCIAL SUPPORT

Like people of almost all ages, the parents of baby boomers are most helped by each other. Among the elderly, these baby boomer parents are the youngest and the best able to give encouragement, practical assistance in times of need, opportunities for sharing, and social support. Many of these people are still alert and healthy, able to drive, relatively independent, and free to be available to one another when needs arise. Friends, neighbors, and relatives in the community can be important resources for both baby boomer parents and the baby boomers themselves who may not always know how to help their parents.

In the coming decade, the giving and receiving of support is not likely to be limited to interactions between people who know each other. Volunteerism is becoming a major trend in society, especially among the elderly. According to psychologist Ken Dychtwald, "volunteering for every manner of helping enterprise—in the community, for political and social causes, for charities—is increasingly becoming a way of life for millions of older Americans."[30] One survey found that more than 30 percent of adults over fifty-five do volunteer work. This permits volunteers to meet people, keep active, be helpful, fulfill a sense of duty, and find personal satisfaction in their activities. This is likely to continue as more baby boomer parents enter the senior citizen ranks.

HELP FROM COUNSELING

Until recently, counselors have given little attention to the special challenges of counseling older people.[31] Even today, few counselors work with this unique group, in part because older people are less inclined to go for counseling help.

But this is changing. Baby boomers do not have hangups about seeing counselors, and many of their parents have observed how counseling can be helpful. To work with this older group, a counselor should be sensitive to the unique problems of baby boomer parents, highly competent, able to focus on short-term approaches to therapy, willing to be adaptable in the use of counseling methods, and sensitive to the importance of empowering the elderly to deal with stress and to solve personal and interpersonal problems.

Be prepared to deal with some negative attitudes toward counseling and some distrust, especially if you are younger. Some of your counselees may want help in relating to their baby boomer children. If you are the same age as those children, or younger, your older counselees may wonder if you really can understand or help. Countertransference and transference issues are likely to arise at some time. It may be true that at least for the next decade or so, the best people to counsel with parents of baby boomers are counselors who have both competence and gray hair.

As baby boomers approach their fifties and sixties, there will be increasing need for specialists to counsel with older people. This could be one of the most fulfilling and potential-filled areas for Christian counseling as we move into the future.

NOTES

1. Lee Smith, "What Do We Owe to the Elderly?" *Fortune* (March 1989), 54–62.

2. Including the suggestion that she read two books: Miriam Galper Cohen, *Long-Distance Parenting* (New York: Signet, 1989), and Selma Wasserman, *The Long Distance Grandmother* (Point Roberts, Wash.: Hartley and Marks, 1988). Also relevant and written from a Christian perspective is a book by Stephen and Janet Bly, *How to Be a Good Grandparent* (Chicago: Moody, 1990).

3. Marguerite Kelly, "Bringing Up Parents: Children of Divorce Can Adjust to Parent's Move," *Chicago Tribune*, August 25, 1991.

4. Melinda Beck, "Trading Places," *Newsweek* (July 16, 1990), 48–54.

5. Paul Light, *Baby Boomers* (New York: Norton, 1988), 265.

6. As we noted earlier, the majority of baby boomers live in the United States, Canada, Australia, or New Zealand.

7. R. L. Butler and M. I. Lewis, *Aging and Mental Health*, rev. ed. (St. Louis: Mosby, 1983).

8. Jane E. Myers, "The Mid/Life Generation Gap: Adult Children With Aging Parents," *Journal of Counseling and Development* 66 (March 1988). For a more complete discussion see Jane E. Myers, *Adult Children and Aging Parents* (Alexandria, Va.: American Association for Counseling and Development, 1989).

9. This is the theme of an excellent volume by Elinor B. Waters and Jane Goodman, *Empowering Older Adults: Practical Strategies for Counselors* (San Francisco: Jossey-Bass, 1990).

10. Harold H. Bloomfield with Leonard Felder, *Making Peace With Your Parents: The Key to Enriching Your Life and All Your Relationships* (New York: Random House, 1983), 26.

11. Tanya Vonnegut Beck, "Forgiving," in Jean Norris, ed., *Daughters of the Elderly: Building Partnerships in Caregiving* (Bloomington and Indianapolis: Indiana University Press, 1988), 207–11.

12. Elaine Cumming and William E. Henry, *Growing Old: The Process of Disengagement* (New York: Basic Books, 1961). This theory stimulated a great deal of discussion and has generally been replaced by other viewpoints. For one interesting commentary see Donald G. Sukosky, "Disengagement and Life Review: The Possible Relevance of Integrating Theological Perspectives," *Journal of Religion and Aging* 5 (No.4, 1989): 1–14.

13. Erik H. Erikson, *Childhood and Society*, rev. ed. (New York: Norton, 1963). In two volumes on counseling women (to appear later as part of the Contemporary Christian Counseling series), psychologist M. Gay Hubbard notes that Erikson's conclusions are based on observations of men. From this it does not follow necessarily that women also are faced with tasks of generativity and ego integrity in the later years.

14. Robert Disch, ed., *Twenty-Five Years of the Life Review: Theoretical and Practical Considerations* (New York: Haworth, 1988). See also Barbara K. Haight, "Life Review: A Method for Pastoral Counseling, Parts I and II," *Journal of Religion and Aging* 5 (vol. 3): 17–41.

15. These are the suggestions of M. A. Edinberg, *Mental Health Practice with the Elderly* (Englewood Cliffs, N.J.: Prentice Hall, 1985) , 163 .

16. Ken Dychtwald, with Joe Flower, *Age Wave: The Challenges and Opportunities of an Aging America* (Los Angeles: Jeremy P. Tarcher, 1989), 277. A recent newspaper report citing studies of baby boomer spending patterns confirms the reluctance of baby boomers to save: Kelley Holland, "Studies Don't See Much in the Way of Baby Boomer Savings," *Chicago Tribune*, August 25, 1991.

17. Waters and Goodman, *Empowering*, 90–91.

18. This is the theme of the book of Ecclesiastes. According to a footnote in the NIV Study Bible, "The basic thrust of Ecclesiastes is that all of life is meaningless, useless, hollow, futile and vain if it is not rightly related to God. Only when based on God and his word is life worthwhile."

19. Gregory A. Hinrichsen, *Mental Health Problems and Older Adults* (Santa Barbara, Calif.: ABC-CLIO, 1990).

20. This is the theme of a book by one of the authors: Gary R. Collins, *You Can Make a Difference: 14 Principles for Influencing Lives* (Grand Rapids: Zondervan, 1992).

21. Michael J. Giewski, Norman L. Farberow, Dolores E. Gallagher, and Larry W. Thompson, "Interaction of Depression and Bereavement on Mental Health in the Elderly," *Psychology and Aging* 6 (1991): 67–75.

22. Waters and Goodman, *Empowering*, 142.

23. We are grateful to Dr. Joseph M. Stowell of Moody Bible Institute for this observation.

24. George Barna, "America 2000: Challenges for the Church," *Evangelical Beacon* 64 (February 1991): 7.

25. Tim Stafford, "The Graying of the Church," *Christianity Today* 31 (November 6, 1987): 17–22.

26. Perhaps the best is by Lissy Jarvik and Gary Small, *Parentcare: A Commonsense Guide for Adult Children* (New York: Crown, 1988). For Christian approaches see Tim Stafford, *As Our Years Increase: Loving, Caring, Preparing: A Guide* (Grand Rapids: Zondervan, 1989); John Gillies, *Caregiving: When Someone You Love Grows Old* (Wheaton, Ill.: Harold Shaw, 1988); and Patricia H. Rushford, *The Help, Hope and Cope Book for People with Aging Parents* (Old Tappan, N.J.: Revell, 1985).

27. These suggestions are adapted from Gary R. Collins, "Caught Between Parents and Children," *Christian Herald* 110 (February 1987): 51–53.

28. Paul A. Cedar, "From the President," *The Evangelical Beacon* 64 (1991): 2.

29. See, for example, Arthur H. Becker, *Ministry with Older Persons: A Guide for Clergy and Congregations* (Minneapolis: Augsburg, 1986), and Horace L. Kerr, *How to Minister to Senior Adults in Your Church* (Nashville: Broadman, 1980).

30. Dychtwald and Flower, *Age Wave*, 158.

31. Among the more helpful publications are books by Bob Knight, *Psychotherapy with Older Adults* (Beverly Hills, Calif.: Sage, 1986), Mary Ann Wolinsky, *A Heart of Wisdom: Marital Counseling with Older and Elderly Couples* (New York: Brunner/Mazel, 1990), and Edmund Sherman, *Counseling the Aging: An Integrative Approach* (New York: The Free Press, 1981). A later volume in this Contemporary Christian Counseling series will deal with Christian approaches for counseling the elderly.

Chapter 14

The Future of Baby Boomers

AGING BABY BOOMERS.

These words seem like a contradiction in terms, but they appear with increasing frequency as the oldest baby boomers approach fifty. Some are already grandparents. Few may have given much thought to retirement or to saving for the future, but as they approach old age, the baby boomers—once again—are likely to make radical changes in the societies where they live.

The baby boomers will be unlike any previous generation of elderly. They will change what has heretofore been the principle stereotype of old people—namely, that they are poor, uneducated, and unemployed. The baby boomers will challenge and strain every existing program and institution concerned with the welfare of older persons. They may well force the rethinking of one of humanity's oldest social contracts: the idea that the working generation will support the old and infirm. . . . There is no reason to think that the baby boomers will be any more docile or malleable in old age than they have been in youth and adulthood.[1]

Economists, demographers, and others who make observations about the future have given some sobering predictions about what lies ahead for baby boomers.

- When the youngest of this generation reaches retirement age, one in five Americans will be older than sixty-five, but few will have tucked away a comfortable nest egg of savings. Government funds, including Social Security, will be limited.
- To curtail medical or other expenses, people will be forced to delay retirement so that early retirement as we know it, will be a unique event; full benefits are not likely to start at sixty-five, and some present-day senior citizen programs will be long gone.[2]
- The society will witness a major attitude shift. No longer will youth be seen as the prime time of life. Baby boomers will convince themselves and the rest of us that maturity is the best period of existence, a time when people can remain active, socially committed, politically influential, productive, sexually involved, and future oriented.
- Older people will be health-conscious and committed to physical workouts. Doctors will lose much of their authority (and income), other professionals will take over many of their duties, and people will take increasing responsibility for treating themselves.[3]
- Compared to previous generations, a larger share of baby boomers will never realize their career goals.
- At present, roughly twenty-six million people are in their peak income years, aged forty-five to fifty-four. When all of the baby boomers pass their forty-fifth birthdays, in 2010, that number will increase by 47 percent to 37.7 million. Their numbers will overwhelm the corporate world with an excess of qualified applicants for top jobs.[4]
- The senior baby boomers will have a staggering influence on consumer spending. Already, the advertising and business fields are shifting their emphasis to focus on baby boom consumers.

- Graying baby boomers, who saved at a rate far lower than
  that of their parents and who had children later, will continue to face the high costs of college for their offspring,
  the need to plan for retirement, and sometimes financial
  responsibility for the health care of their aging parents.
  One Rutgers professor suggests that "the generation that
  was once associated with dropping acid in order to escape
  reality is now going to be dropping antacid in order to
  cope."[5]

Helping aging baby boomers cope is one of the challenges
that counselors and churches will continue to face. As we peer
into the future from our present-day perspectives, we must
continue to ask a basic question: With our awareness of these
emerging trends, how can we most effectively meet the needs
of the baby boom generation?

VOCATIONAL-FINANCIAL TRENDS

Baby boomers have a "sense of futurelessness," according
to social psychologist Robert Jay Lifton. Most hope that life
for themselves will be better in the future, but they do not
have many expectations for the world in which we all live.
More than half of the respondents in one recent survey expressed the belief that life in the twenty-first century will be
dirtier, harsher, harder, grimier, and gloomier than the world
of today.[6] If the future holds little hope for improvement, then
why not live for today, with a short-term perspective and a
willingness to leave money saving and hard decisions until
later?[7]

Like others in the work force, baby boomers have seen numerous changes in the workplace. Some of these
changes—like flexible hours, shorter work weeks, more opportunities for women, and the freedom to work at
home—have been welcomed. Others are harder to evaluate.
Futurists Marvin Cetron and Owen Davies suggest that for
the 1990s and beyond, we will be living in a decade of pink
slips, especially as manufacturing and middle management
jobs disappear. "Most of the new jobs that appear, not just in
the 1990s, but from now on, will fall into only two categories:

the ones you don't want and the ones you can't get—not, at least, without extensive preparation."[8] The job market will move away from manufacturing and into more service and information processing positions. Wages and job opportunities will continue to go down for unskilled and uneducated workers; the demand for specialists will continue to increase. This will make life increasingly difficult for the millions of baby boomers who are far removed from the still-popular yuppie image of their generation. Particularly disadvantaged will be the young baby boomers who face a job market overcrowded with highly competent people. The younger baby boomers may have to face the prospect of salaries that are lower, positions that are less fulfilling, and promotions that are harder to get.

Experts tend to agree that baby boomers will face financial pressures in the future. Some, especially those who are older, will inherit significant financial benefits from their families, although this boost in wealth may have to wait because older people are living much longer than they did in the past. More common among baby boomers will be families who do not inherit much of anything and who are forced to struggle with higher living costs, less than robust economic conditions, a lack of savings to fall back on, and increasing medical costs[9]—especially for older baby boomers and for those in the sandwich generation. To prepare for retirement, younger people should be saving more and consuming less, financial experts agree, but for many families saving seems almost impossible, and cutting back is difficult.[10] It is not surprising to read that "compared to parents at the same stage in life, baby boomers are in financial trouble."[11]

Counselor training in the past has focused on personal stresses, family problems, and interpersonal conflicts. These issues will persist and perhaps get worse as the baby boomers grow older, but Christian counselors and their churches will have to give additional help in the areas of financial and vocational counseling. At present there is little evidence that this important need has attracted the attention of Christian people helpers,[12] even though these stresses affect and are influenced by every other aspect of life, including personal stability and spiritual growth. Life can be miserable when expenses and debts are high and when work is meaningless, low paying, or not available.

FAMILY TRENDS

In the next century, will there be war between the generations? The idea may seem preposterous, but some futurists have predicted that generations in the future will compete vehemently with one another for limited resources and opportunities. While moderate voices speak of "intergenerational coalitions" rather than intergenerational wars, others suggest that already "a battle is brewing that threatens to divide the nation and set generation against generation for decades to come." The wars will occur, predicts aging expert Ken Dychtwald, as "the old refuse to retire and make room for the young in the workplace, as middle aged and older Americans come to dominate politics, as the young find the burden of supporting the older generation to be crushing, and as the baby boomers approach a later life in which they rightly suspect that they will have to do without the traditional benefits of pensioned retirement."[13]

Economic issues may or may not lead to war between the generations, but we can predict with certainty that economic struggles will contribute to dissension in many homes. Conflicts over money have long divided families, and there is no evidence that things will get better in the future. As we have seen, money problems could get worse, and these may be supplemented by other types of family pressures.

Consider busyness, for example. Television, relatively inexpensive air transportation, FAX machines, computer modems, and other technologies have opened our minds and our lives to a barrage of stimulating ideas, people, activities, and pressures. The family has become saturated with stresses and stimulation, according to one recent writer.[14] We have so many demands, options, values, pieces of information, and pressures that many families feel overwhelmed, fractured, and endlessly busy. Believers read in the Bible about teaching God's commandments to our children when we sit at home, walk along the road, lie down, and get up (Deuteronomy 6:7). But some of us rarely sit down together. We rush from one thing to another with scarcely any communication between family members.

As they get older, baby boomers will be faced with parents who live longer, children who stay at home longer, and their own retirements that will be delayed longer. Family members will travel more than they did in the past, the divorce rate will stay high, blended families will continue to be common, and families will probably be affected both by the continuing women's liberation movement and the new men's movement.

How will all of this relate to Christian counseling and the church? Researcher George Barna notes that there will be persisting family frustration and loneliness in the future, and he makes the startling observation that many baby boomer children are likely to find acceptance in street gangs. "For thousands of adolescents, gangs are a response to the dissolution of the traditional family. Membership in a gang provides the only place where some young people find they can get a fair hearing and response to the daily pressures, doubts and struggles they face."[15]

Instead of wringing our hands in despair, Christians must be aware of the pressures and changes that baby boomer marriages and families face; we must champion the benefits of permanent monogamy and of intense family relationships; we must acknowledge the reality of gangs and provide alternatives to help young people face the pressures of growing up in the midst of fractured and dysfunctional families. In what has been called a postmodern world, filled with postmodern families,[16] we must find innovative ways to meet family needs, even when these take us far from our counseling rooms and beyond the confines of traditional psychotherapy. The preceding chapters have attempted to show how some of these innovative approaches can be applied.

VALUE TRENDS

When future historians look over the last half of the twentieth century, they will see a host of startling events that changed the course of history and the lives of those who have lived in the baby boomer era. The tyranny and collapse of communism, the Kennedy and King assassinations, Watergate, the Vietnam and Persian Gulf wars—all are benchmark events that affected millions.

It might be harder for historians to determine what events led to the radical shifts in values that have occurred during the past several decades. Old ideas about truth, purity, commitment, honesty, faithfulness, reason, and progress have all changed and, in many minds, have become obsolete. The roots of these changes undoubtedly are complex, but one writer has suggested (can he be serious?) that the single event which most changed our values was the invention of the remote control television channel changer. In the past, television "required us to do nothing more than sit and dutifully surrender to one chunk of network programming at a time," but the channel changer altered all of that. Now, with the barest expenditure of energy, anyone can skim from channel to channel and from idea to idea.

> The sheer profusion of choice and our ability to move so easily from one to another, undercuts the authority and impact of any particular message. The speed of the channel changer technology allows us to restlessly glance over scores of realities, while making it even more difficult to believe in the special importance of any one.
>
> More and more, in this media-saturated world, we live as if we were carrying our remote control channel changers in our pockets all day, hyper-aware of all the choices available to us, not only about what to watch on TV, but what to believe in and how to lead our lives. This awareness of the multiplicity of possible realities, along with the skepticism that authority and tradition have anything to tell us about how to tune in to the events of our lives, is the hallmark of . . . uncertainty and identity search. . . .
>
> Around the globe we've all become aware of too many different possibilities—other political and economic systems, other cultures, other beliefs—to subscribe to a few hand-me-down ideologies from the past.[17]

Perhaps no previous generation has experienced an upset of traditional values to match the changes that have come during the past four decades. Baby boomers have been influenced by television, a society that increasingly advocates free choice and individual rights, a variety of entertainment possibilities that strip away reality, and academic-based movements such as cultural relativism and deconstructionism. But baby boomers have also felt the freedom to challenge long-established moral standards. They are both the recipients and the creators of an upturned mixture of morals, standards, and values possibilities.

Is it surprising that many baby boomers are confused about their values and without firm commitments to much of anything? "They learn Traditionalist values from the most powerful people in the country, Rejectionist values from their parents—and no values worth mentioning from the endless procession of packaged sports figures and rock stars that have replaced the heroes of earlier generations." Theirs is a world that tends to prefer openness in place of critical thinking, self-fulfillment instead of self-denial, alternative family lifestyles rather than traditional families, a better quality of life in place of a higher standard of living, independence and self-reliance in contrast to interdependence and mutual caregiving, and working to live instead of living to work. Somehow, from this conflicting array of ideas, they are having to synthesize a workable and coherent value system of their own.[18]

At one time counselors assumed that their work was value free and neutral in terms of moral standards, but few people believe this anymore. Research confirms that values are shared in all of counseling, and there is convincing evidence that as therapy progresses, the counselor's values often are passed on and accepted by the counselee, even when there is no conscious awareness that this is taking place.[19] When counselors have confused, ever-changing, and inconsistent values, this confusion is passed to counselees.

In an age of value shifts and uncertainty, there is a monumental need for individuals whose values are relevant to contemporary society but based firmly on the unchanging rock-solid truths of biblical revelation. Many baby boomers struggle with value-related issues, but they rarely darken the door of a church. These are people whose confusion can be lifted and whose lives can be anchored through counseling with Christian counselors who know what they believe and why, and who can reflect these values in their counseling work. The need for such Christian counselors is likely to expand as the baby boomers get older and discover that their shifting values lead to anxiety and instability.

SOCIAL-ENVIRONMENTAL TRENDS

In the 1960s, baby boomers were known for their optimism and social activism. They were intent on changing the world and convinced that they could make things better.

But something happened on the way to middle age. Some of their heroes fell (or were felled), and they learned that government, religion, big business, and the media could not be trusted. Things did not get better; they seemed to get worse. The generation that expected to have a special place in society found that opportunities were limited and their world was crowded. Instead of relieving problems, the baby boomers were causing them: increased suicide, marital unfaithfulness and divorce, venereal disease, higher housing prices, domestic violence, cut-throat competition to reach the top. "The hope of the sixties, when the generation thought that it just might change the world, turned into a generational malaise of frustration and anxiety."[20] It is not surprising that optimism gave way to pessimism and that altruism was replaced by a me-first narcissism.

This is beginning to change. We have seen this repeatedly as we have worked on this book and observed baby boomers shifting away from the social apathy of the fifties and back to greater involvement in contemporary issues. Already, observers are referring to the new We Generation that is waking up, frequently embracing more traditional values, and determining to do something about gangs, crime, the mistreatment of children, sexual abuse, homelessness, AIDS, and drug problems.

In their eye-opening study of American values, researchers James Patterson and Peter Kim painted a grim picture of what we believe and of how we live. But their book ended with an upbeat report about the number of people who are willing to get involved in causes that will make things better. As we have noted, the research was not limited to baby boomers, and we cannot be sure that people who say they are willing to volunteer actually would volunteer. Even so, 58 percent of the respondents said they would be willing to volunteer to help prevent child abuse, improve education, fight illiteracy, "do something meaningful about homelessness," or help clean up the environment. One hundred million potential volunteers are willing to get involved, the researchers concluded, but no one is leading the cause or tapping the storehouse of energies waiting to work.[21]

Two issues rise above all others in stimulating interest and involvement: education and environment. The issues may be different in other baby boomer countries, but in the United States there is widespread belief that our system of education is poor and desperately in need of improvement. Fifty percent of surveyed Americans expressed a willingness to give more time and even more tax money if this would bring genuine school improvement.

Among baby boomers and baby busters, however, there appears to be even greater concern about improving the environment. It is the one issue that attracts people of all political persuasions, that arouses the interest of both older and younger baby boomers, and that ties this generation with the baby busters who follow. Throughout the country, grassroots organizations, local activists, and national environmentalist groups are attracting record numbers who want to dispose of toxic wastes, ban chemicals that harm the ozone layer, reduce acid rain, protect the wilderness and other undeveloped areas, clean up neighborhoods, and cut down on pollution. An estimated 78 percent of us recycle cans and newspapers, 76 percent have tried to cut the household use of energy, and about half have given money to an environmental organization.[22] Now that the Cold War is over and our preoccupation with defense is subsiding, no issue attracts more interest—especially among baby boomers and baby busters—than concern about saving the environment.

When he created the human race, God gave us instructions to "fill the earth and subdue it. Rule over the fish of the sea and the birds of the air and over every living creature that

moves on the ground" (Genesis 1:28 NIV). Instead, we have pol-
luted the world, gobbled up its resources, and neglected our
God-given responsibilities to take care of his creation. Like anyone else, Christians have reason to be involved in environmental issues, but these have not been at the top of the church's
agenda, and they rarely concern counselors. Churches have
put greater priority on the Great Commission and on discipleship. Most of us would agree that this is as it should be. Counselors deal with pressing personal and interpersonal problems,
and environmental issues seem far removed from the minds
of most of our counselees.

If we are to have an impact on baby boomers, however, we
must understand and seek to address their concerns. We must
demonstrate that the Bible speaks to contemporary concerns
about education, the environment, and other emerging issues
that will increasingly concern the We Generation of baby
boomers and baby busters. For many Christians, we must start
by learning about the issues and by finding ways to harness
the new baby boomer volunteerism so this can advance the
cause of Christ and his kingdom.

SPIRITUAL AND RELIGIOUS TRENDS

Religion is making a comeback, at least among baby
boomers. The generation that watched the Jesus People appear
and largely disappear two or three decades ago is now returning to church, showing a massive new interest in spirituality,
and seeking to find God.

In their most recent *Megatrends* book, John Naisbitt and
Patricia Aburdene cite religious revival as one of the ten trends
that will be prominent as we move through the nineties.[23] Revival does not necessarily mean a return to the church,
however. Many still see the church—especially the liberal
church—as dead and irrelevant to baby boomer needs and concerns. Those baby boomers who do attend church prefer
congregations that are theologically more conservative, highly
relevant, respectful of female leadership, in tune with contemporary music, and in touch with baby boomer thinking and
terminology.

Of greater interest to many baby boomers is a spirituality that emphasizes experience, mysticism, and getting in touch with the soul. This is not a spirituality that involves repentance, forgiveness of sins, worship of the triune God, or a commitment to discipleship and evangelism. Instead, this spirituality looks to a god within, described with terms such as "the Life Force," "the Cosmic Energy," "the Creative Surge," or "the Pool of Unlimited Power."[24] It is an I-centered religion in which each person is free to find a spiritual source of strength within.

This kind of spirituality presents the church and Christian counselors with both a challenge and an opportunity. We are challenged to dispute such doctrinal error with kindness, gentleness, and firmness. That will not be easy in an age when the Bible's authority is not accepted and its teachings are widely refuted. Many baby boomers are not even interested in rational discussions or in apologetic arguments. These contemporary seekers want answers to their problems and experiences that make a difference in their lives. But Christians know that even resistant baby boomers can be moved by the power of consistent prayer and by the Word of God that is sharper and more powerful than any two-edged sword.

But if baby boomers present Christians with a spiritual challenge, they also offer an opportunity to present Jesus Christ as the only one who can fill the spiritual void within. In our churches and counseling rooms we need to present a clear biblical message that is meaningful to baby boomer minds but consistently faithful to biblical teaching. We must show how Christ can meet needs and relate to the struggling baby boomers and busters who seek our counsel.

In reaching these individuals, we may have to use contemporary marketing methods, such as advertising, respecting the privacy of newcomers even as we seek to make them feel welcome, or presenting the Gospel in a format that is attractive and interest catching. This does not mean giving a watered-down Christianity that never mentions sin or calls for commitment. Instead, we present both the costs and benefits of walking with Christ and growing in a relationship with the Savior and with other believers.

LOOKING AHEAD

As they have moved through life, baby boomers have touched and impacted almost every segment of society. Education, the media, advertising, business, medicine, the family, sexuality, women's (and men's) rights, religion, the economy, politics—all have been influenced by baby boomers, and there is no indication that this will change as the generation gets older. On the contrary, as the baby boomers move through their forties and fifties, they will be at the peak of their earning capacity and potential for making an impact. Advertisers are well aware of the need to focus their efforts on this significant consumer group. Educators recognize that more mature students are willing to fill classrooms and work on their degrees. Creative entrepreneurs are finding ways to cash in on baby boomer interests and fads. Astute politicians are well aware of baby boomer conservatism, neotraditionalism, interest in environmental issues, and distrust of politicians. And churches that are alive and growing almost always make the effort to understand and speak to baby boomer concerns.[25]

Counselors are sometimes the last to alter their methods and efforts to keep abreast of changing times. But the baby boomers who have influenced every other part of society are putting their mark on people-helping professions. This generation wants brief therapy, not the long drawn-out methods of the past. They want workable answers instead of discussions of ids, archetypes, and unconditional positive regard. "Don't get too formal with me," one baby boomer said as we were completing this chapter. "I'd rather play tennis with a counselor and talk about my problems later." Some are open to reading books, taking computer-administered psychological tests, watching video dramatizations, and discussing their most intimate problems in group settings. Now, more than ever before, we need innovative approaches to counseling if we are to reach and help baby boomers.

But Christian counselors and church leaders must be cautious lest we are so intent on meeting baby boomer needs that we are swayed away from biblical values and established doctrinal truths. The same New Age thinking that attracts baby boomers can easily slip into the church and seep out from our pulpits. The humanistic assumptions and values that pervade so much of contemporary counseling can be embraced uncritically by Christian therapists who fail to realize that their efforts may be in contrast with the core of the Gospel. In a compassionate desire to be tolerant and open to all ideas, we can tone down the reality of sin, the need for repentance, the costs of discipleship, and the Christian insistence that Jesus Christ is the only way to a true knowledge and relationship with God, despite the widespread baby boomer belief that all religions are equally valid.

Christians who work with baby boomers can have firm beliefs without being rigid and intolerant, clear values without stifling creativity and innovation, unique methods of counseling without violating biblical principles, an emphasis on experience without abandoning clear biblical thinking, and relevant, interesting worship services without draining the Christian message of its vitality and call for commitment.

Effective Christian counselors will not ignore this constantly changing population. Already they comprise a significant segment of our counseling caseloads, and our own ranks are being filled with baby boomer counselors. It is they who will take our field and mold the future of Christian counseling as it moves into the next century.

The future belongs to the baby boomers—the future of the church, the future of counseling, and the future of the society. If the past is any indication, that future will be challenging and filled with surprises. Christian counselors will have a significant role to play in working with baby boomers well into the new millennium.

NOTES

1. Landon Y. Jones, *Great Expectations: America and the Baby Boom Generation* (New York: Coward, McCann and Geoghegan, 1980), 312–14.

2. Jim Lynch, "Retirement's Golden Age May Be Over," *Chicago Tribune*, May 12, 1991.

3. Jerry Gerber, *Lifetrends: the Future of Baby Boomers and Other Aging Americans* (New York: Macmillan, 1989), 16.

4. Judith Waldrop, "The Baby Boom Turns 45," *American Demographics* (January 1991), 22–27.

5. Peter Kerr, "Retailers Play to Graying Baby Boomers' Youth Myth," *Chicago Tribune,* September 1, 1991

6. James Patterson and Peter Kim, *The Day America Told the Truth* (New York: Prentice Hall, 1991), 217.

7. It would be inaccurate and unfair to claim that all baby boomers think in this way, but evidence suggests that such thinking is common. See, for example, Paul C. Light, *Baby Boomers* (New York: Norton, 1988), 143.

8. Marvin Cetron and Owen Davies, *American Renaissance: Our Life at the Turn of the 21st Century* (New York: St. Martin's Press, 1989), 247.

9. This is true in the United States where medical costs are extremely high; it is less true in the other three baby boomer countries (Canada, Australia, and New Zealand) where government programs help to protect families from astronomical medical costs.

10. "Downward Mobility is Stalking the Baby Boomers," *Business Week* (January 28, 1991), 22.

11. Light, *Baby Boomers,* 11.

12. In the secular world, Bolles's *What Color is Your Parachute?,* a book about job-switching methods, has become a perennial best-seller that is updated frequently. But how many counselor training programs have courses on vocational counseling? Is there significance in the fact that the planners of Word's Contemporary Christian Counseling series thus far have been unable to find a qualified author to write a book on vocational counseling from a Christian perspective?

13. Ken Dychtwald, with Joe Flower, *Age Wave: The Challenges and Opportunities of an Aging America* (Los Angeles: Jeremy P. Tarcher, 1989), 63, 3. Cetron and Davies also talk about intergenerational wars in their book, *American Renaissance,* 41–45.

14. Kenneth J. Gergen, *The Saturated Self* (New York: Basic Books, 1991). See also, Gergen, "The Saturated Family," *Family Therapy Networker* 15 (September/October 1991): 26–35.

15. George Barna, *The Frog in the Kettle: What Christians Need to Know About Life in the Year 2000* (Ventura, Calif.: Regal, 1990), 73.

16. Christian counselors may disagree with many of the conclusions, but to better understand trends in both the society and in family therapy, most of us could benefit from reading two or three of the articles in *The Family Therapy Networker* (September/October 1991). This issue is devoted to a discussion of "The Postmodern Family."

17. Richard Simon, "From the Editor," *The Family Therapy Networker* 15 (September/October 1991): 2.

18. Cetron and Davies, *American Renaissance,* 277.

19. Everett L. Worthington, Jr., "Religious Counseling: A Review of Published Empirical Research," *Journal of Counseling and Development* 64 (March 1986): 421–31.

20. Jones, *Great Expectations,* 330.

21. Patterson and Kim, *The Day America,* 230–34.

22. Ibid., 234.

23. John Naisbitt and Patricia Aburdene, *Megatrends 2000: Ten New Directions for the 1990's* (New York: Morrow, 1990). We are somewhat reluctant to cite the book because the authors' New Age orientation permeates the entire chapter and leads them to make statements that we consider to be both biased and at times in error. Nevertheless, the book does document the renewed interest in spirituality, especially among baby boomers.

24. Donald G. Bloesch, "Lost in the Mystical Myths," *Christianity Today* 35 (August 19, 1991), 22–24.

25. Doug Murren, *The Baby Boomerang: Catching Baby Boomers as They Return to Church* (Ventura, Calif.: Regal, 1990).

Bibliography

Anderson, Kerby. *Future Tense: Eight Coming Crises of the Baby Boom Generation*. Nashville: Thomas Nelson, 1991.

Anderson, Leith. *Dying for Change*. Minneapolis: Bethany, 1991.

Arterburn, Stephen, and Jack Felton. *Toxic Faith: Understanding and Overcoming Religious Addiction*. Nashville: Oliver-Nelson, 1991.

Barna, George. *The Frog in the Kettle: What Christians Need to Know About Life in the Year 2000*. Ventura, Calif.: Regal, 1990.

Bellah, Mike. *Baby Boom Believers*. Wheaton, Ill.: Tyndale House, 1988.

Bernbaum, John A., and Simon M. Steer. *Why Work? Careers and Employment in Biblical Perspective*. Grand Rapids, Mich.: Baker, 1986.

Bloomfield, Harold H., with Leonard Felder. *Making Peace With Your Parents: The Key to Enriching Your Life and All Your Relationships*. New York: Random House, 1983.

Bocknek, Gene. *The Young Adult: Development After Adolescence*. Monterey, Calif.: Brooks/Cole, 1980.

Cargan, Leonard. *Marriages and Families*. New York: HarperCollins, 1991.

Cetron, Martin, and Owen Davies. *American Renaissance: Our Life at the Turn of the 21st Century*. New York: St. Martin's Press, 1989.

Conway, Jim, and Sally Conway. *Traits of a Lasting Marriage: What Strong Marriages Have in Common*. Downers Grove, Ill.: InterVarsity, 1991.

Dobson, James C. *Love for a Lifetime: Building a Marriage that Will Go the Distance*. Portland, Ore.: Multnomah, 1987.

Dychtwald, Ken, with Joe Flower. *Age Wave: The Challenges and Opportunities of an Aging America*. Los Angeles: Jeremy P. Tarcher, 1989.

Engstrom, Ted W., with Norman B. Rohrer. *The Fine Art of Mentoring*. Brentwood, Tenn.: Wolgemuth and Hyatt, 1989.

Finzel, Hans. *Help! I'm a Baby Boomer*. Wheaton, Ill.: Victor Books, 1989.

Friesen, DeLoss D., and Ruby M. Friesen. *Counseling and Marriage*. Waco, Tex.: Word, 1989.

Gerber, Jerry. *Lifetrends: The Future of Baby Boomers and Other Aging Americans*. New York: Macmillan, 1989.

Gergen, Kenneth J. *The Saturated Self: Dilemmas of Identity in Contemporary Life*. New York: Basic Books, 1991.

Goldenberg, Herbert, and Irene Goldenberg. *Counseling Today's Families*. Pacific Grove, Calif.: Brooks/Cole, 1990.

Gordon, Jacob, and Richard Majors. *The Black Male: His Present Status and His Future*. Chicago: Nelson-Hall, 1991.

Hart, Archibald D. *Counseling the Depressed*. Waco, Tex.: Word, 1987.

————. *The Hidden Link Between Adrenalin and Stress*. Dallas: Word, 1988.

Hendrick, Susan S., and Clyde Hendrick. *Liking, Loving, and Relating*. 2d ed. Pacific Grove, Calif.: Brooks/Cole, 1992.

Hurding, Roger F. *The Tree of Healing*. Grand Rapids, Mich.: Zondervan, 1985.

Jandt, F. *Win-Win Negotiating—Turning Conflict into Agreement*. New York: Wiley, 1985.

Jarvik, Lissy, and Gary Small. *Parentcare: A Commonsense Guide for Adult Children*. New York: Crown, 1988.

Jones, Landon Y. *Great Expectations: America and the Baby Boom Generation*. New York: Coward, McCann and Geoghegan, 1980.

Kalter, Neil. *Growing Up With Divorce: Helping Your Child Avoid Immediate and Later Emotional Problems*. New York: The Free Press, 1990.

Kinder, Melvyn. *Going Nowhere Fast: Step Off Life's Treadmills and Find Peace of Mind*. New York: Prentice Hall, 1990.

LaBier, Douglas. *Modern Madness: The Emotional Fallout of Success*. Reading, Mass.: Addison-Wesley, 1986.

Leinberger, Paul, and Bruce Tucker. *The New Individualists: The Generation After the Organization Man*. New York: HarperCollins, 1991.

Light, Paul C. *Baby Boomers*. New York: Norton, 1988.

Littwin, Susan. *The Postponed Generation: Why America's Grown-Up Kids Are Growing Up Later*. New York: Morrow, 1986.

Lowry, L. Randolph, and Richard W. Meyers. *Conflict Management and Counseling*. Dallas: Word, 1991.

McMinn, Mark R. *Cognitive Therapy Techniques in Christian Counseling*. Dallas: Word, 1991.

Myers, Kenneth A. *All God's Children and Blue Suede Shoes: Christians and Popular Culture*. Westchester, Ill.: Crossway, 1989.

Morrison, Peter, *Changing Family Structure: Who Cares for America's Dependents?* Santa Monica, Calif.: Rand Corporation, 1986.

Murren, Doug. *The Baby Boomerang: Catching Baby Boomers as They Return to Church.* Ventura, Calif.: Regal, 1990.

Naisbitt, John, and Particia Aburdene. *Megatrends 2000: Ten New Directions for the 1990s.* New York: Morrow, 1990.

Norris, Jean, ed. *Daughters of the Elderly: Building Partnerships in Caregiving.* Bloomington and Indianapolis: Indiana University Press, 1988.

Patterson, James, and Peter Kim. *The Day America Told the Truth.* New York: Prentice Hall, 1991.

Peck, M. Scott. *The Different Drum: Community Making and Peace.* New York: Simon and Schuster, 1987.

Postman, Neil. *Amusing Ourselves to Death: Public Discourse in the Age of Show Business.* New York: Penguin, 1985.

Russell, Cheryl. *100 Predictions for the Baby Boomer: The Next 50 Years.* New York: Plenum, 1987.

Saltzman, Amy. *Downshifting: Reinventing Success on a Slower Tract.* New York: HarperCollins, 1991.

Sell, Charles M. *Transition: The Stages of Adult Life.* Chicago: Moody, 1985.

Sherman, Doug, and William Hendricks. *Your Work Matters to God.* Colorado Springs: NavPress, 1987.

Sherman, Edmund. *Counseling the Aging: An Integrative Approach.* New York: The Free Press, 1981.

Sloat, Donald E. *The Dangers of Growing Up in a Christian Home.* Nashville: Thomas Nelson, 1986.

———. *Growing Up Holy and Wholly: Understanding and Hope for Adult Children of Evangelicals.* Brentwood, Tenn.: Wolgemuth and Hyatt, 1990.

Smith, Darrell. *Integrative Therapy: A Comprehensive Approach to the Methods and Principles of Counseling and Psychotherapy.* Grand Rapids, Mich.: Baker, 1990.

Stafford, Tim. *As Our Years Increase: Loving, Caring, Preparing: A Guide*. Grand Rapids, Mich.: Zondervan, 1989.

Steinmetz, Suzanne K., Sylvia Clavan, and Karen F. Stein. *Marriage and Family Realities: Historical and Contemporary Perspectives*. New York: Harper and Row, 1990.

Tavris, Carol. *Anger: The Misunderstood Emotion*. New York: Simon and Schuster, 1982.

Towns, Elmer. *How to Reach the Baby Boomer*. Lynchburg, Va.: Church Growth Institute, 1990.

Wallerstein, Judith S., and Sandra Blakeslee. *Second Chances: Men, Women and Children a Decade After Divorce*. New York: Ticknor and Fields, 1989.

Waters, Elinor B., and Jane Goodman. *Empowering Older Adults: Practical Strategies for Counselors*. San Francisco: Jossey-Bass, 1990.

Willard, Dallas. *The Spirit of the Disciplines: Understanding How God Changes Lives*. San Fransisco: Harper and Row, 1988.

Wolinsky, Mary Ann. *A Heart of Wisdom: Marital Counseling With Older and Elderly Couples*. New York: Brunner/Mazel, 1991.

Worthington, Everett, Jr. *Marriage Counseling: A Christian Approach to Counseling Couples*. Downers Grove, Ill.: InterVarsity, 1989.

Wright, H. Norman. *Marital Counseling: Biblical, Behavioral, Cognitive Approach*. New York: Harper and Row, 1981.

Zinn, Maxine Baca, and C. Stanley Eitsen. *Diversity in Families*. New York: HarperCollins, 1990.

Zunker, Vernon G. *Career Counseling: Applied Concepts of Life Planning*. 3d ed. Pacific Grove, Calif.: Brooks/Cole, 1990.

Index